Developing High-Performance People

Developing High- Performance People

THE ART OF COACHING

Oscar G. Mink, Keith Q. Owen, and Barbara P. Mink

ADDISON-WESLEY PUBLISHING COMPANY

Reading, Massachusetts • Menlo Park, California • New York
Don Mills, Ontario • Wokingham, England • Amsterdam • Bonn
Paris • Milan • Madrid • Sydney • Singapore • Tokyo
Seoul • Taipei • Mexico City • San Juan

The publisher offers discounts on this book when ordered in quantity for special sales. For more information please contact:

Corporate & Professional Publishing Group
Addison-Wesley Publishing Company
One Jacob Way
Reading, Massachusetts 01867

Mink, Oscar G.
   Developing high performance people : the art of coaching/Oscar G. Mink, Keith Q. Owen, and Barbara P. Mink.
       p.   cm.
   Includes bibliographical references and index.
   ISBN 0-201-56313-4 (alk. paper)
       1. Employees—Training of.   2. Mentors in business.   3. Employee motivation.
   4. Performance.   I. Owen, Keith Q.   II. Mink, Barbara P., 1945- .   III. Title.
   HF5549.5. T7M557   1993
   658.3′14—dc20   92-36017
                                                                        CIP

Cover design by Simone R. Payment
Text design by Wilson Graphics & Design (Kenneth J. Wilson)

ISBN 0-201-56313-4

Text printed on recycled and acid-free paper.
5 6 7 8 9 10 11-CRW-98979695
Fifth Printing, September 1995

CONTENTS

PREFACE

Writing this book has been problematic, not because of the normal difficulties of writing, but because the world has been changing so very rapidly. This is the third version of the book. As we examined the earlier versions, we realized that both were written from what we have come to call a *control and dominance* paradigm. Once we saw the lack of value for future generations of leaders, of yet another book stressing control, we repented. However, repentance often comes with a price—we had to reshape much of our thinking. We had to unlearn our own habit of writing from a control paradigm and then learn how to write from what we refer to as an *empowerment and collaboration* paradigm. We hope we have succeeded in fully conveying the power of collaboration in a complex world. You, the reader, must be the final judge.

We feel a sense of pride in our accomplishment. We hope you will be pleased as well. We have all spent many years coaching, counseling, and mentoring others. We know that the model works and, if applied as suggested, will produce powerful results. The principles we espouse are based on research and work on the job. But the following pages definitely don't answer all the questions you will face. Keep an experimental frame of mind, and as William Edward Hickson said, "If at first you don't succeed, try, try again."

ACKNOWLEDGMENTS

All of the leaders, managers, supervisors, associates, and teachers who have influenced our lives have our heartfelt thanks and appreciation. Most important, we thank our mentors, coaches, counselors, and teachers. We are especially grateful for those many wonderful people who have brought the concept of competence "alive" for us. We have clearly been blessed. We are truly humbled by your love and concern. We hope this simple work will be yet another way of thanking you for caring. Also, for the many hands that have made this work possible, we appreciate you and your support. For your patience, we thank you, Kate, for giving us time to get the dirt out of our conceptual plume!

CHAPTER 1

Coaching: The Art of Encouraging Others to Experience Their Power

INTRODUCTION AND RATIONALE

Learning in the workplace is more critical than ever before. Leaders who wish to compete in today's global markets must emphasize the demand from customers for meeting or exceeding their expectations. Changing customer demands and accompanying market opportunities constantly challenge employees to acquire new knowledge, skills, and attitudes—to be competent in both process and content. Coaching is increasingly important as a process to enhance learning in organizations. In today's organizations, those who survive and prosper will be those who learn how to learn at the individual, team, and organizational level. The ability to transfer skills effectively becomes critical to remaining competitive as an organization. In today's environment of comparatively rapid change, good coaching provides a foundation for continuous improvement.

GOALS

In this chapter we begin our exploration of the many facets of the coaching role. Our goals are to deepen your

- Understanding of the coaching role
- Awareness of the values that influence good coaching
- Commitment to develop your competencies as a coach

COACHING: A ROLE WHOSE TIME HAS COME

Four things are happening today that make the art of coaching so important.

1. Employee knowledge and skills frequently become obsolete in the course of a calendar year. Technology changes so fast that many people find themselves

1

incompetent. This seems to be especially true for the middle-level person who has been in a managerial role for some time.

2. Diversity and complexity increase daily in the workplace. People with different cultural backgrounds and different learning backgrounds are entering the workforce in increasing numbers. As the difference among workers grows larger, greater competence at working with individual differences will be required.

3. There appears to be a skilled labor shortage. The number of skilled people entering the job market is actually decreasing relative to the number of new technical and professional jobs that are being created.

4. There is a decline in the competence level (knowledge, skills, and attitudes) of people who are entering the workplace for the first time. New employees often do not have the necessary competencies to succeed in today's jobs.

To deal with these changes, we must become experts at transferring the skills, knowledge, attitudes, and values so essential to success. We need to do so with greater speed than ever before. Developing people in a short time frame will be what separates the successful organization from the unsuccessful organization. People need training and development in a variety of areas. To meet the challenge, each person must become an expert coach and support the learning of others in the workplace.

WHAT IS COACHING?

To begin our journey, we define the term coaching. **Coaching** is the process by which one individual, the coach, creates enabling relationships with others that make it easier for them to learn. The coach helps other people set and achieve performance goals at levels higher than those at which they are currently performing. This process occurs in such a way that it creates stronger people who have a greater appreciation for themselves and their capacity to couple their personal competence with effort and produce good results. The coaching process is an empowering process.

There are a number of key words and concepts in this definition. For one thing, coaching is a *process*, not an event. Learning is a process that requires practice and repetition and time. Likewise, the process of people empowering themselves takes time because people acquire skills and knowledge incrementally and through different media at different rates. Application and reflection need to occur after each step.

A second key word in the definition is that of **empowerment** itself. In essence, coaching is the transfer of knowledge, skills, and/or values and attitudes from the coach to the learner. Through the coaching relationship, learners are enabled (empowered) to perform new tasks, to do more than they were doing, or to do something entirely different, or even to perform at a higher level of complexity. For example, when a programmer coaches a manager suffering from technical obsolescence by teaching her how to program in a new language, then the manager is empowered—capable of directing an entirely new set of work activities, that is, programming in a new language.

The programming example depicts a coach enabling a learner to improve job performance. The coach may do this by helping learners acquire new skills, knowledge, and/or values and attitudes. These changes help learners experience themselves differently and help them change the way they view themselves from a self-limiting view to a more self-enhancing view. When people combine knowledge and a set of related skills with personal effort and then succeed at appropriate tasks, they increase their belief in their own ability to achieve and enhance their sense of exercising control over their own lives, which is empowerment.

A third key concept of the definition is *relationship*. Coaching is a relationship between people, the coaches and the learners. If the context of coaching is a team or group setting, the essential transformation still takes place at the individual level. Relationships between individuals become the essential component of coaching. Successful coaching is based on mutual trust, acceptance, and respect, and focuses first and foremost on individuals, and second on the behavior change or new learning.

A fourth key concept implied in the definition is the concept of *transformation*. One outcome of coaching relationships is that the learner is able to perform at increasingly higher and more complex levels. This involves freeing oneself from the repetitive patterns of old learnings, which may be firmly imbedded in the unconscious, and adopting new mental operations—new mental models or structures that guide performance at work. In fact, one way the coaching relationship can be judged is by evidence of the learner's transformation. This mental transformation may be quantitative, as in when the learner is able to do more of what she was doing in the past. It may also be qualitative, as in when the learner is enabled to do something different, or when the learner leaps from one level of performance to an entirely different level using a new mental model. A direct outcome of great coaching is learners who take charge of their own learning. They can self-organize their learning around increasingly more difficult and complex arenas of performance. We say they operate at a level of **metalearning**. They have mastered the art and science of recognizing which of their values, goals, or contextual influences are governing their learning and performance. When required to do so, they manage those influences in ways that produce the desired or intended outcomes.

PRESCRIPTION VERSUS EMPOWERMENT: A SHIFT IN PARADIGM

This is an age of transition, a time during which we are moving from one economic era to another, from one way of viewing management to another, it is hoped, more productive manner. If coaching is the transfer of skills, knowledge, values, and attitudes from the coach to the learner, then how is this relationship best conceptualized?

In the past, the coach/manager was viewed as the person who established goals, developed work plans and schedules, devised control systems, and monitored performance to ensure that goals were met. Work roles were prescribed in order to increase the likelihood that a person's behavior conformed to what was expected or required from that role in a particular business. This was a prescriptive mode of thinking about coaching. Philosophically, it was deterministic, control-oriented, and specific. It sacrificed the holistic endeavor and ignored variation in process and influencing conditions at the workplace. As a result, poor quality in products and services was produced by those who blindly pursued their work as though they were extensions of a machine.

Globalization has produced quality-based competition. Now leaders must change their practices, and the work environment must change to enable continuous improvement or experience-based learning. The prescription model, by definition, is ineffective. Performance tends to conform to expectations, and people tend to do just what's prescribed. As work requirements change, the prescriptive model makes it difficult to respond. Appropriate responses require change. To continue to produce quality products or services, a whole new set of procedures and rules must surface. The prescription model makes this difficult, if not impossible, because it

1. Reduces individual initiative

2. Lessens the likelihood of a person finding errors in the process

3. Constrains the employee from initiating needed corrections

Can one person prescribe excellence in achievement from another person and achieve sustained continuous improvement? Apparently not. Excellence prescribed will not produce excellence in performance. Ask any parent of a struggling teenager who has lost her self-confidence how well prescriptions and exhortations work! Goals prescribed by one person are not necessarily powerful drivers for another.

Typically, little positive change comes from imposed demands for excellence. A new view is necessary for us to keep pace with the incredible rate of change in the technical and socioeconomic environments of today. In this new view, responsiveness or adaptability to the changing world is required. How do we best transfer skills from one person to the next? How do we get people up to speed in a variety of roles with a variety of demands? We believe the solution lies in the ongoing enhancement of every employee's mastery of her own work and in each employee's learning how to acquire new skills.

The empowerment viewpoint is growing in acceptance. We are not using the term *empowerment* as it has become popular in the literature of the late 1980s. We don't believe anyone empowers anyone else. We do believe that people need to experience, at the personal level, an organization climate that allows each person to *discuss openly* and without fear of reprisal any aspect of organization life that mitigates against their individual performance or the performance of their work team or unit. Equally critical is having permission to *express feelings* related to job experiences. When managers see their role as one of facilitating empowerment in others, their behaviors should change from prescribing behaviors to releasing behaviors that support every individual's potential to achieve at the highest possible level. To do this, managers must help employees see opportunities for improving performance and create the means by which improved performance can occur. This includes providing the psychological climate and appropriate tools.

Table 1.1 depicts some of the differences between the two views.

TABLE 1.1
PRESCRIPTION VERSUS EMPOWERMENT

The Prescription Model	The Empowerment Model
Gives goals	Develops consensus about goals
Defines roles	Lets roles evolve
Writes procedures	Lets procedures evolve
Controls behavior	Emphasizes quality as a way of life
Evaluates performance	Focuses on ways to improve processes
Directs	Collaborates
Relies on extrinsic motivation (e.g., fear)	Increases initiative and internal motivation

WHY WE WROTE THIS BOOK

In our experiences as consultants, trainers, and teachers, we have observed firsthand the effects that today's tremendous social changes are having on the ability of people to perform their jobs. The pace of change is leaving people behind, not to mention the work teams and organizations in which they are expected to produce satisfactory results. The ability to acquire concepts, improve processes, and transfer skills in quick, yet effective, ways becomes more critical with each passing day. In the future there will be only two types of businesses—those that have failed and those that have emphasized continuous learning. Learning in the workplace requires the acquisition of competencies that enable organizations to operate as intelligent or adaptable entities. Organizations, work teams, and individuals need to be capable of adaptation and transformation. The entire structure of economic enterprise will be based on the continuous learning of people involved in the workplace. The only constant seems to be change. The key debate is not whether change occurs but whether it is induced by environmental pressure alone or whether it may also be induced by leadership. We believe leadership can induce transformation.

There are many modes for effecting the transfer of concepts and skills and improving processes, but the quality personal coach can be one of the most effective means for doing so. We think of this person as an avuncular figure—a brother or sister of a parent—teaching the niece or nephew how to dribble a basketball, repair a lawn mower, write an essay—patient, friendly, supportive, confrontive, instructive, encouraging, and persuasive. This avuncular figure is not bound by role of parent and is free to provide comfort and support without the added dimension of formal power and control. This person's sense of seeing achievement in the child is not weighted by expectation, guilt, and pride. The effectiveness of the coach is due not so much to the coach's technical expertise as to the coach's role in helping learners see that their limits are self-imposed and that growth is possible. The relationship between the coach and the learner is crucial to the learner's willingness to confront and go beyond her current limits. Our hope for this book is that you will use it and, in the process, become more effective in this important role.

THE LAYOUT OF THE BOOK

Chapter 1 presents the need for the role of coaching, given the great changes that are shaping work and the workforce. The remainder of this book is divided into five parts. Each part develops an essential set of tools that will help you become an effective coach.

Part 1: What Is Coaching? looks at the role of coaching. Chapter 2 examines the role of coaching in detail. The relationship between coaching, counseling, and mentoring is discussed. This is followed by a brief look at the skills of coaching. This discussion concludes by providing a model of performance. If you use this model when coaching, you can be a more effective coach.

Part 2: Creating a High-Performance and Productive Climate examines the essential elements of high performance. Chapter 3 introduces you to the concept of the high-performing productive environment. Chapter 4 develops the skills for building a foundation on which high performance is possible. Finally, Chapter 5 shows you how to build high-performance productive climates.

Part 3: The Tools of High-Performance Coaching looks at what effective coaches do to enhance feelings of empowerment in their associates. Chapter 6 reviews some key elements of adult learning and development. Chapter 7 provides a detailed discussion of how to become a high-performance coach in your own environment, with information and tools that will support you in your efforts to become a more effective coach.

Part 4: When Coaching Is Not Enough takes a look at failure and provides the tools you need to deal effectively with failure or personal defeat. Learning how to manage guilt and shame is critical. Chapter 8 introduces the notion that often coaches act to renew individuals who have reached points of quiet desperation in their growth and development. People sometimes fail. As a coach you can play a significant part in determining how the person responds to failure. Learning to mourn failure can lead to future success. Chapter 9 examines how to help people deal with and let go of failure so they can begin the process of healing and renewal.

Part 5: Endings and New Beginnings explores the further reaches of the concept of coaching that is developed in the book through various cases. This part of the book is more conceptual and theoretical. Chapter 10 extends the discussion begun in Chapter 2 about the ingredients of performance and organizational learning, and provides applications of some of the critical concepts developed in the book.

HOW TO USE THE BOOK

At the conclusion of each chapter is a set of activities. You may use these activities to develop the skills of the high-performance coach. The activities are of two varieties. *Discovery Activities* help you develop awareness of your current skills, knowledge, and values as they relate to being an effective coach. *Growth Activities* enable you to practice the skills that are characteristic of an effective coach. Also, we have included a glossary. There you will find more detailed definitions of all bold-faced words.

There are two ways to read the book. You may read it straight through, working sequentially from one chapter to the next. Or you may find it more beneficial to choose chapters that deal with areas in which you want to develop at this time. Either way will work. We recommend that you begin by reading the first two chapters. You will then understand our particular view of coaching, and you will more fully appreciate the model of coaching on which the book is built.

AN ACTIVITY ABOUT DISCOVERY AND GROWTH: DISCOVERING YOUR VALUES ABOUT COACHING

Purpose

Coaching effectiveness is built on a foundation comprised of

- Your values, which organize your personality, including how you think and problem solve

- Your skills

- Your job knowledge, as shown in Figure 1.1

FIGURE 1.1
COACHING EFFECTIVENESS

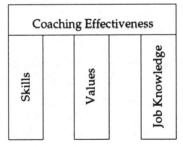

Of these three pillars, values is perhaps the most important. You can have all the skills and job knowledge in the world, but that won't make you an effective coach if your values are inconsistent with the role of coach. Ultimately, what you do when faced with a coaching opportunity is determined by your values.

All behavior is a reflection of a person's values. Your true values are reflected in the actions you take. In fact, this is how value is defined. A value guides action. Values are reflected in our beliefs about what is and isn't worthwhile. If you want to know what your values are, observe your behaviors. Every action reflects a set of choices that you make

- To be aware of the choice or to deny it

- To be aware of alternatives or to be locked into only one

- To take action or not to take action

- To do this and not that

This book introduces many new skills. To apply these skills in the best possible way, it is important that you examine the values revealed in your behavior, and that you strive to develop and enhance those values that will enable you to learn. To become the most effective coach possible, you need to approach the experience of learning in the same way that those whom you coach must approach the experience of learning—with openness, a receptivity to change, and a willingness to work hard to create change. The goals of this activity are to help you

- Develop awareness of your most important values

- Understand the gaps between what you say you value and what you really value

- Position yourself to begin working through and eliminating those gaps

- Become aware of when you are and are not producing desired outcomes or results

Directions

The Core Beliefs Inventory consists of thirty-two pairs of statements. Choose which statement within each pair is most typical of you in most situations, most of the time.

Core Beliefs Inventory

1. H During my spare time, I have no trouble finding things to do.
   P During my spare time, I often have trouble finding things to do.

2. S I feel very sure of myself.
   D I am usually unsure of myself.

3. T My managers/supervisors have, for the most part, been very helpful.
   M My managers/supervisors have, for the most part, shown a lack of understanding.

4. O I allow my feelings to show.
   C I don't allow my feelings to show.

5. H I have been very lucky so far.
   P Luck has not played a role in getting me where I am.

6. D I am sometimes overcome by feelings of loneliness and worthlessness.
   S I generally feel comfortable, even when I am alone.

7. M I doubt the honesty of people who are more friendly than they have to be.
   T Just because people are friendly doesn't mean they are dishonest.

8. O I frequently expose myself to new learning opportunities.
   C I find there is little time to learn new things.

9. H I am generally happy.
   P I am generally unhappy.

10. D My friends don't need me as much as I need them.
    S My friends need me just as much as I need them.

11. T Most people will admit their mistakes, even when it would be just as easy to blame someone.
    M Most people try to blame someone else to cover up for their own mistakes.

12. O It is easy for me to listen to feedback without becoming defensive.
    C I find I often become defensive when I listen to feedback.

13. H I get a great deal of fun out of my life.
    P I rarely seem to find life much fun.

14. S When someone thinks badly of me, this is of no great cause for concern.
    D When someone thinks badly of me, I worry about it.

15. M It is mainly fear of being caught that keeps people honest.
    T People are basically honest.

16. C I find it very hard to deal with conflicts.
    O I find it quite easy to deal with conflicts.

17. H Most problems can be solved if one takes action.
    P It often doesn't do any good to even try to solve problems.

18. S When criticized wrongly for something I did not do, I do not feel guilty.
    D When criticized wrongly for something I did not do, I still feel a bit guilty.

19. T Most people are nice.
    M Most people are objectionable and have hidden motives.

20. C If I disagree with another person, I tend to keep quiet.
    O If I disagree with another person, I tend to let that person know.

21. H Things generally work out for the best.
    P Things just naturally have a way of going sour.

22. S I sleep well at night, no matter what.
    D I often have trouble sleeping at night.

23. T I am very critical of other people's work.
    M I am generally very accepting of other people's work.

24. O I readily share my personal views on just about everything.
    C I am very selective with whom I share my personal views on certain topics.

25. H During ordinary difficulties, I generally keep up hope.
    P It is hard for me to keep up hope, even during ordinary difficulties.

26. S When one small thing after another goes wrong, I go on as usual.
    D When one small thing after another goes wrong, I feel overcome.

27. T People generally do what they say they are going to do.
    M You generally have to check up on others because they rarely do what they say they are going to do.

28. C I feel very uncomfortable telling others what I like about them.
    O I feel very comfortable telling others what I like about them.

29. H Generally, I am a person of great faith.
    P Generally, I am a person of little faith.

30. D I often feel guilty about even small mistakes.
    S I rarely feel guilty, even when I make mistakes.

31. T Most people are inclined to look out for others.
    M Most people just look out for themselves.

32. O My friends say that I am easy to get to know.
    C My friends say that I am hard to get to know.

Scoring and Interpretation

Count the number of H's and P's you circled and record the number in the blanks below. The total of H + P should equal eight. Likewise, total the number of S's and D's you circled, the number of T's and M's, and the number of O's and C's. Subtract the number of P's from the number of H's; the number of D's from the number of S's; the number of M's from the number of T's; and the number of C's from the number of O's. The differences can range from +8 to –8. Transfer the difference to the scoring profile.

H: _6_ – P: _2_ = _4_

S: _7_ – D: _1_ = _6_

T: _7_ – M: _1_ = _6_

O: _5_ – C: _3_ = _2_

Scoring Profile

Pessimism | – | Hope
-8 -7 -6 -5 -4 -3 -2 -1 0 +1 +2 +3 (+4) +5 +6 +7 +8

Doubt | – | Confidence
-8 -7 -6 -5 -4 -3 -2 -1 0 +1 +2 +3 +4 +5 (+6) +7 +8

Mistrust | – | Trust
-8 -7 -6 -5 -4 -3 -2 -1 0 +1 +2 +3 +4 +5 (+6) +7 +8

Closed | – | Open
-8 -7 -6 -5 -4 -3 -2 -1 0 +1 (+2) +3 +4 +5 +6 +7 +8

Interpretation

Hope. This scale measures the degree to which you expect the best from life. Research tells us that those who expect the best from themselves and others more often obtain the best than do those who are pessimistic. The most effective coaches tend to be very hopeful.

To increase your sense of hope you could

1. Comment on the positive parts of a plan or idea before suggesting problems or revisions.

2. Attend funny movies and "belly laugh." See something funny in normal everyday situations.

3. Watch your speech pattern. Say "I choose to" or "I am going to" instead of "I have to."

Self-Confidence. This scale measures the degree to which you believe that you can, by your own efforts, influence future events, that you will do well in what you try, and that you feel as smart and as capable as others. Effective coaches tend to be self-confident as opposed to being full of self-doubt.

To increase your sense of confidence you could

1. Before beginning a task, decide if it is one you really want to do well or merely complete to a satisfactory level.

2. Make a list of your strengths and skills. Keep it up to date. Use it as a check when someone gives you "constructive criticism" concerning your "faults."

Trust. This scale measures the degree to which you trust others and have confidence in their good intentions. Effective coaches are essentially trusting. This belief in others acts as a self-fulfilling prophecy.

To increase your sense of trust you could

1. Take what people say at face value. Believe that what people say is what they mean. Do not look for hidden messages and motives.

2. When making agreements, put in sanctions or natural consequences. Do not use punishment after the fact. If agreements are not kept, let the natural consequences follow, but do not add punishment.

Openness. This scale measures the degree to which you are willing to self-disclose yourself to the world. The most effective coaches are willing to share, as well as to listen.

To increase your sense of openness you could

1. Start each day by deciding to learn something new.

2. Express what you are thinking and feeling at the time of an event or conversation.

Reflection

1. What are your core beliefs?

2. What do your scores suggest about you and your view of the world?

3. What effect do these beliefs have on you and on your ability to coach others?

PART 1

What Is Coaching?

The major goal of this section is to develop a shared view of what the term coaching means. Once this task is completed, we focus on the various meanings of the coach's role. An assessment tool to help you determine how to increase your personal effectiveness as a coach is in Appendix A. We suggest that after reading Chapter 2, you complete that instrument. It is also helpful if your associates rate themselves on these same skills. This may reveal competency gaps that you and your associates may not have noticed and that need to be addressed.

C H A P T E R 2

What Is Coaching?

PURPOSE

Experts project that successful organizations in the 1990s will be responsive, flat, and entrepreneurial (Peters and Waterman, 1982; Peters and Austin, 1985). Although we may not place a lot of confidence in exact predictions of the future, things do seem to be changing at an ever-increasing rate. In such a dynamic environment, people and organizations must have the skills and knowledge necessary to create and adapt. In short, they must have the ability to learn, and they must have the ability to empower others. Coaching becomes an increasingly important skill given this reality. This chapter provides an in-depth look at this important leadership skill.

GOALS

The goals of this chapter are to help you understand

- The role of coaching in the broader context of performance in the organization.

- That coaching is a developmental process that depends on the learner's current skills, aptitudes, and concerns, and on the current level of use of the skills needed.

- That coaching is not optional. Coaching is an absolute necessity because people's performance must match the demands of jobs that are changing to adapt to changes in technology development, process improvements, and customer demands—internal and external.

- Where you are now in terms of your own development as a coach.

WHAT IS COACHING?

The term *coaching* often produces a mental image of a football or basketball coach. Depending on what the coach actually does, this analogy may or may not be adequate for the purposes of this book. This is because the head coach is usually a general manager or chief executive officer responsible for running an entire program. In reality, a head coach may spend almost no time actually empowering players to become better performers.

When we think about the art of coaching, we have a different image. The main function of the coach is to encourage and enable others to become more competent and to empower themselves to seek ways continuously to improve those work processes they can influence. The image of the quarterback coach or the offensive line coach is somewhat more accurate. The focus of these two coaches is narrower than that of the lead coach. These coaches focus on values, knowledge, and skills that result in intelligent self-directed performance. They can play the positions, but they can't play in the game. Instead, they enable others to play, through teaching, observing and correcting performance, and encouraging constant improvement through teamwork and coordination of people and activities.

These individuals work daily with their players to improve their performance by providing the knowledge and skills they need to execute their roles to perfection. What does the line coach do? Initially, the line coach teaches players to execute various blocking schemes from a technical perspective. This teaching involves training in how to use the hands, body position, movement of the feet, and a host of other subskills, all of which must be developed to execute a block properly.

As a next step, the line players learn how to block as a unit. The coach teaches a pattern of blocking in which all line players are expected to execute blocks in relation to each other. They play in a coordinated fashion, or as a team. As a third step, players learn how to execute a specific pattern of blocking in response to a specific offensive move by an opponent team. If the coach is successful, each player knows what to do—even under conditions never before encountered. The line players are empowered to continue to vary skills and combinations thereof and learn new skills and patterns of play through personal and collective initiative—empowering themselves. These line players have established internal control, learning capacity, and stewardship with regard to their roles and performance.

From the empowerment point of view, coaching is a special kind of relationship between the coach and the coached. It is a relationship in which the learner permits and encourages the coach to influence her performance. A coach cannot make a player excel—a coach can only encourage or release the player's potential to excel. Whether the coach succeeds depends on her ability to create the conditions under which a sense of personal control of results produced may occur.

With these scenarios in mind, we can begin to delineate the elements of an effective coaching relationship. We define **coaching** as a relationship between two people in which one person finds ways to enable and empower the other person to perform at increasingly higher levels or in a different role. So what does this require?

- What *qualities* are inherent in a relationship that lead to a belief that each person can influence the results produced through timely combinations of personal skill and effort?

- What *values* do effective coaches bring to their relationships that enable others to empower themselves?

- What *skills* do effective coaches bring to their relationships that enable them to succeed in the empowerment process?

- What are the *characteristics* of these special relationships?

Some answers to these questions may help us gain insight into coaching as a process. First, let's take the broadest view: What general qualities can be observed in effective coaching? There are three qualities of this special coaching relationship:

- *Clarity.* A coach creates a context in which achievement and excellence are seen as real possibilities. Everything the coach does clearly communicates the possibility of accomplishment.

- *Coherence.* A coach demonstrates by example what she hopes the learner will learn. Everything the coach does or says reflects commitment to excellence and goal achievement.

- *Openness.* There can be no coaching without listening and observing, without sharing and giving, without an attitude of flexibility and willingness to experiment, without valuing free and informed choice, valid information, and collaboration.

Good coaching requires the coach to create a context that enables and facilitates learning. It becomes necessary to create and live a clearly developed, understandable value system that is coherent and observable by the learner. The learner must share this value system.

Coaching Is Value Laden. The coaching role is similar to the avuncular role—warm, friendly, concerned, and free from the constraints of formal role power. Coaches value growth in other people. Coaches value winning and being the best through hard work, self-discipline, and personal responsibility. Eric Fromm provides a useful way of thinking about the values inherent in coaching in *The Art of Loving* (1956). He says that loving involves caring for the growth of the other person and doing what is necessary to release that person's potential for growth. In order to nurture growth, the coach must know the learner; must be willing to concentrate on what the learner is doing and needing; must be willing to be committed to the relationship; must know that growth is often a painful, drawn-out process; and finally, must have the courage and discipline to do the right thing at the right time.

Coaching Is the Ability to Care.   And this caring must be genuine—real. Caring is demonstrated through the proper application of a range of skills, qualities, and values, including patience, persuasion, dedication, hard work, preparation, and spending whatever time it takes to find the uniqueness in another person. Finally, a good coach reflects outwardly an inner world in which she clearly values the unconditional worth of another human being—respect for life.

Good Coaching Involves Team Work and Shared Effort.   The essential elements of successful coaching are observable in good learning environments. Coaching is a partnership. Both the coach and the learner must work at the task with persistence. There must be a level of trust in the relationship that enables team effort. This trust centers on competence, personal disclosure, and keeping simple social agreements—agreements to meet, study, prepare, experiment, and learn.

Good Coaching Involves Leadership.   A leader influences others. Coaching requires patience, friendly persuasion, and unfeigned love. One role of the coach is to empower the learner to go beyond current beliefs about personal limitations. This means that the coach is often in the position of encouraging others to try something new. Even when producing poor results or unintended outcomes, people are often reluctant to change. The complexity of changes varies, and the more complex the change, the more effort required by the learner. And the more risk perceived, the more the learner's fear increases. The effective coach understands how to encourage the learner to try despite self-doubt and fear.

Good Coaching Requires Structure.   You can't help a person feel empowered in an arbitrary or highly random environment. Rather, the situation must be such that the coach and the learner have quality interactions and a reliable process for experimenting with new learnings. The learner and the coach must be able to identify the relationship(s) among the newly acquired knowledge and skills, the learner's personal efforts, and the improvements or variations in results produced.

Good Coaching Also Involves Management.   By this we mean that effective coaching is no accident. It is built on an unflinching commitment to preparation. This preparation involves such things as analyzing the tasks to be mastered, designing effective means of teaching these tasks, getting the resources needed to teach them, and anticipating future learning needs. *The emphasis falls on learning how* *to learn.* This involves the use of how-to skills (metaskills): self-directed learning, resources for obtaining information, and study skills within a business environment—observing others, effective use of technical manuals, and goal-setting and problem-solving processes.

As you can see, coaching is a complex process. One goal of coaching is helping others learn how to do something they can't yet do. The best coaching helps people determine why something should be done, what is to be done, how to do it right, when to do it, where to do it, and how much it should be done. This process may involve providing verbal, behavioral, and attitudinal (value) information as a means of dealing with temperament in skill acquisition, as well as procedures for ensuring that learning has indeed taken place and can continue to take place. The essence of helping another person acquire new competencies requires that you as a coach recognize that valid information includes the feelings that are associated with the facts. These findings, when accurately expressed, often reflect the values, attitudes, and beliefs that are critical to the behavior changes required by the knowledge and skill being taught.

THE COACH AS PEER

In most organizations, work takes place in a team setting. In an effective team, members share the responsibility for accomplishing a shared goal or purpose. In the context of the work team, the manager, as well as team members, plays many roles. One role is that of coach. Good coaching produces a process by which one individual enables another individual to (1) perform at a higher level some task or process, or (2) to perform well in some new role or job. Coaching implies personal commitment to a quality learning process. Good coaching requires good working relationships.

During our work with people in an array of organizational settings, we have observed that the role of coach becomes effective when the participants relate to each other as equals. Typical superior-subordinate relationships, where power, dominance, and control are issues, disallow good coaching. Therefore, we think of coaching more in terms of a peer relationship or **mateship**—we're all in this together—than a supervisory relationship. This is because of our belief that the essence of coaching demands a relationship between one who wants to share expertise and one who wants to learn. This is most possible when people

1. Are willing participants in a relationship

2. Put trust in one another's competence

3. Deal with value issues

4. Access feelings as a part of valid information

You cannot make someone learn and grow; you can only facilitate learning or release the potential for learning. This is why we like to think of coaching as peer coaching done by associates. And this is why we refer to the learner in the coaching relationship as the *associate* and the teacher as the coach.

COACHING AS LEADERSHIP

In many but not all instances, effective coaching involves effective leadership. Leadership is usually defined as the ability to get things done through other people. Although this definition may have limitations when applied to coaching relationships, many skills used by effective coaches are also demonstrated by effective leaders. For example, coaches often have to

1. Create and/or share a vision of future performance

2. Direct the activities of learners

3. Foster confidence in learners

4. Share risks and accept mistakes as a necessary part of learning

Often learners do not believe they can execute a task or reach a goal. In these instances, the coach must persuade the learners that their goals are attainable, and that learners can attain goals important to them. However, keep in mind that the coach may not be able to perform at the same level as the learner. Often the coach cannot show the learner how to travel the required learning path; the coach can only encourage the learner to venture where she has not ventured before. How does a coach do this? We have found that the best coaches help learners see what is possible. Good coaches foster belief in the learners that they can achieve their goals. Coaches help learners envision pathways that can be traversed. Coaches encourage associates to try a bit harder, to reach a little deeper, to walk the extra mile.

The coach leads by envisioning with the learner what is possible. The best coaches also demonstrate a level of courage to risk within their own arenas of competence, and the learner can both share and emulate that courage to risk.

COACHING, COUNSELING, MENTORING: WHAT'S THE DIFFERENCE?

Many terms are used to describe aspects of the leader-associate relationship. It is especially instructive to think about the subroles of coaching, counseling, and mentoring and to identify the ways in which they differ. In so doing, we can gain a better understanding of what the larger process of managing is all about.

TABLE 2.1

SOME DIMENSIONS OF COACHING, COUNSELING, AND MENTORING

Dimensions of Process				
Process	*Time*	*Content*	*Focus*	*Typical Operations*
Coaching	Short to Intermediate	Job-related learning	Learning and/or development for the current or future job	Helping improve or transform individual and team performance through learning and workscape design
Counseling	Varies; typically short term	To remedy motivational or attitude problems	Remedial or developmental; Any area of a person's life space	Active listening; Exploring feelings and ideas; Breaking frames of reference; Examining values, goals, and variables that create unsatisfactory or satisfactory personal outcomes
Mentoring	Mainly long term	Career; Family role; Current performance that is future-related	Typically developmental; Often covers all life structures—current and future	Creating career opportunities; Encouraging extensive programs of development—degree programs, certification, professional licensing; Fostering and supporting career decisions

One way to think of the three subroles is in terms of time. The manager's long-term role is to help develop those people with talent and interest in learning. In the intermediate run, the goal is to develop competent associates who perform at high levels of excellence. In the short run, the manager's role is to remove environmental and interpersonal barriers to learning and high performance, thus creating the conditions that support the person in choosing to experience her power.

Coaching best describes those processes that take place over a relatively short to intermediate time span. For example, a new employee is hired and is gradually trained to perform a particular job. Or a new team is formed, and members teach each other the various aspects of their jobs so that all understand the roles of the different team members and how these roles work together. Or a manager may need to acquire a new set of technical skills, and an associate may coach her during the learning process.

Counseling involves relatively short-term interventions designed to remedy problems that interfere with the employee's job performance. These short-term problems are usually considered to be motivational or attitudinal. We are not referring to what happens when employees are told by supervisors to improve or get out, but rather to when an individual is having trouble succeeding and a respected peer helps the person see ways to overcome problems by trying some new behavior.

Mentoring describes processes carried out over a long time span. A mentor is most helpful in facilitating overall career growth and personal advancement. The mentor influences the associate by virtue of her ability to open doors to opportunity. We believe that good mentors deal with the complete life space and life structure of the mentee—family, career, and current work role.

Actually, there is little difference among the three subroles when considered without the perspective of time. At every moment, you as a manager, team leader, or team member are concerned about helping associates realize their potential by learning new skills, confronting poor attitudes, or clarifying their values. Sometimes, this concern may manifest itself in the form of teaching; it may be revealed in your efforts to remove personal and organizational barriers, or it may be revealed in your attempts to provide opportunities for career advancement.

In short, as a manager, team leader, or team member, you should make every effort to see that your associates have the tools to grow and to be all they are capable of being. When you are successful in this endeavor, your associates succeed, you succeed, and your organization succeeds. This is why we like to think of the role of coach as that of aiding individuals to release and experience their personal power. As a coach, you are providing your associates with the tools they need to transcend current limitations and grow.

Many of us don't mind seeing ourselves as mentors or coaches because this seems to be a normal kind of behavior. However, we don't necessarily like to see ourselves as counselors because that smacks of having to deal with negative feelings and possible conflict situations. The roles are not really that different. Most counseling is developmental, not remedial. After all, those whom you coach often experience problems with learning. If a person is going to succeed, you must be fully available to that person to work with feelings about negative experiences. No organization or work unit can attain high-performance levels unless valid information—including feelings—can be openly shared without fear of reprisal.

TO COACH OR NOT TO COACH: THE NECESSITY OF COACHING

You may be wondering if you really need to learn the skills of coaching. In our view, you have no choice—not if you want to succeed. Most people are managers, leaders, or associates of someone. The output of others, as well as your own output, is vital. All people must know how to perform. To address this point more clearly, think of your organization as an "accountability hierarchy." Managers and supervisors have a number of people working for them. What these other people produce determines their success. Managers and supervisors are responsible for results, but they do not have direct control over associates' outputs. The output of your associates is a function of their own abilities and motivations, the organizational context, and your personal effectiveness as a coach in other words, you exercise positive influence over your success by helping others acquire job competencies. It is therefore important to know (1) what coaching is, (2) how to coach, (3) when to coach, and (4) how much coaching to do. This book can empower you to coach effectively and thereby improve your own probability of succeeding with your career.

Even if you have no responsibility for the work of others, you still need to learn how to coach effectively. This is because the economic challenges facing today's organizations truly threaten their continued existence. You need to be able to coach so you can help your team keep pace in the rapidly changing world; you must know how to rapidly transfer your skills to others. People become technologically obsolete more quickly than ever before; when building a work team, there are fewer technically qualified competent people on whom to call. As you can see, whether or not you hold an official leadership role, your own and your organization's future depend, in large measure, on your ability to coach.

PERFORMANCE MODEL FOR COACHES

Theoretical Background

The approach we take in this text, developed over a period of time, is called **Reality Performance Management (RPM)**, our general theory of motivation and performance. Briefly, we believe that people will perform at high levels when they

- *Can.* Individuals perform if they have the capacity to succeed. These individuals have the right tools to do the job. A supportive psychological climate exists.

- *Want.* Individuals achieve those goals that are important to them or on which they place value.

- *Are Willing to Try.* Individuals work hard to succeed to the extent to which they believe they will succeed. This belief is generated from past successes.

When these three aspects of performance are well developed and when constraints are minimal, people consistently perform up to their potential. On the other hand, poor performance is a symptom of a deficit in one or more of these three elements. If a person is not competent, she may fail; if a person doesn't value the reward resulting from success, she may fail; and if a person doesn't believe that acting leads to the goal and doesn't even try, she may fail.

High-performance coaching requires that the coach create a supportive environment. Generally speaking, high performance is elicited in environments that provide

- *Opportunity.* The chance to perform valued activities

- *Incentive.* The availability of a valued reward

- *Feedback.* The availability of information about the effectiveness of one's performance with respect to the agreed-on goal or goals

If the environment of the individual and her aspirations is supportive, she will be empowered to succeed; if it is not, the individual's chances of success are diminished.

The role of coach can be important in teaching the competencies, stimulating the desires, and encouraging the beliefs that encourage a person to succeed. High-performance coaching refers to the set of competencies required to create high performance.

The Performance Model in Figure 2.1 depicts the relationships between the primary dimensions of field thinking, when applied to performance.

FIGURE 2.1
PERFORMANCE MODEL. © COPYRIGHT OSCAR MINK, APRIL 1992.

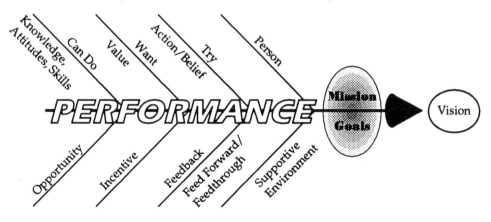

Vision provides the overall direction and alignment for the entire system—the *why*. The mission and goals denote what products and services we provide for whom. The bones on the fishbone interrelate the Person/Supportive Environment interaction. Performance strengthens as the interactive effect moves from left to right to create a human system in which the whole clearly exceeds the sum of the parts.

Figure 2.2 emphasizes the input side of a high-performance system. The performance potential generated by an appropriate balance between the person's Can/Want/Try performance component and the workscape parallels opportunity,

FIGURE 2.2
PERSON-ENVIRONMENT INTERACTION. © COPYRIGHT OSCAR MINK, MAY 1992.

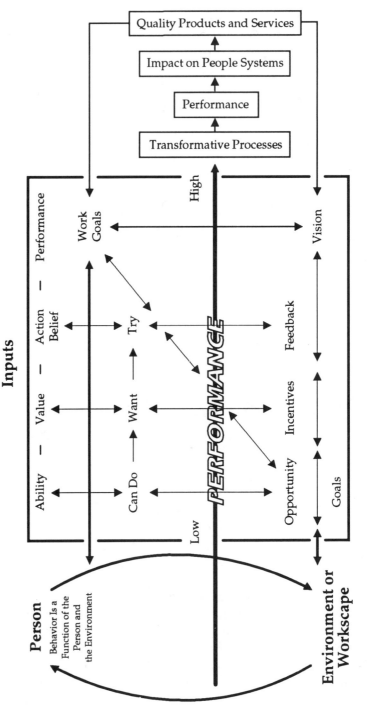

incentives, feedback, and vision. Together, these components generate a performance potential, which, when taken through transformative processes, produces a performance output that impacts all human-system components—person, group, and organization. These, in turn, make use of appropriate materials, tools, and technology to produce quality products and services.

COACHING AS A TOOL FOR DEVELOPING OTHERS

Patience is one key skill of the effective coach. Learning takes time; excellence takes more time. For example, when a new person is hired, that person, at a bare minimum, is expected to perform at the level required to succeed in completing assigned tasks. She must do so within an established time frame and at a standard or level of quality that meets or exceeds customer expectations. Yet it takes time for a newly hired employee to progress through the learning curve. This is why new hires are often on probation for the first few months. How many rookies start in an NFL game? Not many! The reason is that it takes a lot of training to get even talented players to be competitive within the framework of a particular team, its strategy (offense), and its culture. Coaching is a developmental process in which people are systematically trained to execute the complex skills required to perform the job right.

Why is coaching a developmental process? To answer this question satisfactorily, we turn to the ample research conducted in the area of adapting to change. For ten years, the Research and Development Center for Teacher Education at the University of Texas at Austin has studied the process of adopting new practices, innovations, and planned change. In the process of developing the **Concerns Based Adoption Model (CBAM)**, this team of researchers introduced two new concepts to explain how people change: Stages of Concern (SOC) and Levels of Use (LOU).

Stages of Concern

Stages of Concern (SOC) refer to the change in feelings and perceptions over time as a person first becomes familiar, and then comfortable in practice, with a change. Initially, a person facing a change feels uncomfortable and lacks confidence. As the person becomes familiar with the innovation, her attention changes to focus on the task itself. After a while, the individual finally masters the change, acquires the skill(s), and focuses attention on adapting the change to make it a tool for herself. There are seven stages of concern in the CBAM (Hord, Rutherford, Huling-Austin, and Hall, 1987).* These stages are illustrated in Figure 2.3.

---

* Adapted from Hall, 1976. Hord, Rutherford, Huling-Austin, and Hall, 1987. Original concept from Hall, Wallace, and Dossett, 1973. The concept of stages of concern about an innovation was originally developed by Francis Fuller, educational psychologist, the University of Texas at Austin.

FIGURE 2.3
STAGES OF CONCERN

Order	Stages
Last	6 Refocusing
↑	5 Collaboration
	4 Impact/Consequences
	3 Management
	2 Personal
	1 Information
First	0 Awareness

In the **Awareness Stage (0)**, there is little concern about or involvement with the innovation. A typical expression of concern about the innovation at Stage 0 would be, "I am not concerned about it (the innovation)."

The **Information Stage (1)** involves a general awareness of the innovation and interest in learning more detail about it. The person seems not to be worried about self in relation to the innovation. There is an interest rather in such substantive aspects of the innovation as general characteristics, effects, and requirements for use. A typical expression of concern about the innovation at Stage 1 would be, "I would like to know more about it."

In the **Personal Stage (2)**, an individual is uncertain about the demands of the innovation, personal adequacy to meet those demands, and her own role within the reward structure of the organization. There is also uncertainty about decision making and consideration of the potential conflicts with existing structures or personal commitments. Financial or status implications of the program for self and colleagues may also be reflected. A typical expression of concern about the innovation at Stage 2 would be, "How will using it affect me?"

The **Management Stage (3)** is characterized by the focus of attention on the processes and tasks of using the innovation and the best use of information and resources. Issues related to efficiency, organizing, managing, scheduling, and time demands are utmost. A typical expression of concern about the innovation at Stage 3 would be, "I seem to be spending all my time in paperwork."

In the **Impact/Consequences Stage (4)**, attention is on how innovation affects the associate's immediate sphere of influence. The focus is on the relevance of the innovation for associates; evaluation of associate outcomes, including performance and competencies; and the changes needed to increase associate outcomes. A typical expression of concern about the innovation at Stage 4 would be, "How is my use affecting my associates?"

The **Collaboration Stage (5)** focuses attention on coordination and cooperation with others regarding use of the innovation. A typical expression of concern about the innovation at Stage 5 would be, "I am concerned about relating what I am doing with what other managers are doing."

In the **Refocusing Stage (6)**, the emphasis is on exploration of the more universal benefits from the innovation, including the possibility of major changes or replacement with a more powerful alternative. The individual has definite ideas about alternatives to the proposed or existing form of the innovation. A typical expression of concern about the innovation at Stage 6 would be, "I have some ideas about something that would work even better."

Figure 2.4 presents the seven stages of concern along with examples of typical expressions of concern about the innovation.

FIGURE 2.4
STAGES OF CONCERN: TYPICAL EXPRESSIONS OF CONCERN ABOUT THE INNOVATION

	Stages of Concern	*Expressions of Concern*
I M P A C T	6 Refocusing	I have some ideas about something that would work even better.
	5 Collaboration	I am concerned about relating what I am doing with what other managers are doing.
	4 Impact/Consequences	How is my use affecting my associates?
T A S K	3 Management	I seem to be spending all my time in paperwork.
	2 Personal	How will using it affect me?
S E L F	1 Information	I would like to know more about it.
	0 Awareness	I am not concerned about it (the innovation).

Levels of Use

Both the person's feelings and her use of a new skill change over time. The CBAM research team identified several distinct changes in behavior or Levels of Use (LOU) that display a measurable progression over time from nonuse, to mechanical use, to refined use, and finally, to mastery of a particular competency, as illustrated in Figure 2.5.

FIGURE 2.5
LEVELS OF USE

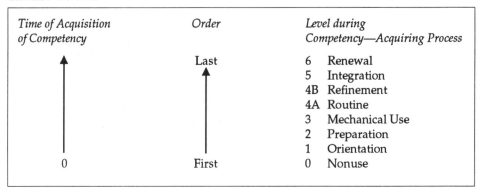

Time of Acquisition of Competency	Order	Level during Competency—Acquiring Process
	Last	6 Renewal
		5 Integration
		4B Refinement
		4A Routine
		3 Mechanical Use
		2 Preparation
		1 Orientation
0	First	0 Nonuse

Although similar to the Stages of Concern, the Levels of Use are different in that they refer to user *behaviors*, rather than feelings. In addition, the user's Level of Use may differ from her Stage of Concern, often lagging a little behind.

At the **Nonuse Level (0)**, the potential user is not involved with the innovation and is doing nothing toward becoming involved. A typical expression of this level of use might be, "Yes, I've heard of it, but I just don't have time to learn any more about it right now."

At the **Orientation Level (1)**, the user is taking action to learn more detailed information about the innovation. The user at this level might be heard to say, "I'm looking at materials pertaining to the innovation and considering using it sometime in the future."

At the **Preparation Level (2)**, the user decides to use the innovation by establishing a time to begin. You might hear her saying, "Since I'll be using it in September, I'm identifying right now what I'll need and when I should begin to set things up."

At the **Mechanical Use Level (3)**, the person using the innovation is grappling with how to organize and manage the program to establish a basic effectiveness with it. The user's effort is focused on the short-term, day-to-day use of the innovation with little time for reflection. The user is trying to master the tasks required to use the innovation. You might hear a user at this stage say, "I'm just trying to keep things going as smoothly as possible every day. There still seem to be so many problems to work out."

At the **Routine Level (4A)**, the user's implementation of the change has stabilized. Few operational changes are being made, and little thought is being given to improvements or the impact of the innovation. A person at this level of use might say, "The new system is going smoothly. I don't anticipate any changes in the way we are doing it any time soon."

At the **Refinement Level (4B)**, the user is evaluating the impact of the innovation on her immediate customers or clients and varies the use of the innovation accordingly. A manufacturing manager at this level might say, "I take some time each day to talk to shipping and receiving and customer service to find out what they like and dislike about the changes we have made and why."

At the **Integration Level (5)**, the user is changing procedures based on consultations with colleagues in order to increase the effectiveness of the innovation and improve coordination. A typical comment at this level might be, "We have found that customer satisfaction is improved when several of us coordinate our efforts in using this system."

Finally, at the **Renewal Level (6)**, the user seeks major modifications or new alternatives to the innovation in order to achieve increased impact on clients or customers. An example of this person's attitude might be, "I'm seriously considering replacing this system with another one, or combining it with some new approaches that I think would be far more valuable for my customers."

Figure 2.6 presents the seven Levels of Use along with examples of typical statements by users at each level. Figure 2.7 is a flowchart for identifying an

FIGURE 2.6
LEVELS OF USE: TYPICAL STATEMENTS ABOUT THE INNOVATION

Level of Use		Typical Statement
6	Renewal	I'm seriously considering replacing this system with a new one, or combining it with some new approaches that I think would be far more valuable to our customers.
5	Integration	We have found out that customer satisfaction is improved when several of us coordinate our efforts in using the system.
4B	Refinement	I take some time each day to talk to shipping and receiving and customer service to find out what they like and dislike about the changes we have made and why.
4A	Routine	The new system is going smoothly. I don't anticipate any changes in the way we are doing it any time soon.
3	Mechanical Use	I'm just trying to keep things going as smoothly as possible each day. There still seem to be so many problems to work out.
2	Preparation	Since I'll be using it in September, I'm identifying right now what I'll need and when I should begin to set things up.
1	Orientation	I'm looking at materials pertaining to the innovation and considering using it sometime in the future.
0	Nonuse	Yes, I've heard of it, but I just don't have time to learn any more about it right now.

FIGURE 2.7
FLOWCHART FOR DETERMINING LEVEL OF USE

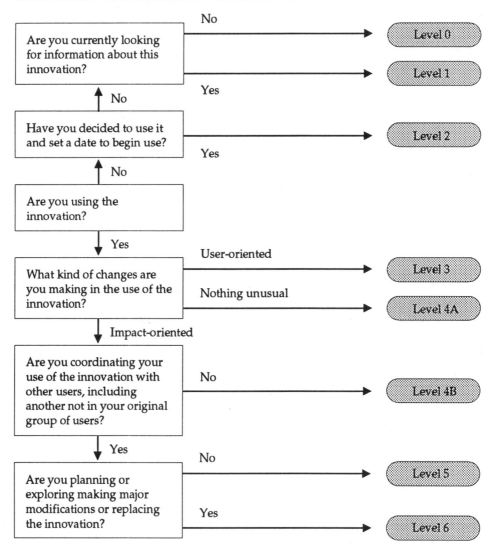

Excerpt from: Loucks, S.F., Newlove, B.W., and Hall, G.E. *Measuring Levels of Use of the Innovation: A Manual for Trainers, Interviewers, and Raters.* Austin: Research and Development Center for Teacher Education, University of Texas, 1975.

individual's current Level of Use. As you can see, any time a person enters a new situation, she must progress in both the behavioral and feeling dimensions through a series of stages related to the content and process of change. These stages are developmental—occurring whenever people experience change—and progressive, which means earlier stages must be resolved before later concerns can be resolved. As a manager/supervisor responsible for growing high performers through the use of coaching skills, you must always strive to understand where the person is in her own growth cycle and to adapt what you are doing to match the stage of concern and level of use.

By developing an awareness of where the learner is in the process of learning, you can tailor instruction to the needs of the learner. Different strategies are appropriate for individuals at different stages of learning.

Level	Intervention Strategy
Level 0: Nonuse	• Tell the person about the job. • Allow the person to express any misgivings she may have.
Level 1: Orientation	• Share descriptive information. • Sell the benefits versus the costs. • Help clarify learner's problems and concerns.
Level 2: Preparation	• Provide encouragement. • Establish realistic and simple achievement goals. • Answer all questions.
Level 3: Mechanical Use	• Reward effort. • Help the learner solve problems. • Correct mistakes. • Build an expectancy of success.
Level 4A: Routine Use	• Reward achievement. • Expand understanding. • Ask questions.
Level 4B: Refinement	• Reward refinement.
Level 5: Integration	• Allow freedom to innovate. • Make the learner a teacher. • Provide growth opportunities.
Level 6: Renewal and Innovation	• Allow time to explore innovations. • Reward creativity.

You can apply the CBAM methodology in two ways: (1) to monitor your own development as a coach, and (2) to track the development of your associates when you are coaching.

To manage and monitor your own development, use the High-Performance Coaching: A Behavioral Checklist," Appendix A, as a guide. Take it now, then use the Contracting for Change model at the end of this chapter to plot your personal development. After you finish this book and complete the various Activities for Discovery and Growth, use the Coaching Checklist again to review your progress.

Stages of Concern (SOC), Statistical Process Control (SPC), and Customer Complaints: A Sample Case Study

As a manager, you have been charged with introducing statistical methods to monitor variation in your area of customer complaints. You have to balance your own learning and applications with the diverse concerns of your associates.

Considering the SOC conceptual framework, you could expect to proceed through phases of understanding. See Figure 2.8.

FIGURE 2.8
STATISTICAL METHODS

	SOC	Things You Might Think or Feel
Time ↓	*Personal*	I've never been good at math! Back to grade school! How can I coach statistics when I don't get it myself? What's going to become of me and my job?
	Task	I'm starting to get the hang of it, but it's tough. It's very hard to do without occasionally checking the formula and going by the book.
	Impact	I wonder how this will affect our productivity. Are my associates benefiting from SPC? Are there other applications?

Recognizing this, you can accommodate your own concerns and seek the support or resources you require. The first step toward getting your needs met (solving the problem) is knowing what your needs are (defining the problem). So, in response to the first chart, you could seek the interventions in Figure 2.9.

You can apply SOC and LOU to the coaching process on two levels:

1. *Coach.* Learning and coaching process for herself. As the individual coach goes through SOC and LOU she learns and applies the theories.

2. *Coach/Associate Relationship.*   As the coach works to help the associate become competent with a new innovation, she can gauge when to use what technique. The coach understands the process that the associate will go through in learning the new innovation. The coach can then be more sensitive to the associate's needs and concerns and is better able to respond to their development.

FIGURE 2.9
POSSIBLE COACHING INTERVENTIONS

	SOC	Things You Might Think or Do
Time	*Personal*	Take a diagnostic math test. Get someone to coach you. Get a good workbook. Learn. Practice. Study carefully the seven basic statistical tools. Master one at a time. Make sure the environment supports you in these learning endeavors.
	Task	These notes and formulas on 3 x 5 cards make use possible. What a lot of work to figure out the best way to chart customer complaints. The **Pareto chart** really helped everyone.
	Impact	Our customers reps are really happy campers! These new graphics on the types of customer complaints and response times really helped our team. Engineering and manufacturing have used our data to make a valuable design package. We've gone six months now without a product failure.

Finally, your ability to empathize with your employees' experiences increases as you master the complicated skills of coaching.

AN ACTIVITY FOR DISCOVERY AND GROWTH: CONTRACTING FOR CHANGE

Purpose

Contracting for change is designed to help you develop your coaching skills. The following form will help you focus your thinking on what you want to learn and what you need to do to accomplish this purpose.

Directions

Complete the form below and keep it handy for reference as you work to improve your effectiveness as a coach. You may wish to discuss your completed form with a more experienced coach, or with someone you've found helpful or supportive in the past.

Self-Contracting Form

Areas in Which I Need to Improve

Specific Learning Goals

Barriers to Learning   Strategies to Overcome Barriers

_____

Action Steps   Completion Date

_____

THE EMPOWERING PARADIGM

Why a New Paradigm?

The world has changed, and to be competitive in a global economy, organizations must change the way they view traditional management functions. The old models and assumptions underlying those models are now obsolete. Traditional management approaches emphasized control, dominance, and prescription, but new approaches must emphasize acknowledgment and empowerment. It seems clear that traditional notions of control provide no guarantee that workers will produce, if for no other reason than the old notions of control are too slow to provide a meaningful assessment of quality, quantity, and responsiveness.

As yet, there is no consensus about what the new organizational paradigm must be. Nevertheless, we can glimpse some of its outlines. One fundamental element of a new model is the belief that people are most effective when they act autonomously within a value framework of common social interest. Every associate is a member of a larger whole. The actions of individuals affect the whole, just as the actions of the whole affect the individuals. Enlightened social interest, a concept originated by Alfred Adler, means that a person or an organization should not act unilaterally for the sake of self-aggrandizement. Rather, people should act in concert with one another so that both individuals and larger social units are bettered as a result. In such a model, it is imperative that people continuously learn and grow. To help their associates do this, coaches must change the relationships between themselves and those whom they coach.

To learn and grow continuously, people must be acutely aware of the assumptions that underlie their decision-making processes, and of the intricate relationship between assumptions and actions. They must realize that assumptions provide nothing more than a map to guide action and that, as a map, assumptions are both incomplete and dynamic. If assumptions remain static in a dynamic environment, they quickly become useless as a guide for action.

To learn and grow continuously, it is also necessary that the relationship between coach and associate, between organization and employee, become one of mutuality. Coaches can no longer prescribe action. Prescription does not enable people to respond creatively to a complex environment, nor to improve those processes created to manage the environment. Rather, they must be participants in looking at reality, critically examining the assumptions being made about that reality, and then changing the model and, therefore, the actions that flow from it.

Empowerment versus Control.   Our world today offers a premium for organizations that learn quickly. How long does it take to get an idea from conception to market? When people and work teams act in an empowered way, they are able to make rapid adaptations to their changing environment. However, in organizations and work teams in which people are controlled from without—by policies, procedures, and accountability requirements—learning takes longer. Why? Because associates are unable to act autonomously—they must continually obtain permission to act. They are more motivated toward achieving some predetermined standard than they are toward striving for quality.

In the learning organization, associates are able to make decisions and share a common vision for making those decisions. They are enabled to learn and to adapt more quickly and with greater creativity. In such systems, a greater premium is placed on highly competent people.

Open versus Closed.   Learning systems are essentially open systems. Openness is required for learning because data are required for learning—the willingness to examine assumptions underlying actions, and so forth.

Holistic versus Elemental.   Another aspect of learning is the ability to see things in relationship. The revolution called "just-in-time manufacturing" came about because innovators in this area saw manufacturing as a loop that started with the supplier, continued through the manufacturing phase, culminated in a delivered product, and initiated a new order for supplies. When seen as a loop of interlocking processes, the manner in which manufacturing is managed changes. Time is seen as a resource in such systems. Anything that increases time in the process should trigger a search for how to improve the process. However, when seen as discrete tasks bearing little relationship to one another, then each system runs independently of the others, and the whole remains out of harmony. Effective coaches help their associates recognize the interdependence of processes. They talk about such interdependence, and they model it.

Flexible versus Rigid.   Assumptions are pragmatic tools to help one deal with a range of situations without having to reinvent the wheel every time. Still, assumptions have only limited usefulness and should therefore be evaluated regularly as to their validity. Learning how to learn is the ability to understand the limited usefulness of one's assumptions and the willingness to let go of them and build new ideas when needed.

Autonomous versus Scripted Action.   Many organizations attempt to "script" the behavior of associates to control it. Although this control may have some usefulness in a stable environment, it is less relevant in today's dynamic environments. To be responsive, associates must have the power to act quickly and with authority.

Action by Consensus versus Unilateral Action. Too often, managers make decisions that affect the whole team without taking the time to seek the cooperation of those who must carry them out. Successful coaches seek consensus before making decisions, for this consensus is fundamental to effective teamwork.

This paradigm shift also changes how organizations view coaching. The old approach to coaching emphasizes the coach's authority and control over the employee; the new approach emphasizes partnership between the coach and the associate.

Productivity and quality are increasingly the domain of committed individuals and/or work teams striving to do their best in a supportive environment. This means managers have to empower their employees to perform at ever-increasing levels of productivity. The process of coaching involves discovering the actions that empower and enable employees to contribute to productivity in an environment that encourages excellence.

What Is Coaching? Two Paradigms. In terms of the control-dominate-prescribe paradigm, coaching is an activity in which the manager trains and guides employees' activities. In terms of the acknowledge-empower paradigm, coaching is a committed partnership between the associate/team and the coach, who serves as a catalyst for performance at the highest possible levels.

The Coach and the Coached. The relationship between a coach and an associate is very different under the new paradigm. Coaching takes place because there is a demand for it. Most people want to be coached, especially when there is a vision of excellence. The coach becomes an integral component of this quest, even though she is rarely able to outperform those who are coached.

In short, for coaching to take place, a shift must occur in the way that the fundamental relationship between the coach and the associate is defined and experienced. In the old paradigm, managers decided and players implemented; in the new paradigm, managers are agents of learning who help people understand how to exceed their current limits. Coaching is the eyes and ears of the relationship, enabling those coached to see what could not be seen, to do what could not be done, to achieve what could not be achieved.

What Is Empowerment?

According to Webster's *Third New International Dictionary*, to empower means to give faculties or abilities to do something. This definition could imply control by another person, but we emphasize the concept of enabling people to create something significant. Empowerment is the process by which a manager enables people in a work team to produce results by providing the necessary environment. Coaching, in our terms, is a process by which the manager empowers individuals and teams by providing whatever support is needed. Coaching is the essential managerial activity that leads to the development of a high-performance (empowered) climate.

The Coach Role in an Empowerment Paradigm

In the new paradigm, the coach and the associate form a partnership with the goal of helping the associate, as an individual or as part of a team, exceed previous performance limits. The role of coach is that of *nurturer* in this case. Just like the mother and father nurture bonding and then separation, the coach nurtures bonding (involvement) and separation (autonomy) in the learner. In normal adult development a mentor is both mother and father and has the role of initiating the person into the rites of autonomy and/or membership in the community. When this is missing in an adult's development, that person's development is arrested. When it is present, the person usually fulfills his or her potential.

The coach is like this nurturer. The coach is not necessarily perfect, but a coach cares about the associate; and he cares about that associate's success in being all that he can be. So the coach nurtures what is good and points out what is not effective. All information is provided to help the associate exceed his present performance limits. The coach provides a new way of seeing a particular aspect of performance and thus opens doors that had been closed.

Mayeroff in *On Caring* (1971) speaks of being at home in this world as one meaning of being healthy. People who are at home feel a sense of belonging, but they also feel a sense of commitment to that which is home. In this sense the coach's role is to create a "home" for the associate. There are two aspects to being at home—one is needing and the other is being needed. The coach needs the associate and communicates this need, and the associate needs the coach. The recognition and acceptance of this relationship between needing and being needed makes coaching, and thus empowerment, possible.

What Are the Dimensions of the Empowering Process?

Coaching creates a climate. When the work environment is perceived as a partnership, different kinds of assumptions about work have to be made. One is obvious—in a partnership, people are equals in most respects. They differ in the roles they play. The coach has one role, the associate has another. One is not more important than the other, for one does not exist without the other. So one way the manager creates a partnership is by relating to the employee as an associate who is involved in a joint journey toward the attainment of excellence.

It is within this matrix of partnership that the processes of empowerment unfold. Jack O. Gibb in his book *Trust* (1978) provides a useful discussion of these processes. He sees a partnership as an opening up between two people. This opening up focuses on various concerns over time. Initially, the issue of trust is foremost. Can trust be created in this relationship? The coach must demonstrate trustworthiness by revealing intentions and proving the ability to do what he or she claims to be able to do.

When the trust barrier is passed, openness occupies the foreground. The coach then provides insights and shares observations with the associate about issues and situations the associate must understand. Of course, the associate must listen.

Openness leads to realization and performance. **Realization** is that process during which the coach and the associate work together toward shared purposes. Through this process of working together the true partnership between the coach and the associate develops, a phase Gibb refers to as *interbeing*.

The Outcomes of Empowerment

Empowerment is desirable and produces something meaningful, if not measurable. What happens when an employee becomes empowered? At the most fundamental level, an empowered associate is a free person, free to discover and to grow from experience. Empowerment is the liberation of the individual's soul to be all it can become.

A free person understands **responsibility** in the sense that she is accountable, able, and willing to act and to accept the consequences of that action. In this regard, it can be said that an empowered associate understands that fear, in essence, results from the irrational belief that she can control all environmental events. Fear stems from the contrast between the illusion of safety and the reality that we are faced with tragedies in life essentially out of our control; however, by our own choices to act or to refrain from acting we gain more control of our lives. In an empowering relationship, the coach leads by example and when necessary helps the associate experience this essential lesson. In the process of learning, the associate develops a sense of **self-efficacy** or ability to control results produced by her skill and effort.

An empowered person understands that power comes from within, not from without. People who are not empowered believe that power lies outside their grasp. Thus, they tend not to act from their souls, but from a need to avoid punishment. Their actions are fear-based. The empowered associate, however, understands that power is an agreement between two people based on mutual trust. Such an individual is coachable because he or she lets go of the need to control. The person lets go because he or she understands that power comes from within. This individual has nothing to fear from letting go; indeed, she has everything to gain.

Courage is also the outcome of empowerment. Courage is the willingness to act despite uncertainty and opposition. Rollo May (1975, p. 12) says courage is a paradox in that, while we must be fully committed to what we believe in, we must also be aware of the possibility that we might be wrong.

An empowered person is a committed person. Even though she might be wrong, the empowered person is willing to engage totally in what she believes. We may not be able to will ourselves to have insight and understanding, but we can will ourselves into total absorption in what we *believe* to be important. This willingness to let go and to get totally involved enables the empowered associate to produce and create—the ultimate outcome of empowerment. It gives her the courage to be productive and confidence that if she applies herself and exercises her skill, she can achieve the goals she selects and thus succeed in her current job as well as in life.

PART 2

Creating a High-Performance, Productive Climate

P art 1 explores the role of coaching in detail. Part 2 examines the context in which it is possible to create excellent performance. The context both contains and enables the communication of role expectations.

Chapter 3: The High-Performance, Productive Environment. This chapter explores the nature of high performance and the qualities of the environment that promote learning. We will

1. Look at the kinds of factors that produce high performance

2. Explore the attributes of a climate that encourages empowerment

3. Demonstrate how you might go about creating this environment

Chapter 4: Developing Empowering Relationships. How do you, the coach, go about facilitating the establishment of the technical aspects of the high-performance environment? This chapter reviews the processes of setting goals, establishing performance standards for goal achievement, and facilitating self-regulation from the empowerment perspective.

Chapter 5: Laying the Foundation for the High-Performance Environment. Here we discuss how the coach facilitates the creation of a climate in which self-regulation and empowerment are possible. Climate creation is a key dimension of how a coach can demonstrate true ownership of process.

Many traits or characteristics are associated with the concept of empowerment. One focuses directly on the relationship between quality outcomes in life and the belief held by the person—based on reinforcement history—that she can couple her ability and skill with physical and mental effort and produce desired outcomes or results. This belief is exemplified by assuming personal responsibility for life's results as opposed to projecting blame onto someone or something else such as luck, chance, fate, or task difficulty. An internal **locus of control** is characterized by giving oneself permission to act, as opposed to seeking permission from external sources. We are empowered when we generate energy internally, as opposed to importing energy from the surrounding environment.

An empowering organizational climate expresses permission, protection, and collaboration—an organizational "can do" attitude. Leaders provide a sense of approval and support for any associate making a decision. Through recognition and encouragement, leaders manifest permission and support for self-management, including interventions initiated by an associate that impact leaders. The organization's leaders need and want all associates to have and to exercise control over the critical tasks in their jobs. By doing so, leadership provides another building block in supporting internal control for empowered people.

The organization itself becomes empowered when its employees have the power to develop solutions and the permission to act in relation to those solutions. This permission can be explicit or implicit and is based on goal alignment. It is much easier to have an empowered environment when the goals of the organization are aligned with the goals of its individual employees. This goal alignment replaces a "we/they" mentality with an "us" mentality. With goal alignment and an "us" mentality, empowered employees perform. All topics related to performance can be discussed. Discussion, reflection, and critical examination help the person, team, and organization reach more challenging goals.

People who value openness in relationships with other human beings encourage full participation in the enterprise. Conformity and not rocking the boat were frequently valued in the organization of the past. In an empowered organization, people place value on learning and the ability to analyze and solve problems. In addition, both employees and the organizational structure, policies, and operating principles support and promote creativity and innovation. This encouragement of creativity and innovation is manifested in employee attitudes such as, "I am the best person for my job," "I have the authority to get my job done," "I am confident that I can do my job," "My associates communicate to me that I am the best person for my job," "I feel I can talk to anyone I need to in order to do my job," "I feel I have received the necessary training for my job," and "I can take the risks necessary to do my job well." Individuals and organizations experiencing empowerment are set free. They become captains of their own fates. They work with the knowledge that they are capable and are responsible for the success of their own self-energized quests.

OPEN ORGANIZATIONS: A PARADIGM FOR UNDERSTANDING "THE HUMAN SIDE OF ENTERPRISE"*

A useful way to think about the context in which coaching takes place is in terms of the *open organization paradigm*. From this perspective, three characteristics— integrated wholeness, internal responsiveness, and external responsiveness—may be used to describe an entire organization and its subsystems. The *open organization model* examines these characteristics at individual, group, and organizational levels. It also indicates the interchange among them. See Figure 3.1.

At the Individual Level:

- Unity relates to self-concept, which is organized by personal values.

- Internal responsiveness refers to awareness of one's wants and needs, and permission to fulfill them.

- External responsiveness relates to interaction with others that produces mutually beneficial results.

At the Group or Team Level:

- Unity involves concern with and commitment to team goals or purpose, supported by shared values.

- Internal responsiveness means group members are aware of one another and are sensitive to other member's needs and wants.

- External responsiveness refers to cooperative interaction with groups or components within the organization.

At the Organization Level:

- Unity involves organizing according to purpose and having a sense of where the organization is headed—vision.

- Internal responsiveness involves cooperative interaction between the different components within the organization.

- External responsiveness refers to the way the organization interacts with the community—its vendors and the quality of products and services provided to customers.

---

* Doug McGregor's classic book, *The Human Side of Enterprise*, concerns the critical aspects of healthy work environments. In his now famous Theory X and Theory Y, McGregor emphasized the values that underlie our assumptions about people. He saw Theory X as those values that cause one to believe that workers must be driven or directed by others. Theory Y values, on the other hand, assume that a person is self-directing and self-motivated and simply needs a supportive environment and clear goals to perform well.

FIGURE 3.1
OPEN ORGANIZATION MODEL

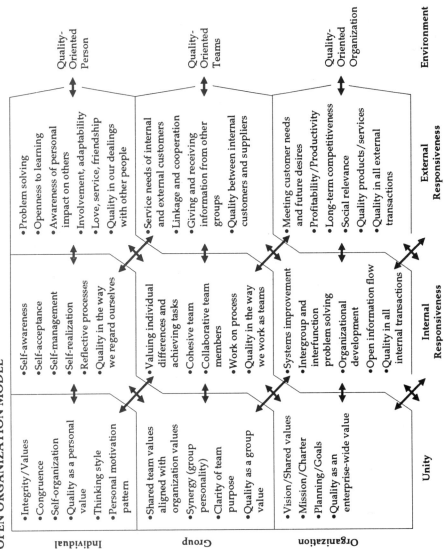

The right-hand edge of the open organization model represents the concept of overall openness at all levels.

In terms of this model, then, the context in which coaching is most likely to be effective is in an open organization, which has a high degree of alignment between values and goals, of internal responsiveness, and of external responsiveness at organizational, group/team, and individual levels. If, however, any one of these processes is dysfunctional, the whole cannot function effectively. The chapters in this section can help you create an environment that nurtures learning.

SYSTEMS THINKING: FROM A FIELD THEORIST'S PARADIGM—VINTAGE LEWIN

Lewin (1969) viewed social systems (families, work teams, or organizations) as existing in a quasi-stationary state, with equilibrium being maintained by system-balancing forces that create and restrain against disequilibrium. This notion as applied to the human body involves such things as blood sugar balance, cell hydration, and body temperature, and such stress reactions and counteractions as the adrenal glands' secreting adrenaline in an emergency and noradrenalin reestablishing a balance after the emergency. Those who raise tropical fish are familiar with the critical nature of maintaining appropriate pH balance and temperature ranges in the tank, along with other requirements for filtering the tank water.

To demonstrate an application of field thinking, Lewin developed a method called **Force Field Analysis**. This method can be applied to the problem of improving associate performance with internal customers. The model in Figure 3.2 reflects the basic components of all systems: Context (work environment), Inputs, Processes, Outputs (products), and Impact (CIPPI). This model gives a framework for identifying and understanding the various forces at play in any system. Human systems are basically open systems, meaning that energy exchanges or interfaces with other systems occur on the boundaries. Energy permeates boundaries in exchange with the surroundings. The outputs of the system impact on a broad spectrum of the business outputs. For example, Chevron Exploration and Production Services (CEPS) Company is a high-technology company that provides concentrated information products and services, especially software. They service the entire spectrum of the oil industry from geophysical exploration through production. In order to enhance the potential for learning to occur in their organization, they had each person in a key leadership role go through a self-evaluation on eighteen key dimensions of leadership. They completed self-assessment forms including the 16PF (Sixteen Personality Factors—a personality test developed by Raymond Cattell and Associates) and the LMJD (Leadership Management Job Dimensions Survey, developed by Oscar Mink and Keith Owen of the Somerset Consulting

FIGURE 3.2
AN OPEN SYSTEMS MODEL

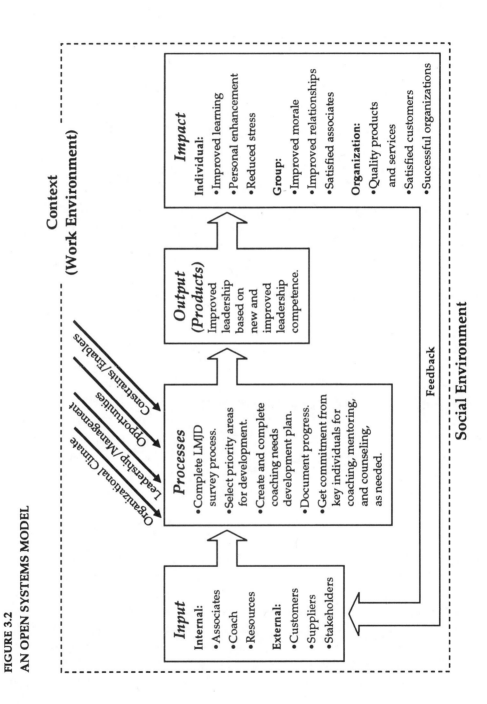

Group), which targets eighteen dimensions of competencies critical to leadership. The CEPS leadership group also asked all associates—peers, subordinates, and current supervisors—to complete the LMJD. Each person was given a series of comprehensive reports targeting leadership competencies that could be developed further should the recipient choose to do so. The output of this process had potential impact on

- The individual
- The work teams they can influence
- The organization
- Customers
- Vendors

To continue to develop your thinking about what makes up a high-performance system, we need to discuss some notions about environment. Chapter 3 discusses environment and performance.

C H A P T E R 3

The High-Performance, Productive Environment

PURPOSE

If you have chosen to read this book, you probably want to know how to improve performance—yours and others'. If you are responsible for achieving goals through your efforts and those of others, you will find this chapter especially useful. The performance of all members of any work group impacts your personal achievement; similarly, your performance impacts your associates' achievements.

This dynamic places you in an interesting position. Your destiny as well as the destiny of your associates is inextricably intertwined: Their performance affects you; your performance affects them. There are, however, tools available to you that allow you to maximize your chances of achieving success—both on your own and by being involved in another's learning. These tools include understanding the ingredients of the high-performance environment and the methods for creating such an environment.

What does the high-performance environment look like? What values and attitudes influence high performance? In this environment, how do people feel? How do they behave? The concept of **climate** refers to context—the values and attitudes held about people that create the strategies and unwritten rules of behavior. These strategies tell members of a particular environment what actions encourage and support others. Climate imposes constraints on performance. Leaders must carefully scrutinize the work climate to remove hidden constraints on performance.

GOALS

The specific goals of this chapter are to

- Increase your understanding of the ingredients required for creating a high-performance climate

- Encourage you to work with others to create a high-performance climate

- Reflect on values that govern strategies required for a high-performance climate

- Provide you with methods and tactics for actually creating a high-performance environment

INGREDIENTS OF THE HIGH-PERFORMANCE, PRODUCTIVE ENVIRONMENT

There are many ways of looking at something you wish to understand, many frameworks. A framework is useful because it helps you structure your thinking and understand the situation better. However, we often forget that other frameworks are possible. We get stuck in the frame of reference in which we personally operate and, in the process, limit our ability to create and innovate. Joel Barker (1985) calls this "paradigm paralysis."

In this chapter, we explore two traditional ways of looking at the climate or context of high performance. Each is significant in its own right, but when considered alone neither offers the insight they provide when they are combined to form a new unified whole. Our approach derives from the *field theory* thinking of Kurt Lewin. The first part of our framework uses the personality psychologist's way of looking at behavior—the trait view. The second uses the behavioral psychologist's view—the behavioral view. Finally, we combine these views to offer a third, more holistic or field thinking, paradigm.

THREE WAYS OF LOOKING AT HIGH PERFORMANCE

The Individual/Trait Viewpoint of High Performance

Individual psychologists approach high performance by studying the individual differences associated with excellence. This perspective has often been called the *trait perspective*. From this perspective, high performance is an individual attribute. Accordingly, some people have the potential to achieve and some do not. Thus, the task of the organization is to choose people who have the ability and the desire to achieve.

Many books describe the characteristics of the high performer. For example, writers like Charles Garfield (1986) have studied people who were identified as high performers. These writers discovered that high performers have several characteristics (traits) in common.

1. *Achievement Orientation.* High performers have a great desire to achieve because they have developed a dream about what they want for themselves.

2. *Self-confidence.* High performers have a positive mental attitude that allows them to act with high levels of confidence.

3. *Self-control.* High performers have a highly developed sense of self-discipline.

4. *Competence.* High performers have developed the specific ability or competence to achieve in their chosen areas.

5. *Persistence.* High performers have a bias toward action. They are "can do" people who are willing to work hard continually to achieve their goals.

From this point of view, you can identify and select people capable of high performance simply by understanding their psychological makeup. Unfortunately, the tools available for such selection are only partially successful for identifying such individuals.

The Behavioral/Environmental Viewpoint of High Performance

The behavioral point of view is also useful in understanding high performance. From this point of view, the challenge of achieving improved performance is simply a matter of eliciting and then reinforcing the right behaviors. High performance is achieved through the systematic management of rewards and punishments. The organization's task is thus to create an environment that elicits and then rewards the desired behaviors.

Several influential books discuss the behavioral approach to achieve high performance. For example, *The One-Minute Manager* by Ken Blanchard provides a design for improving high performance. The manager assesses current performance, develops a plan for the associate, provides feedback, and delivers rewards and punishments depending on the outcome produced by the associate.

Extensive research on the necessary conditions for social learning has identified five ingredients of the high-performance environment.

1. *Climate.* The social or interpersonal world needs to be positive, supportive, and conducive to risk taking. Sufficient trust must be present to provide the context for executing simple social agreements and action plans. A positive, trusting social climate encourages learning (skill acquisition) and problem solving. It instills in the associate a sense of confidence in her ability to learn and to perform at the level that meets expectations of both self and others.

2. *Direction.* The high-performance environment helps establish clear goals and informs people about the required standards in achieving these clear goals. This environment provides both the performer and the learner with clear performance guidelines.

3. *Opportunity.* Once the goal is established, the individual must have the opportunity to perform the correct behavior. This includes the provision of

whatever tools, materials, processes, training, education, or development are needed. Individual skills and abilities already present must be identified and applied.

4. *Consequences.* Every behavior produces a range of consequences or results. Some results match desired outcomes and are considered positive. Other results create a mismatch with desired outcomes and are considered negative or are ignored. Then feedback about the consequences (results) of behavior as they relate to the established goal or problem must be provided.

5. *Incentives.* Finally, the person must receive a valued incentive (or payoff) for positive behavior and a negatively valued outcome (no payoff) for negative behavior.

From this point of view, the role of the manager is simply to manage behavior by managing the processes that elicit the desired behavior and by delivering the consequences of that behavior. This example describes the prescriptive approach to management that characterizes many contemporary work environments.

Most managers probably adopt one or the other of these models, often to their own detriment. For example, one consequence of relying too much on a trait explanation is that managers tend to overestimate the effects of these factors on performance, while ignoring the environment they have created. Thus, they often blame failures on individuals rather than asking themselves if the environment facilitates performance. In reality, it may be their own management style or the assumptions they make about people and work that inhibit individual and group performance.

On the other hand, when managers emphasize the environmental explanation alone, they may also experience failure. Too much attention to the external environment and not enough attention paid to the values, attitudes, and skills of the people managed, or to the culture of the organization, can also produce poor results.

Modern organizational psychology has shown that neither of these points of view is sufficient to achieve high performance. To understand high performance, a much broader view is required.

The Person-Situation/Interactionist Perspective, or Applying Systems Theory to Human Systems

In modern organizational psychology, the concept that behavior is determined by both personal factors and environmental factors has taken hold. Behavior is a function of the person and the environment in interplay. Because high performance is a function of this interaction, this view is called the *interactionist* or *person-situation perspective*. Every event or action in a human system has an impact on someone somewhere else in the system.

When you adopt this point of view, you accept the premise that high performance is a process of creating environmental conditions that enable high performance. At the same time, you must choose and develop associates who both can and want to perform at the highest possible levels and who expect that coupling their skills with effort will produce positive results. When you examine, simultaneously, all potential forces, and work with these forces to improve both process and performance, you are engaged in a field thinking paradigm. Kurt Lewin,* the father of social psychology in the United States, first applied this methodology to performance problems.

A MODEL OF HIGH PERFORMANCE

From the person-situation point of view, high-performance people develop as a function of the person, the environment, and the interaction between the person and the environment. High performance results when the interplay between you and your world optimizes your potential to perform.

To understand high performance you must understand how some of these diverse interactions might occur. Since we have briefly discussed the person and the environment, it is instructive to think about their interaction. Can you imagine a situation in which you could get sustained high performance from people without their having formed some kind of positive attachment to or identification with the environment? Of course, we can easily imagine situations in which people are coerced into performing through fear and constant monitoring, but it is harder to imagine circumstances under which self-directed people would engage in sustained effort in the absence of such an attachment, especially in a determined effort to achieve continuous improvement.

Recently we have come to understand more clearly what it takes to create positive identification with and commitment to the organization. In order to develop a positive identification with the organization in your associates, leaders must

- Demonstrate an alignment between personal and organizational goals

- Show people how they can meet their needs

- Show concern

- Help create mutual trust and respect

- Demonstrate personal competence

---

* See K. Lewin (1969) for initial reading. His thoughts also influence this book through such other authors as Argyris, O. Mink, and Ron and Gordon Lippitt.

- Behave in a consistent or dependable manner

- Respond meaningfully to individual needs

Positive identification with the organization releases in individuals the willingness to work hard. The associate involvement also increases commitment.

You can do a number of things to promote positive identification with the environment.

- Demonstrate that you are worthy of your associates' respect by acting with personal integrity.

- Involve your associates in the decision-making, learning, and problem-solving processes.

- Establish conditions under which collaboration can occur.

- Get others involved in setting goals, defining problems, and discovering solutions to those problems.

An often-replicated finding from social psychology indicates that if you can get people involved in a collaborative process, their level of commitment to that process will increase. Their attitudes toward others and the organization will become more positive.

Table 3.1 depicts our notions of a model of a high-performance environment.

TABLE 3.1
THE HIGH-PERFORMANCE ENVIRONMENT

	Ability	Value	Action	Performance
Person	Can Do (Skills and aptitudes)	Want (Attitudes and desire)	Try (Belief about ability to succeed)	Goals (Desired outcomes)
Environment	Opportunity (Clear expectations)	Incentive (Valued rewards)	Feedback (Respond to outcomes)	Vision (Meaning, focus, direction, actions)

Stated in another way, high performance is possible only in situations in which there is a match between the person and the performance environment. One purpose of coaching is to help create this match.

THE CULTURAL VIEW OF HIGH PERFORMANCE

The interplay of individuals and the organization (its values, purposes, systems, and processes) over time leads to the development of the organizational culture. In our view, culture is the set of interconnecting, yet largely unwritten, rules that organize behavior. This unwritten or silent language affects perceptions and guides individual and collective behavior. These unwritten rules define what anthropologists call the *workscape*. The workscape can be productive or it can be unproductive. In a productive workscape, the rules encourage and support high performance; in an unproductive workscape, the rules encourage and support inferior performance. Because few existing bureaucracies emphasize competence and individual development, most organizations produce mediocrity.

When one looks into the nature of the productive workscape, several characteristics are evident. The following processes represent six key dimensions of the high-performance workscape:

1. *Vision, Shared Purpose, and Leadership.* The productive workscape is held together by the glue of a shared vision, shared purposes, and goals. Vision, shared purpose, and goals depict *why* we exist. People are there because they value the purposes of the organization or team. The leadership of the team or organization serves to provide focus. The shared purpose and the leader's actions must be consistent. A leader's actions must reinforce the purposes and values of the group and reflect the overall vision of the organization. The leader's role is to consistently identify, discuss, and integrate the team's purpose and vision with the organization's purpose and vision.

2. *Shared Values and Teamwork.* In a productive workscape, people trust and accept one another. They work together to accomplish a shared purpose and establish shared values through trust and understanding of others.

3. *Individual Autonomy and Freedom.* In the productive workscape, the work to be done and the people with the expertise to do it are more important than structure or position. Structure may even be invented in order to place the customer (internal or external) at the top, ensuring that all employees support customers with quality products and services. There is little concern with status and a lot of concern with sharing skills and teaching. People are willing to work hard because they identify with the job.

4. *Positive Relationships Characterized by Feedback and Problem Solving.* In a productive workscape, people are focused on performance, not on status or hierarchy. Again, the goal is central, not someone's position or authority. In such a climate there is give and take, shared learning, and continuous searching for ways to improve products and services.

5. *Management of Focus.* Productive workscapes support meaningful goal accomplishment. People have the tools they need to succeed, the opportunities to succeed, and supportive management to help identify and remove or reduce constraints so they can produce quality products and services. All leaders must work to provide the practical requirements of achieving purpose—labor, materials, tools, training, methods, and so on.

6. *Work Structure.* In productive cultures, people know what the right thing to do is. They know what skills are required for accomplishment and how to use them autonomously. In such cultures, personal causation is a reality and people believe they count. Also in productive cultures, associates know both what is expected of them and how to use feedback to improve performance. That is, work is defined in terms of specific processes and productivity outcomes.

Productive cultures become understandable. Everyone knows what to do and why to do it. Further, they know the right thing to do at any moment. Productive cultures become coherent or unified. Everything goes together and supports the main purpose of the organization. Words and deeds correspond with purpose. Such cultures also are open. They are aware of and responsive to the changing nature of internal and external reality; therefore, they frequently examine what is and is not working and let go of what is no longer relevant and acquire new ways of doing things.

To summarize, then, when you have the right people who share the same values, goals, and purposes, and give them opportunities and incentives to excel in a supportive environment in which they feel free (empowered) to contribute as a team, then the workscape will be productive.

CREATING THE HIGH-PERFORMANCE ENVIRONMENT

As a coach/manager you play a key role in creating the workscape of productivity. So how do you go about creating the high-performance environment? The suggested strategies that follow are a result of our personal experiences in creating such environments and of our studies and observations of successful leaders and coaches. We believe we understand much of what they do so well from observing and interpreting the impact of their coaching practices. Reflect on these ideas and our illustrations: identify notions that might work for you, and then experiment by applying the principles and observing the results. Did the result produced match the result intended? If so, great! If not, reexamine the goal and try a new experiment. First, we look at the "pillars" of the high-performance environment; then, we describe some processes that have proven effective.

Twelve Pillars of the High-Performance Environment

There are twelve pillars of high-performance climates. When in place, these pillars help create an environment that encourages performance through involvement, self-management, commitment, and a sense of autonomy and empowerment.

Pillar 1—Shared Vision.   Develop a shared vision for your team or organization. Let others know what your personal vision is. *Vision* describes the ultimate purpose of a group. It provides a frame of reference within which to organize work behavior. Vision says to everyone, this is why we are here, this is who we are, this is what we produce, in terms meaningful and understandable to the group.

However, it is not enough just to develop a vision. You must also get people to own the vision, to share it, and to commit to it. Involving others in forming the vision encourages sharing and commitment. To get others to share in your vision, you need to communicate openly and be responsive to inquiries and suggestions. Involving others with you in creating meaning enables the team to achieve its purpose(s). All associates need to become a part of the vision and to share an understanding of its importance to them personally and to their work group and the organization.

Pillar 2—Shared Values.   Develop shared values for the team and the organization. Vision is to ends as values are to process. There are many ways to achieve a goal, some of which you may value, some of which you may reject. For example, some colleges value winning football games so much that they have motivated recruits to attend their universities with illegal inducements, such as money and cars. What a value statement! "Winning is more important than obeying the rules of the land." If you want your team to live by a certain set of values, then you must develop those values together, with each person contributing to them. You have to model norms to your associates through your own actions and techniques. Living according to agreed-on values will produce positive consequences and experiences.

Values and related assumptions are critical to achievement. Often, values are not openly discussed at work, and thus remain obscure. The values that guide an employee's behavior must be shared, defined, and experienced by the work group. They then form a basis or foundation for actions that produce consistent and necessary results—quality in products and services, productivity, and continuous improvement. If there is a difference in values, then time must be taken to search for a super-ordinate value, a statement or concept that serves to bridge the seeming differences.

Pillar 3—Goals.   Together, develop goals that are both important (worthy), specific, and constant with the emphasized values. Goals are the ideal guides for short-term outcomes or objectives that define the achievements needed to realize the vision and attain the purposes of the team. Every team member should have performance goals. We have found that teams with individual and team goals outperform those without goals or with goals that are too vague.

Pillar 4—Focus. Provide focus by developing processes that help team members act in ways consistent with the team's *mission*—the goods and/or services that you provide and to whom. The shared values and work goals you have mutually agreed on, team structure, other components of the cultural or symbolic system (leadership style, staffing, skills, strategy, science and technology, systems), political considerations (for example, career concerns, life-style and family, and task interactions), and person-organization needs, provide the context for performance and desired outcomes. All of these provide opportunities for you and the team to focus your associates' attention on what is really important. For instance, if you want every team member to identify shared values crucial to the task(s), you could identify these values through team discussions focused on the behavior of the team. When assessing how the team is doing, you and the team would discover and examine the underlying or governing values that either enhance or inhibit team performance. There is, however, another aspect. This is what you do when you as team leader or manager provide the emotional and technical support that is so crucial for your own achievement and the achievement of others.

Pillar 5—Desire for Productivity. Leaders and managers must make clear that they value and want productivity. They must assure that pursuing accomplishment is meaningful. They do this by communicating the value of both productivity and the associates. When associates know they are in a productive situation and that they are valued, then they will use their knowledge and work hard.

Pillar 6—Support for Accomplishment. When associates see that leaders provide them the tools, money, equipment, time, resources to produce, and the markets to buy/use their outputs, they will work hard.

Pillar 7—The Right People. Make sure people can succeed. If you want your team members to act a certain way and to perform at a certain level, you must make sure that they are able to do so. Each person must be competent to perform in her own roles. "Hire for quality, train for excellence." Hire the best people you can hire, then coach them to perform according to the requirements of the job, the team, and the organization.

Pillar 8—Teamwork. To achieve the synergies possible when sharing a dream, people must work together. Trust and mutual acceptance and creative use of one another's differences seem to be the foundation stones on which shared values emerge and effective teamwork is built. As coach/leader of the team, you are the key person in setting the standards for trust and mutual understanding and the acceptance and use of various individual talents.

Pillar 9—Empowerment and Autonomy.   The antithesis of empowerment is prescription and unilateral action. For people to realize their potential, and thus for the team to realize its potential, each person must feel free to contribute to team goals as most appropriate to that individual, and to negotiate openly with leaders and other associates. An adaptive team does not function according to strictly defined procedures; rather it is flexible, creative, and responsive to customer needs and desires. To achieve their potential, people must feel empowered to act with volition. This means they must feel free to contribute what they alone can uniquely contribute. It also means that they must be able to discuss every aspect of their work or the team's work and express every relevant, meaningful feeling.

Pillar 10—Leadership.   Human systems—companies, religious organizations, schools, teams, people—need leadership. People in general say we simply need better leadership. In what sense might this be true? The successful coach must lead by providing a climate or context that enables every person on the team to contribute fully. This might mean teaching someone a new skill, it might mean encouraging the person to try something she has been afraid to try, it might mean listening to someone share her grief, or any one of a hundred other things. No matter what it takes to enable people, the coach/team leader must ensure that the conditions supporting empowerment exist.

Pillar 11—Feedback, Feedthrough, and Problem Solving.   Provide people with accurate information about what they are doing in relation to performance goals. Every successful coach is adept at giving people feedback about their behavior versus their performance goals. Feedback and feedthrough provide information about the extent to which a person's actions are consistent with stated expectations (feedback) and with stated goals and values (**feedthrough**). Successful coaches, parents, teachers, and managers have in common the ability to give people effective feedback. Feedback is effective when the recipients desire information, listen, and, if need be, change their actions to improve results. Because improvement needs to be continuous—a learning process—valid information about performance, customer satisfaction, and values needs to be continuous.

Pillar 12—Rewards.   People who have incentives they value normally provide the needed effort. People work hardest when their efforts allow them to get what they want, need, and value. No leader or coach can motivate another person. People are motivated to the extent that their efforts lead to outcomes they desire and value. The high-performance environment must provide the opportunity to achieve these outcomes.

ACTIVITIES FOR DISCOVERY AND GROWTH: SUCCESS STRATEGIES FOR CREATING THE HIGH-PERFORMANCE ENVIRONMENT

Now that you have the conceptual tools you need to create a high-performance environment, you need to implement these ideas! To get started on becoming an excellent coach, work through the following activities. Your associates will learn what is important by doing and by reflecting on their actions. You will learn how to become an excellent coach by doing and then reflecting on your experiences. If you are confused by a problem, ask associates to challenge your thinking and suggest alternatives. Often this process will enhance your learning.

Activity 1
The Peak Performance Environment:
A Snapshot of Where You Are Now

Purpose

This activity provides a tool for systematically examining your environment. To what extent are the keys discussed in place in your environment? The goals of this instrument are to

1. Help you diagnose your current work team

2. Pinpoint areas of strength and weakness

3. Facilitate the change process

Directions

Your work environment either facilitates or inhibits high performance. This forty-item survey assesses what we currently know about high-performance environments.

1. Rate your current environment's performance on each item in the profile.

2. Sum the scores for each dimension and plot the totals on the Performance Potential Profile graph.

The Organizational Performance Potential Profile

Circle the number that represents where your organization is now in relation to each item.

Rating Scale

1	2	3	4	5	6	7	8	9
Not Typical				Somewhat Typical				Very Typical

Dimension 1: Clarity of Vision

1 2 3 4 5 6 7 8 9   1. The purpose of our work is clear and shared.

1 2 3 4 5 6 7 8 9   2. Everyone knows what the purposes of the team are.

1 2 3 4 5 6 7 8 9   3. There is consensus among team members regarding the team's vision.

1 2 3 4 5 6 7 8 9   4. The vision is frequently discussed among the team.

1 2 3 4 5 6 7 8 9   5. The team vision is the focus of all our activities.

Dimension 2: Clarity of Values

1 2 3 4 5 6 7 8 9   6. The values of the team are clearly defined.

1 2 3 4 5 6 7 8 9   7. Team members know the values.

1 2 3 4 5 6 7 8 9   8. The team members all share the values of the group.

1 2 3 4 5 6 7 8 9   9. Management behavior is clearly consistent with the accepted team values.

1 2 3 4 5 6 7 8 9   10. Group norms encourage people to do their very best.

Dimension 3: Clarity of Mission

1 2 3 4 5 6 7 8 9   11. Each team member can state clearly what product or service we provide and for whom.

1 2 3 4 5 6 7 8 9   12. Each member of our team is committed to our mission.

1 2 3 4 5 6 7 8 9   13. Our shared values are compatible with our mission.

1 2 3 4 5 6 7 8 9   14. Our performance focuses on our mission.

1 2 3 4 5 6 7 8 9   15. Our customers understand our mission.

Dimension 4: *Goal Clarity*

1 2 3 4 5 6 7 8 9   16. We have established clearly defined goals and objectives.

1 2 3 4 5 6 7 8 9   17. Everyone on this team knows what she must do to succeed.

1 2 3 4 5 6 7 8 9   18. The goals we are expected to accomplish are clearly consistent with team values.

1 2 3 4 5 6 7 8 9   19. We frequently discuss how we are doing in terms of living up to our values.

1 2 3 4 5 6 7 8 9   20. Everyone knows how the team's goals contribute to the success of the organization.

Dimension 5: *Providing Focus*

1 2 3 4 5 6 7 8 9   21. There is a great deal of open sharing regarding how to achieve our team goals.

1 2 3 4 5 6 7 8 9   22. My job contributes to the success of the team.

1 2 3 4 5 6 7 8 9   23. We all work together in order to achieve team success.

1 2 3 4 5 6 7 8 9   24. When a problem arises, it is solved immediately.

1 2 3 4 5 6 7 8 9   25. Team members have clearly defined roles that clearly relate to team purposes.

Dimension 6: Developing Competence

1 2 3 4 5 6 7 8 9   26. My manager/supervisor makes sure that I am able to perform the work expected of me.

1 2 3 4 5 6 7 8 9   27. I have the resources I need to do my best.

1 2 3 4 5 6 7 8 9   28. I train myself before I am expected to produce results.

1 2 3 4 5 6 7 8 9   29. I am free to do my job using the best methods available to me.

1 2 3 4 5 6 7 8 9   30. I am given many opportunities to learn and grow in my work.

Dimension 7: Success Feedback

1 2 3 4 5 6 7 8 9   31. I am well trained to accomplish the goals expected of me.

1 2 3 4 5 6 7 8 9   32. I am held accountable for the goals I am expected to accomplish.

1 2 3 4 5 6 7 8 9   33. I get feedback about my performance on a regular basis.

1 2 3 4 5 6 7 8 9   34. The feedback I get helps me perform better.

1 2 3 4 5 6 7 8 9   35. If I make a mistake, I am shown how to perform more effectively.

Dimension 8: Incentive

1 2 3 4 5 6 7 8 9   36. Excellent performance is recognized and rewarded.

1 2 3 4 5 6 7 8 9   37. I am given many opportunities for earning rewards for high performance.

1 2 3 4 5 6 7 8 9   38. The rewards I get are directly tied to the goals I am expected to achieve.

1 2 3 4 5 6 7 8 9   39. My manager/supervisor expects me to perform at the highest possible level.

1 2 3 4 5 6 7 8 9   40. In this team, poor performance is recognized and improved.

Scoring Grid

Clarity of Vision	Clarity of Values	Clarity of Mission	Goal Clarity
1. __	6. __	11. __	16. __
2. __	7. __	12. __	17. __
3. __	8. __	13. __	18. __
4. __	9. __	14. __	19. __
5. __	10. __	15. __	20. __
Totals __	__	__	__

Providing Focus	Developing Competence	Success Feedback	Incentive
21. __	26. __	31. __	36. __
22. __	27. __	32. __	37. __
23. __	28. __	33. __	38. __
24. __	29. __	34. __	39. __
25. __	30. __	35. __	40. __
Totals __	__	__	__

Now plot the Total ratings from the Scoring Grid to the Performance Potential Profile. The height of the bar reflects the overall strength of your environment at this time.

Performance Potential Profile

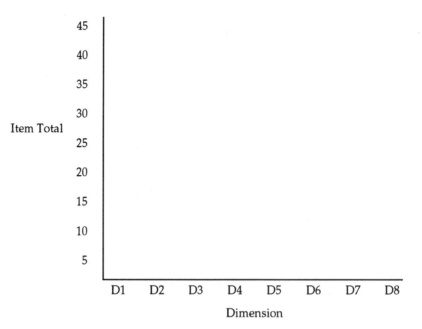

Interpretation

1. What are the most important areas of need facing your team at this time?

2. What are the consequences of this situation in terms of team functioning, problem solving, and relating?

3. Is this an acceptable condition at this time?

4. What changes seem to be needed at this time?

5. What are the first steps in this change?

Activity 2
Developing Team Values and Philosophy

Purpose

Underlying the organization's stated vision/mission is a set of assumptions or values about what is important and worth living for. These values consciously or unconsciously act as a framework for defining the vision/mission, deciding what is attainable, and even defining reality. That is why it is so important for the coach and the team to clarify and define their values. The goals of this activity are to

1. Develop core team values

2. Write a managerial/team philosophy statement that reflects these values

3. Build commitment to these values

Directions

Step 1: Scenario of the Future.   Develop a scenario of a preferred future for the organization, and from this identify the values that undergird this hoped-for state.

Step 2: "Prouds and Sorries."   Have team members think about those experiences in their personal life history that have made them feel proud and those experiences that have led them to feel sorry. Follow the procedure outlined below.

1. Record your "prouds and sorries." (e.g., Charles: "Our team was successful in achieving zero defects over a six-month period.")

2. Go back through these statements and clarify the values you see reflected there. (e.g., Leader: "Charles seems to place a high value on 'achievement' and 'teamwork.' What did you hear?")

3. Third, think about the values. What kinds of behaviors would be typical of your team, team members, or you if these values were to become an integral part of day-to-day working together?

Processing

Answer the following questions.

1. What are the core values of your team going to be?

2. What values currently seem to be guiding behavior in your team? That is, what behaviors are typical (normative) of your group now, and what values are revealed in these behaviors?

3. If you discover any discrepancies in your hoped-for and expressed values, what has to be done to develop a culture in which the new values are the norm?

Identifying Core Team Values

Core Values	**Behavioral Implications**
We believe in . . .	We operate such that . . .

Activity 3
Developing Your Purposes

Purpose

The most typical characteristic of really successful organizations is the presence of a vision or mission with which people identify and to which they are passionately committed. The goals of this activity are to

1. Develop a clear sense of your group's mission, and

2. Communicate this to the group, that is, identify with the team's stated goals.

Directions

Think about what the major output of your group is or should be. What goods or services do you provide and for whom? If your group is within a larger organization, think of your team as a provider of goods or services to other groups in the organization. What do you provide these groups? What is your group's mission in view of this relationship to other groups in the organization? For example, the mission of an information services group might be to provide quality information in a timely manner to other divisions in a company.

Write your mission statement, and then share it with your subordinates. At the same time, get team members to write what they perceive the team's mission to be. Allow them to share their views. Get their reactions and listen to them describe how to make the mission a more vital representation of what your group is accountable for.

Processing

When you have written and discussed the mission, think next about how to make the mission the starting point for all that the team does. How do you get people to identify with the mission and to perceive it as their own? To facilitate this process, answer the following questions:

1. What is the main output of your team?

2. Who are your customers?

3. What does it mean to provide excellent service to your customers?

4. What is your mission? Write your mission statement in your own words.

Identifying the Team Mission

Key Customer(s):

Key Output(s) provided these customers, e.g., services, products, information, interactions:

Standard of measuring the team's success:

Mission of the team:

Activity 4
Building Commitment to a Shared Value System

Purpose

It is one thing to develop a list of values; it is another to build a climate in which the values become a reality. The purposes of this activity are to

1. Help you think through the steps needed to build a shared commitment to the team's values

2. Encourage people to behave in a way that is consistent with the stated (internalized) values

Directions

Here, you must walk a fine line as leader and as facilitator. On the one hand, the values are not an option; on the other hand, people conform best to values they have freely chosen. These steps may prove helpful to you and your team:

1. Discuss in your team what the new values are to be.

2. Look at the current values. Remember, openness is important in any team, and if you punish people for telling the truth then they will not tell the truth. Record the norms and the behaviors that reveal values at work.

Current Values	Norms	Business and Behavioral Implications
A.	A.1.	List: • Questions you might ask to confirm this norm. • Things you might hear people say or see them do.

3. Ask team members to think about how to build in the new values. Ask them how they can help you do this.

New Values	New Norms	Business and Behavioral Implications
A.	A.1.	List: • Questions you might ask to confirm this norm. • Things you might hear people say or see them do.

4. Make a plan to develop these new values that recognizes the unproductive norms identified above. You may accomplish this by developing processes that allow you to monitor what is going on and to keep your team on track. For example, regular team problem-solving meetings may effectively facilitate problem solving and productive norm development.

Activity 5
Setting Your Course

Purpose

Your success as a coach depends on whether everyone in your group makes a commitment to shared goals. The goals of this activity are to

1. Develop a process for setting goals that tie into the team's core values

2. Get team members involved in the goal-setting process

3. Facilitate development of strategies that tie into goals

4. Facilitate goal accomplishment

Directions

For each core value, develop a list of possible goals. For example, if excellent service is a value, then translate this into an achievable goal statement. A useful process is to ask team members to write suggestions as to how they would like to develop their goals. Goal statements are statements of "ideal" outcomes in a broad general sense.

Once this has been done for each value, team members share their ideas one at a time, without comment, until all the ideas have been listed. These potential goals are then discussed and evaluated.

Prioritize the remaining items following this discussion and develop an achievement plan for each high-priority goal. The plan should state

1. What is to be accomplished

2. Under what conditions

3. When it is to be accomplished

4. The standard of attainment expected

5. Who is responsible

6. What it will cost

7. How success will be evaluated

Example:
By July 15 [when: (3.)],
when answering a phone call [conditions: (2.)]
concerned with product performance service [what: (1.)],
each person will get back to the customer with an answer
or plan within one hour of the call [standard: (4.)].

Processing

Answer the following questions:

1. What are the core team values?

2. What would your team be doing if it were to focus on these values?

3. How can you measure attainment?

4. What is the best strategy you can develop at this time?

Strategic Values and Goals

Values Goal	Strategy	Accountability	Cost	Time
(What)	(How)	(Who)	(Who Pays)	(By When)

Activity 6
Creating Focus

Purposes

One key pillar of high performance is the ability of the organization to stay focused on what is important. The goals of the following activity are to

1. Help you develop structures and processes that enable you to focus the team's energy on core values and goals

2. Help you use this focus to achieve high performance

Directions

How do you ensure that your team focuses on accomplishing what is important? So much activity is really just passing time, a sure pathway to failure. You want a team on task in a productive manner. In this activity, we offer suggestions about how to create structures and processes that allow you to stay focused on what is important.

Suggestion 1: Form Employee Involvement Teams. This process gets your team members involved in solving problems related to performance. These teams build focus by recognizing and eliminating unfocused activities.

Suggestion 2: Start Goal-Setting Incentive Programs.   Help employees set challenging goals, individually or collectively. Goals focus activity on what is important and provide a framework for evaluating individual and team performance.

Suggestion 3: Identify and Eliminate Unfocused Activities.   Always be ready to examine each and every activity that you and your associates perform. Are these activities contributing to accomplishment? If not, then such activities must be recognized and eliminated. A good technique is to ask your internal and external customers some questions to evaluate your performance: What's good now? What needs improvement? What needs to be stopped? What needs to be implemented?

Suggestion 4: Implement Change as Soon as Possible.   Once you identify problem areas, strive to eliminate them as soon as possible. When you allow unproductive behavior to persist, it becomes a norm that takes over the team.

ON COMMITMENT—THE PSYCHOLOGICAL FOUNDATION FOR CHANGE

What is commitment? What are the consequences of making a commitment? The challenge for us now is to develop a useful perspective or model. A good learning goal for you as a coach is to discover how to use commitment to enable people to become more effective.

To understand what commitment is, why it is so important, and how you can increase the commitment of team members, let's start with definitions. **Commitment** has been defined as the attribution of importance to an as yet uncreated future. From this definition, we see that one important element of commitment is attribution. **Attribution** is the psychological process of explaining the causes of events we experience during the course of our daily lives. For example, should we successfully attain some important goal, is our success a function of our skill, intelligence, and effort, or is it a function of luck and the level of difficulty of the task? How this attribution is made plays an important role in our personal learning and development. If we attribute our successes to skill, intelligence, and effort, we come to expect to succeed, even when we are failing. If, on the other hand, we attribute our successes to easy tasks and luck, even when we happen to be succeeding, we come to expect eventual failure. In the long run, our attribution affects our willingness even to try.

Commitment is the process of assigning a positive probability of occurrence to something that has not yet happened. In other words, most people commit to something when they believe, in their heart of hearts, that something has a probability of happening that they believe to be greater than zero. Leader credibility is important in eliciting this belief. Leader judgment is vital in making the decision to encourage this commitment on the part of others.

A second key term in the definition of commitment is *importance* or *real value*. What is important is what one values. A person tends to act in a manner consistent with her core values. A person's true values are revealed in that person's actions. When a person values something or someone, she exerts effort on behalf of that thing or person. So in terms of our definition, commitment means that the person values something.

A third key term in our definition is *future*. In the context of work goals, future is what people value when they are committed to something that doesn't even exist. For example, when two people are married, they stay married as long as they attribute value to the ideal of that marriage. That ideal doesn't exist; it is simply a dream. Yet it (the dream) enables a couple to work through whatever may be happening today, even when they are disagreeing about how much money to save or about some other real issue.

So, commitment is the willingness to work in the present toward an ideal that doesn't exist yet, because you believe in that ideal or because you believe in the person who is espousing that ideal. The key here is that you are willing to exert more effort toward achieving what you value and believe you can achieve.

How to Build Commitment

So how do you coach so as to build commitment? Obviously, coaching involves a strong element of leadership. For one thing, to build commitment among your associates, you have to be able to create and communicate in an impassioned way an ideal that your associates can also be passionate about.

Ultimately, however, leadership is not enough. Other things must happen. The ideal cannot be the coach's ideal. It must be owned by all members of the team. The ideal must resonate with a need or value within the hearts, souls, and minds of those you hope will make a commitment to the ideal.

An ideal that has no reality has no significance. Each person must feel as if she can contribute to the realization of the ideal. In short, each person must know what the ideal is and how to contribute to its development. Commitment is not an abstraction; it is a living testimony to a dream.

Success is often difficult to attain. Therefore, another aspect of building commitment is encouragement. To sustain a belief that something is important, you must be willing to risk and be capable of providing encouragement to others, especially when progress is slow or apparently nonexistent. You must believe that the goal is attainable and that each associate is capable of contributing what is required.

Another key to gaining commitment is to promote identification with the roles associates are expected to fill. To promote identification, it is important that people be enabled to fill roles that are right for them.

You can also influence a person to commit by mediating meaning. For example, as a leader you can make sure that each person knows that it is she who creates the important outcomes. Other ways to create meaning are to provide links to outside sources, to get needed resources, to interpret events for associates, and to protect associates from outside interference.

C H A P T E R 4

Developing Empowering Relationships

PURPOSE

As explained in Chapter 3, one key to coaching excellence is involving people in the development of the team or organization mission so that they commit to this mission. This task is partially accomplished by creating the conditions in which people can develop a sense of belonging to the team. The broad goal of this chapter is to show you how you can build positive involvement between you and your associates through *empowering* relationships.

GOALS

The goals of this chapter are to help you

1. Understand the nature of the empowered relationship

2. Discover what kinds of changes you may need to make to be more effective in creating empowered relationships

3. Establish trust in your work group

4. Develop a team in which acceptance of and respect for individual uniqueness are norms, and thus learn to gain the confidence and respect of your associates

5. Cultivate empowering relationships within your team and then create the foundation for high performance

AN INSIDE LOOK AT THE EMPOWERED TEAM

Effective coaching takes place when people feel at home in an environment. Being at home means feeling as if you belong—feeling connected. Home is a place where you feel safe, even as you strive to allow others to feel safe. It is a place where you are accepted, even as you are accepting. It is a place where it is okay to take risks, even as you encourage others to take risks. It is a place to learn and grow, even as you facilitate others' learning and growth. In other words, the ideal home is a place where you are needed and where you need to be—a good place to be.

The beautiful simplicity of open systems theory occurs in the intricacies of interdependence. The people, teams, and other components of an organization all impact on each other as a system. High performance in open systems occurs under conditions of alignment according to common purpose, performance (routines or established operations), and learning—the adding or changing of behaviors or operations to accommodate advances in science and technology in the marketplace. People provide the foundation of these qualities of adaptability. Empowerment starts with and builds on existing strengths of the individual. Macher (1988) identifies four characteristics of people who can and do empower themselves:

1. Technical competence acquired through previous learning from work experience

2. A personal sense that work has real meaning ("What I do matters")

3. The ability to exercise power and authority or influence to make a difference when it matters ("I can make it happen")

4. The ability (and willingness) to build trusting relationships with others ("I am in charge of me in my relationship with you")

One of our goals has been to understand the qualities of a place where people feel at home, a place where they feel empowered to learn and grow. This led us to look at teams and how they function.* Our studies revealed at least four qualities observed in the empowered team. These teams perform at the highest possible level in meeting goals and in the sense of empowerment experienced by team members. These qualities are

1. *Shared Purpose.* Members have reached a consensus on why the team exists; they see the validity and relevance of this purpose in their own lives. They feel included as members of the team. They feel at home. They are focused on what is important.

2. *Shared Values.* Congruence exists between the values expressed by individual team members and the values of the team as a whole. This congruence of values is reflected in the high degree of interpersonal trust and acceptance of individual uniqueness that characterizes the empowered team.

* A more detailed model of team functioning is found in *Groups at Work* by Mink, Mink, and Owen, Educational Technology Publications, 1987.

3. *Overall Openness.* High-quality interpersonal relationships exist. They are characterized by feedback and problem solving. These quality relationships are fueled by healthy, open people who seek to collaborate with others in empowered teams. They create a high degree of shared or mutual influence, of give and take. Members relate to each other as equals. Their interactions reflect quality interpersonal relationships. You will observe that these people communicate freely and honestly. They are not bound by hierarchical structure. People exchange information, solve problems, and give and receive meaningful feedback.

4. *Celebration and Mourning.* Empowered teams share the glory of success and the despair of failure. Then they let go so that they can complete new tasks and goals that fulfill the shared purpose.

These four elements—shared purpose, shared values, overall openness, and celebration—create the context in which coaching, learning, and growing can take place. They provide the backdrop out of which high performance may develop.

WHY RELATIONSHIPS ARE SO IMPORTANT: THE SIGNIFICANCE OF SELF-ESTEEM

To understand more deeply the importance of relationships at work, it will help to consider briefly the relationship between self-esteem and achievement. Self-esteem reflects the degree to which one values oneself. To maintain or gain self-esteem, a person needs to feel useful in important roles—to achieve. One of our basic psychological needs is the desire for a stable and positive self-evaluation (Maslow, 1971).

These self-evaluations are based on information from our internal world (self-talk) as well as from many external sources. Work can be a critical source of information about our achievements. We need to have esteem for ourselves. We also need the esteem and respect of others. Self-esteem requires feedback from others who show us that we are valued and appreciated.

Carl Rogers (1961) urged people who help others to hold them in *unconditional positive regard*. Treating others with positive regard provides a crucial ingredient in emotional health. We form more positive feelings about ourselves in relationships with others who treat us with positive regard. When people meet their needs for esteem and positive regard, they begin to develop a sense of confidence in their ability to control important outcomes in life. They develop more personal power. They make more contributions to the workplace. They become more self-directing. They learn, solve problems, and perform better. They believe in themselves and their own competence. They become self-confident.

Each of these vital personal qualities and resulting behaviors becomes important for achieving success in the workplace. Self-esteem seems to be at the core of personal success.

Those who have studied the development of self-esteem (Carlsmith, 1968; Bean and Clemes, 1978) have identified four components of self-esteem:

1. *Connectedness.* Individuals with good self-esteem are more likely to join in and enjoy being members of a work group because they feel connected.

2. *Sense of Uniqueness.* They accept and appreciate themselves.

3. *Sense of Personal Power.* They feel powerful because they believe in their competence and personal strength.

4. *Sense of Purpose.* They feel as if their lives have meaning and order.

People with these characteristics have learned how to focus on what is important and to see and make meaningful connections among the multitude of ideas, stimuli, and learning opportunities that surround them. These connections form a kind of mental fabric that undergirds and creates models of life. These structures or models of life are cognitive—they become, among other things, mental representations of the various roles a person plays in life, for example, mother, father, husband, associate, and leader, to mention but a few. These roles, when interrelated, provide a framework within which a person chooses and acts—a *life space*.

An individual's self-esteem waxes and wanes according to her success in meeting various role demands. As coach, you play a key role in helping your associates meet these important demands in the social setting of work. For example:

- Developing an effective work team enables your associates to develop a sense of connectedness.

- Empowered individuals, meeting and exceeding what the job demands, develop a sense of uniqueness and competence.

- Understanding and committing to the team's mission enables each individual team member to develop a sense of purpose.

- Collaborating with associates to define, design, and implement strategy provides an opportunity to develop a sense of models for implementation.

People can develop a sense of uniqueness and competence; however, your ability to encourage your associates to build trust, discover uniqueness in each other, and understand the team's mission and strategies for attaining it optimizes the conditions necessary for these individuals to learn and solve problems.

Self-esteem is revealed in a person's behavior. Our beliefs, current knowledge base, and feelings shape the choices we make, and in turn, we gain or lose self-esteem as a consequence of these choices. Self-esteem both determines and is determined by the individual's choices and their effects. Self-esteem can steadily increase or decline. Its formation can be a function of both positive and negative self-fulfilling prophecies. Whether positive or negative, self-esteem acts like an internal compass. If you believe you can, you act like you can; if you believe you can't, you act like you can't. Either way, the belief becomes self-fulfilling. Thus, people who expect to fail, do fail, while those that expect to succeed, do succeed. This effect has come to be known as the Wallenda Factor, in memory of Karl Wallenda, who fell from a tightrope after years of success. The story goes that before he fell, he was thinking about falling instead of walking.

We strive to act in accordance with our own perceptions of reality. We feel psychological tension or dissonance when we act at variance with our own self-perceptions. If we feel incompetent, we will, in order to avoid this state of dissonance, tend to act incompetently. If we feel competent, we tend to act competently.

This self-fulfilling nature of self-esteem is what makes it so crucial for the coach/leader/manager to know how to help encourage the development of an authentic sense of self-esteem—esteem based on positive experiences originating in self-determined goals and values. Success flows from positive experiences: the more the person succeeds, the more that person expects to succeed. Success follows expectations of success. Henry Ford once said, "Whether you believe you can or you believe you can't, you're right."

Self-esteem, whether positive or negative, is self-sustaining. A person with positive self-esteem tends to make choices that reinforce positive esteem, but a person with negative self-esteem tends to make choices that reinforce negative esteem.

William James (1956) believed that self-esteem is the ratio of one's successes to one's expectations. This notion helps us understand the dynamics of self-esteem. For example, if our successes are greater than our expectations, then self-esteem is positive and increases; if, however, our successes are lower than our expectations, then self-esteem is negative and decreases, until we can develop new skills or reframe our expectations. If success and expectations are equal, then self-esteem remains steady.

Our perceptions are critical to our self-esteem; how we perceive our successes and expectations, whether in our own terms or others, objectively or unrealistically, harshly or indulgently, determines how we feel about ourselves.

$$\text{Self-Esteem} = \frac{\text{Success}}{\text{Expectation or Pretension}}$$

Figure 4.1 illustrates the effects on self-esteem of positive and negative experiences relative to positive or negative expectations.

FIGURE 4.1
EXPECTATIONS AND SELF-ESTEEM

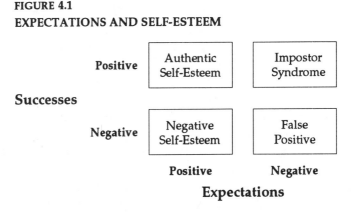

If both results and expectations are positive, then the person can be said to have authentic self-esteem. If results are negative and expectations are positive, then the person can be said to have authentic negative self-esteem. Such an individual would benefit from coaching, both by examining expectations and developing skills to support those expectations. A person who has positive experiences but negative expectations feels like an impostor. When such an individual has a success, her experience is one of "Who, me?" This person feels like a fake—like someone who is out of place. The impostor actively devalues her experience by viewing her success too harshly, or setting her expectations too high, or both. The net effect is that she feels like a phony, even though other people see her as successful and evaluate her positively. She also needs coaching, but in this case, the emphasis might be on enabling that individual either to reexamine her expectations or to reform her perceptions about her success.

Finally, there is the person who has a false positive self-esteem. This person is failing and expects to fail. Ironically, actual failure coupled with an expectation of failure leads to a false sense of negative self-esteem, one that becomes self-fulfilling because the individual doesn't see the relationship between what she expects to get and what she is actually getting.

In short, self-esteem has varied and complex effects on achievement. In light of these effects, it becomes equally clear why one of the most important aspects of coaching is learning how to develop self-esteem in associates.

Table 4.1 displays some of these differences.

TABLE 4.1

CHARACTERISTICS OF POSITIVE AND NEGATIVE SELF-ESTEEM

	Positive ◄─────► Negative	
Behaviors		
• Responsibility	• Accepts	• Avoids
• Feedback	• Accepts	• Gets defensive
• Response to experiences and information	• Open	• Closed
• Mistakes	• Admits	• Blames others
• Risk	• Takes risks	• Avoids risks
• Commitments	• Keeps	• Breaks
• Expresses opinions	• Openly	• Withholds
• Work adjustment	• Good adjustment	• Poor adjustment
Attitudes		
• Self-regard	• Positive	• Negative
• Self-respect	• High	• Low
• Trust	• High	• Low (suspicious)
• Expectations	• Optimistic and hopeful	• Pessimistic and cynical
• Feelings about self and others	• Positive	• Negative
• Ideal and perceived self	• Congruent	• Incongruent
• Feelings	• Accepts	• Denies
• Empowerment	• Feels in charge of own life	• Feels controlled by others

Let's return to the question, "Why are relationships important?" Clearly, self-esteem is an important aspect of achievement and, just as clearly, a product of the relationship between you and your associates. People learn about themselves and develop self-esteem from the feedback they get from significant others. As a coach, you are one of these influential others. Your opinion of an associate counts, your recognition of an associate counts, and your approval and disapproval of an associate count. You affect whether an associate does or does not develop self-esteem.

THE QUALITIES OF AN EFFECTIVE COACHING RELATIONSHIP

Quality work relationships are important. Relationships are part of the commerce of human activity. People relate to one another to meet their needs. But what specifically makes an effective work relationship? Effective relationships enable all parties to meet their needs successfully. Effective human resource development requires meaningful alignment between people's needs and the organization's tasks. Leaders and good coaches share the same challenge: attending to and valuing the relationship between what people need and an organization's task so that human energy for work is released.

At least three sets of needs, all originating in value systems, operate:

1. The personal needs of the people who are responsible for production

2. The needs of the task

3. The needs of the organization to produce quality products and services cost effectively.

Coaches are successful when they help people meet all three kinds of needs. Given this definition, we can characterize effective work relationships by

1. Functional levels of trust

2. Belief in self and positive regard and respect for every other individual in the work environment

3. A degree of openness that permits the exchange of valid information (both facts and feelings)

4. Many opportunities for information exchange and feedback

5. The ability and readiness to identify and solve problems

6. Many opportunities for achievement

7. Necessary resources, including appropriate tools

8. Appropriate incentives for individual and team achievement

Note that self-esteem is not just a consequence of positive human interaction; it is also a product of what one is empowered to do and to accomplish, and how one is treated. As a coach, you can develop effective relationships by understanding the nature of those relationships and the areas that you specifically can influence by virtue of your own values and self-esteem. By modeling this, you can encourage it in others—creating an environment where autonomy, fairness, and justice exist for the benefit of your associates.

DEVELOPING TRUST

What Is Trust?

Trust is the building block on which all relationships develop. The dictionary defines trust as

- "An assured reliance on some person or thing"
- "A confident anticipation in a person or thing"
- "Hope in the future"

These definitions underscore that trust always involves an element of risk. This risk is based on our prediction or judgment of another person's intentions and competence. Trust implies a permeating sense of reliability. When we take risks, most of us feel some distress because we know the worst case may result, and we will then have to deal with the negative consequences of having entrusted ourselves to another person, situation, or event.

Why Is Trust So Important to the Success of the Coaching Relationship?

As a coach, you have a critical role in supporting and encouraging trust in the workplace. In work environments, many people are bruised from past encounters with leaders and/or associates. Many associates are thus reluctant to discuss issues relating to work and the jobs they have to do. Relationships with co-workers (associates) in work environments where very little trust exists tend to be less effective. People avoid risks if the environment isn't safe. They won't be open to learning and problem solving or to trying new or innovative ideas.

Research on the importance of trust in relationships in the last thirty years has focused on three aspects of trust:

- Contractual
- Self-disclosure
- Physical

The following sections explore these concepts and provide an additional perspective.

Contract Trust

Trust is the confident anticipation (expectation) that people will do what they say they are going to do. Psychologists like Rotter (1967) and MacDonald, Kessel, and Fuller (1972) call this **contract trust.** They found **contractual trust** to be an important dimension of trust. People need predictability and order in their environments. When you do what you say you are going to do, you establish with others the confident expectation that their relationship with you is going to be predictable. People who feel safe in their social environments act with confidence.

Contractual trust can be established through making and keeping simple agreements. Examples are

- Scheduling and keeping appointments (meetings, return phone calls, lunch dates, deadlines)

- Setting meeting guidelines (attendance, involvement, roles) and following them

Many environments, however, are seen as unpredictable and undependable. If your experience is that no one comes to meetings on time, why should you bother? It is very hard to generate enthusiasm or commitment to go. To counteract this, a norm of dependability and reliability needs to be established. If your associates see you as keeping your agreements, and they start establishing an environment where this is the norm, people will feel increased trust in their and others' dependability.

Self-Disclosure Trust

Another dimension of trust that also reflects the person's confidence in others is called "**self-disclosure trust.**" Recall your feelings when a person you liked withheld important information from you. You probably found it hard to trust this person; further, you most likely found yourself less and less willing to share your own thoughts and feelings. Traditionally, people use information to control others. If someone withholds information from you, you may well feel manipulated, controlled, or deceived.

The degree of a person's openness provides an important indicator of the trust level in a relationship. Conversely, the lack of openness may signify a lack of trust and an unhealthy relationship. Self-disclosure trust means a willingness to engage in reciprocal sharing and openness. We define self-disclosure trust as the willingness to share relevant information when it is needed. We are not suggesting that complete openness is always a desirable goal in a coaching relationship. Rather, we do suggest that, to build trust, you must demonstrate a willingness and ability to

- Be open

- Share relevant information

- Meet your own needs

- Meet the needs of the team member

- Meet the needs of the organization

We advocate constructive openness relevant to the problem at hand.

Physical Trust

Finally, people like to feel that their physical and psychological environment is safe. This is called **physical trust**. When they are uncertain as to the safety of their environment, they begin to feel vulnerable and to spend as much time worrying about their safety as thinking about their jobs.

This is easy to understand if we consider the concept of self-monitoring, the processes by which people scan their environments to see what is going on and how they should act. When people sense danger in the environment, they prepare appropriately—by avoiding the danger or fleeing the scene. For example, if you criticize someone every time she points out a problem with how a job is done, she will soon stop making valid comments when things go wrong. In the past, when she was open with you, you mistreated her. You've created a psychologically unsafe environment. This affects work performance and invites high levels of defensiveness. Another example—controversial, but powerful—is an unstable organization with layoffs impending. This creates a difficult place for people to work when they don't know if they have a job. Not talking about it makes it worse. Because of the high level or intensity of the personal stage of concern, an organization in this state experiences lower productivity. Failure to hold open discussions with employees is a serious mistake.

If we extend this notion of self-monitoring further, we see that if people feel they have to spend more and more time monitoring their environments to maintain a sense of well-being, then they spend less and less time on constructive and creative problem solving.

Underlying Principles

Two threads tie these three aspects of trust together. The first is **intentions**. Associates trust you if they understand your intentions. That is, they trust you if

- They understand your motives for what you do.

- They believe you are being forthright and honest with them and not attempting to use or manipulate them by withholding information.

- They believe you are really interested in them as persons and have their best interests at heart.

A second thread is **competence**. Associates trust you to the extent you are perceived to be competent to do what you say you are going to do. Even though you may aspire to have the most productive team in your organization, this is possible only to the extent that your associates fully believe you have the skills to achieve the goal you and the team have set for yourselves. We call this the *principle of competence*.

Studies of effective leaders show that **integrity** and competence are the two most important leadership qualities. Associates need to believe you are competent in those areas where you demand trust. When associates believe in your integrity and competence, they are more likely to behave in a dependable fashion; they are more likely to trust your judgments; and they are more likely to listen to your feedback.

Neither of these principles is new, for they lie at the heart of most definitions of maturity (for example, the model used by Hersey and Blanchard in *Situational Leadership*, 1988). A person is mature to the extent that she is able (competent) to do what she intends to do. You will be perceived to be an effective coach to the degree you can create the belief that you are trustworthy. You will succeed in reinforcing this belief when you do what you say you are going to do (exhibit your competence) and when you are open (reveal your intentions). When you demonstrate congruence between intentions, competence, and values, you convey integrity. An interesting observation is that, while we tend to judge ourselves by our intentions, we judge others by their actions.

The real lesson in this is that the greatest potential for misunderstanding lies in not knowing or trusting the intentions of the other person. Likewise, understanding and trust can begin with sharing or clarifying your own intentions and checking out or questioning the intentions of the other person rather than assuming you know.

Trust and Learning

To learn means to be receptive to change because, by definition, learning is a relatively permanent change in current behavior brought about by experience. It is important to realize that, for learning to take place, there must be a confrontation between current behavior and desired behavior. This confrontation is potentially risky because it signifies that current behavior is not appropriate or effective. This confrontation may be self-generated or facilitated by another person, such as when you as the coach confront one of your associates.

There are several possible responses to confrontation. Several years ago, Franklin Ernst (1971) created the concept of the OK Corral, which will be useful here to understand why it is often difficult to facilitate learning (that is, change). According to Ernst, there are two basic life positions, "OK" and "not OK." In a relationship, this means that there are four possible variations of the life position, as illustrated in Figure 4.2.

FIGURE 4.2
THE OK CORRAL

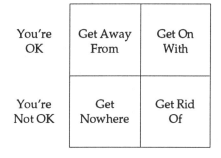

	I'm Not OK	I'm OK
You're OK	Get Away From	Get On With
You're Not OK	Get Nowhere	Get Rid Of

1. *I'm OK, you're OK—"Get on with life!"* In this position, the person feels good about herself and about you. The person is receptive to learning from you because she trusts your intentions.

2. *I'm OK, you're not OK—"Get rid of!"* In this position, the person is basically not capable of trust because she has come to expect others to be untrustworthy. Although on the surface the person feels good about herself, she has trouble entering into productive relationships because of a negative attitude toward others. This person cannot hear feedback about herself.

3. *I'm not OK, you're OK—"Get away from!"* In this position, the person may actually withdraw from you while appearing to be receptive to influence. In actuality, a person in this position does not learn because of not trusting herself. The tendency exists to be passive and dependent on you as boss or expert. This person doesn't have enough self-esteem to empower herself, and requires careful, intensive coaching.

4. *I'm not OK, you're not OK—"Get nowhere."* A person in this life position struggles to survive. Influencing such an individual in a positive manner proves more challenging than most of us can handle in a business environment. Typically, this person does not believe in herself or in you, and she doesn't trust you.

Things You Can Do to Affect the Development of Trust

Your behavior has either a positive or negative impact on the development of trust. You may inadvertently do things that make it hard for people to trust you. And because they find it hard to trust you, your effectiveness as a coach is thereby diminished. Table 4.2 lists some of the things you might do to build trust in your work team.

TABLE 4.2
FACTORS THAT ENHANCE THE DEVELOPMENT OF TRUST

You may enhance the development of trust if you

- Do what you say
- Reinforce people when they offer ideas or opinions
- Disclose your personal feelings
- Listen to others
- Prepare adequately
- Exhibit competence
- Allow people to make mistakes and learn from them

Tools for Building Trust: Listening and Sharing

In a group, information is either shared, denied, hidden, or repressed. Only when information is shared can people do things we associate with effective, mature relationships: plan, make decisions, create, produce, solve problems, and have fun together.

The Johari Window (Luft and Ingram, 1961) provides a useful way of thinking about how the process of sharing and listening to information affects a relationship. The quality and completeness of disclosure of any information in any relationship either enhances or distracts from the relationship. Valid information affecting our relationship may be either known or unknown to me and known or unknown to you. This fact leads to the following four-pane window (displayed in Figure 4.3) for analyzing a relationship. It can be used to analyze interactions between

- Individuals
- Groups
- Organizations
- Societies

It can also be used to analyze relationships of

- Individuals to groups
- Groups to organizations
- Individuals to organizations
- Individuals to cultures

FIGURE 4.3
THE JOHARI WINDOW

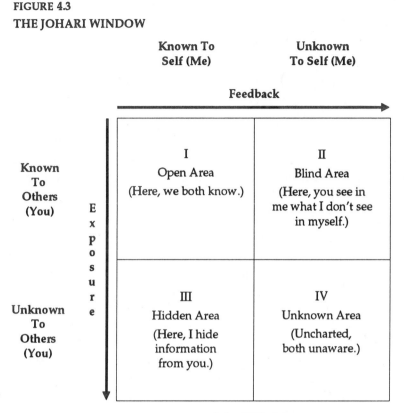

Johari Window

Think of each of these panes as potential energy sources, where the amount of energy corresponds directly to the amount of valid information exchanged. You can see that the effectiveness of the relationship will correspond directly to the size of the open or shared area.

- In the open or shared area, information is shared by both persons or, in the case of a team, all team members. It is therefore available for things that effective teams do well: learn, self-manage, identify problems, solve problems, celebrate together, and grieve together.

- In the blind area, I don't know what you do. If you choose not to tell me, or I will not hear you when you do share, then this information remains unavailable to me for all the shared events. I will continue to produce error in our relationship. I have less energy available for being effective on task because a good portion of it is tied up in being blind to how I'm producing error.

- In the hidden area, I refuse to share things with you. I know them, but you don't. The act of hiding also reduces the level of energy available to us for being productive.

- Finally, in the unknown area, neither you nor I have information. Whatever we have chosen to repress from awareness cannot be used to help us discover how to develop an effective work effort.

The size of the open area can be increased by making a commitment to improve two things: sharing and listening. As I share, the size of the hidden area declines. As I listen and you give good feedback, the size of the blind area decreases. As more valid information becomes available for us, more energy can be focused on productive work.

DEVELOPING ACCEPTANCE

The Sense of Uniqueness and Goal Accomplishment

Trust is essential to learning and problem solving. If you want to be an effective coach, you must be able to build trust in your associates. Trust provides the first positive ingredient necessary for a learning climate.

A second powerful requirement or human social need that enhances learning is the need to feel unique. The ability to meet this need in not innate. Rather, we learn to meet this need primarily through interactions with our social environments. When we are treated as if we are special and unique, then we learn how to experience ourselves in this manner. When we feel unique, we tend to act authentically and are more apt to produce valid information—data and feelings. When we do not learn to feel unique, then we inevitably learn unproductive ways of meeting our needs. Karen Horney (1945) claimed that when people do not learn how to meet their needs in an authentic manner, they instead develop "neurotic" ways of dealing with their needs. The neurotic patterns are characterized by a rigid, compulsive behavioral style, a style of behaving that is routine and automatic. People do not easily see that they need to learn; therefore, they typically do not learn. Horney identified three neurotic styles. She labeled one style the *compliant style*. Compliant people will agree with you in an effort to be seen as acceptable; however, they will not be genuine with you. Such people meet their need for uniqueness by blending in and being pleasing. Often they are in the "You are OK, I am not OK" quadrant.

A second neurotic type is the *aggressive style*. Aggressive people meet their needs for uniqueness by resisting the influence of others. Instead of becoming productive team members, they typically rebel against the norms of the team. This rebellion becomes so negative that they often receive negative recognition or punishment from the group. These people are in the "I'm OK, you're not OK" quadrant.

Horney's third style was depicted as *detachment*. Detached people meet their needs by remaining aloof and uninvolved—in other words, they are withdrawn. In the extreme, these people remain in the "I'm not OK, you're not OK" or "get nowhere" quadrant.

Each of these three styles leads to ineffective results. In a social setting none of these styles meets a person's needs. In summary, many important behavioral differences exist between people who have developed a sense of uniqueness and those who have not. Some of these are presented in Table 4.3.

TABLE 4.3
CHARACTERISTICS OF PEOPLE WHO DEVELOP UNIQUENESS

Those Who Sense Their Uniqueness	Those Who Don't Sense Their Uniqueness
1. Take reasonable risks	1. Will not take any risks
2. Express themselves in a group	2. Remain closed in a group
3. Try new things	3. Avoid trying new things
4. Exhibit flexibility	4. Exhibit inflexibility
5. Accept feedback readily, both positive and negative	5. Resist feedback, positive or negative
6. Can work in a cooperative setting	6. Find it hard to be team players

Things You Can Do to Develop Acceptance

As coach, you are in a powerful position to influence the development of your associates' sense of uniqueness. It is important that you understand what kinds of behaviors threaten people's sense of uniqueness and what kinds of behaviors promote their sense of uniqueness. It has been found that uniqueness develops in an environment in which acceptance and respect are the norms.

As a coach, you communicate to your associates acceptance or rejection because associates are coming to you with problems to be discussed and solved.

- Do you criticize those who dare to share a problem with you, or do you make a genuine effort to help them define the problem and jointly seek a reasonable solution?

- When goals are not being met, do you invite associates to share their ideas about how to work more creatively, or do you threaten them with punishment?

- Do you listen to ideas openly and without judgment?

- When people are doing a particularly good job, do you recognize their efforts and praise what is unique about the work they are doing?

- Do you tolerate differences of opinion?

- Do you permit associates to tell about the things they do not like without getting defensive?

- Do you allow people to experiment with the way they get the work done?

These are ways you either facilitate or inhibit the development of uniqueness in your associates. These behaviors can also promote or inhibit their development of confidence and trust in you. They also facilitate or inhibit the learning process.

How to Build a Person's Sense of Uniqueness

You could use many different tactics to ensure adequate opportunities for people to meet their need for a sense of uniqueness. At the core of each tactic would be opportunities for people to express themselves in an accepting environment. The following are some things you could do to enable people to develop a sense of uniqueness:

1. Provide opportunities for individuals to contribute to the team's goals.

2. Provide opportunities for individuals to design elements of their own jobs.

3. Give people the freedom and responsibility to solve problems that occur during the course of their work.

4. Encourage and reward innovation, creativity, and personal initiative.

5. Acknowledge frequently each individual's contribution to the success of the whole.

6. Notice and acknowledge what is special and unique about each individual.

7. Solicit and apply ideas from team members about how to do a job better, how to improve quality, or how to improve other aspects of the team's performance.

People develop a sense of uniqueness when they feel empowered to be themselves.

ACTIVITIES FOR DISCOVERY AND GROWTH: BUILDING POSITIVE WORK RELATIONSHIPS

The activities in this chapter have been selected to help you encourage empowering relationships. They were chosen because they seem to be adaptable to a wide range of settings.

Activity 1
Developing Yourself: Or, How Well Developed
Is Your Self-Esteem?

Purpose

This discovery exercise will help you understand your own sense of self-esteem and clarify your personal development goals at this time.

Directions

1. Complete the Personal Strength Assessment, rating each item in terms of how characteristic that behavior is of you.

2. Transfer your ratings to the scoring grid following the instrument.

3. Total the scores for each column, then transfer your scores to the Self-Esteem Profile.

4. Think about what you might do to nurture your own self-esteem.

Personal Strength Assessment

1	2	3	4	5	6	7	8	9
Not at All Characteristic				Characteristic about Half the Time				Very Characteristic
		Somewhat Characteristic				Characteristic		

1 2 3 4 5 6 7 8 9	1. Approach others with confidence.
1 2 3 4 5 6 7 8 9	2. Act spontaneously.
1 2 3 4 5 6 7 8 9	3. Solve problems.
1 2 3 4 5 6 7 8 9	4. Make daily plans for learning and growing.
1 2 3 4 5 6 7 8 9	5. Express my feelings and opinions clearly.
1 2 3 4 5 6 7 8 9	6. Am myself in a wide range of situations.
1 2 3 4 5 6 7 8 9	7. Aware of my values and goals.
1 2 3 4 5 6 7 8 9	8. Act with confidence in a wide range of situations.
1 2 3 4 5 6 7 8 9	9. Listen, even under stress.
1 2 3 4 5 6 7 8 9	10. Accept myself and my feelings.
1 2 3 4 5 6 7 8 9	11. Organize my time so I can achieve my goals.

1 2 3 4 5 6 7 8 9   12. Handle conflicts with others.

1 2 3 4 5 6 7 8 9   13. Get close to others and share.

1 2 3 4 5 6 7 8 9   14. Trust myself in a wide range of situations.

1 2 3 4 5 6 7 8 9   15. Think about options in the decisions I am facing.

1 2 3 4 5 6 7 8 9   16. Accept the challenge of decisions and the skills to make decisions.

1 2 3 4 5 6 7 8 9   17. Express caring.

1 2 3 4 5 6 7 8 9   18. Open to both myself and to others.

1 2 3 4 5 6 7 8 9   19. Conceptualize problems.

1 2 3 4 5 6 7 8 9   20. Carry a plan of action through to completion, despite setbacks.

1 2 3 4 5 6 7 8 9   21. Am personal.

1 2 3 4 5 6 7 8 9   22. Am creative, curious, and interested.

1 2 3 4 5 6 7 8 9   23. Organize my learning in a systematic manner.

1 2 3 4 5 6 7 8 9   24. Accept responsibility for myself and my actions.

1 2 3 4 5 6 7 8 9   25. Love and give.

1 2 3 4 5 6 7 8 9   26. Treat myself with respect.

1 2 3 4 5 6 7 8 9   27. Influence others.

1 2 3 4 5 6 7 8 9   28. Act with self-control and personal power.

Scoring Grid

Transfer your scores to the scoring grid and then plot your self-esteem profile.

Skills for Connecting	**Skills for Being Unique**
__ 1. Approaching People	__ 2. Spontaneity
__ 5. Express Feeling and Opinions	__ 6. Authenticity
__ 9. Listening	__ 10. Self-Acceptance
__ 13. Sharing	__ 14. Trusting Self
__ 17. Expressing Caring	__ 18. Openness
__ 21. Personal	__ 22. Creative
__ 25. Love and Caring	__ 26. Self-Respect
__ Total	__ Total

Skills for Having Models

__ 3. Problem Solving

__ 7. Value/Goal Awareness

__ 11. Time Management

__ 15. Decision Making

__ 19. Thinking Skills

__ 23. Learning Skills

__ 27. Influencing Skills

__ Total

Skills for Personal Power

__ 4. Planning

__ 8. Self-Confidence

__ 12. Handle Conflicts

__ 16. Decisions

__ 20. Self-Discipline

__ 24. Responsibility

__ 28. Self-Control

__ Total

Self-Esteem Profile

	10	20	30	40	50
Sense of Connectedness					
Sense of Uniqueness					
Sense of Models					
Sense of Power					

| | 10 | 20 | 30 | 40 | 50 |

Processing

From this self-analysis, pick several areas you wish to strengthen. List these below:

Make a plan to develop your self-esteem.

Activity 2
Acknowledgment, Understanding,
and Selective Recognition

Purpose

Communication is the most powerful tool you have at your disposal for developing self-esteem and empowering people. This exercise helps you develop your associates' self-esteem through the use of communication.

Directions

1. *Acknowledging.* This is the process of affirming others. To do this, practice two skills: nonverbal communication and reflection. You acknowledge nonverbally by observing what others are doing. When you share with another what you have observed, this completes the loop of acknowledgment.

2. *Understanding.* This is the process of mirroring another's feelings and meanings. To do this, practice two skills: acknowledging feelings and mirroring. You acknowledge feelings by affirming the other person's feelings: Are you feeling . . . ? Does it hurt when . . . ? You mirror when you link feelings to experience: Do you feel annoyed when . . . ? Do you get frustrated when . . . ?

3. *Selective Recognition.* The process of praising competent behavior and ignoring incompetent behavior is called **selective recognition.** You recognize positive behavior by specifically describing the behavior, and then communicating what you like about the behavior: I see you as being particularly effective when you. . . .

Practice these three skills often to increase your effectiveness as a coach.

Activity 3
Effective Work Relationships

Purpose

This discovery exercise helps you examine the effectiveness of your current work relationships. Place an *N* on the scale to represent where you believe the team is NOW and an *F* on the scale to represent the desired FUTURE status of the team. Have team members complete this scale also.

When you have completed your ratings, discuss them openly and ask team members to contribute ideas about how to improve the quality of the work relationships within the team.

1. The level of trust in the work team is:

   1   2   3   4   5   6   7   8   9

Extremely   Moderate   Extremely
   Low   High

2. The level of positive regard and respect for each individual is:

   1   2   3   4   5   6   7   8   9

Extremely   Moderate   Extremely
   Low   High

3. The level of openness (sharing of useful information) is:

   1   2   3   4   5   6   7   8   9

Extremely   Moderate   Extremely
   Low   High

4. The extent to which opportunities for information exchange and feedback are present is:

   1   2   3   4   5   6   7   8   9

Extremely   Moderate   Extremely
   Low   High

5. The ability and readiness to identify and solve problems are:

   1   2   3   4   5   6   7   8   9

Extremely   Moderate   Extremely
   Low   High

6. The level of opportunity for individual and team achievement is:

   1   2   3   4   5   6   7   8   9

Extremely   Moderate   Extremely
   Low   High

7. The extent to which resources, including appropriate tools such as computers, are available is:

   1   2   3   4   5   6   7   8   9

Extremely   Moderate   Extremely
   Low   High

8. The degree to which incentives for individual and team achievement are available is:

   1   2   3   4   5   6   7   8   9

Extremely   Moderate   Extremely
   Low   High

ON TEAMWORK: DEVELOPING YOUR WORK TEAM

Teamwork

Why Teamwork Is Important.   Teamwork is the focal topic of this chapter. Teamwork is important for several reasons.

- A majority of work takes place in the context of a team. This is true of many of the new developments in manufacturing such as Computer Integrated Manufacturing.

- Quality programs like Total Quality Management (TQM) require people to work together to set quality objectives and solve work-related problems. Yet, many people assume that quality is a purely technical problem; they forget to develop their employees to be competent to work together as a team. Consequently, the quality program suffers and does not appear to fulfill its potential.

Team Productivity.   The possible relationships between the state of a team and its productivity have often been investigated. By *state*, we mean those conditions that appear to characterize the dynamics of teams. One way this research has been done is to measure some aspect of team dynamics and then correlate this variable with an indicator of team performance levels.

An important quality of a team is its level of cohesiveness. **Cohesiveness** is a measure of the degree to which team members like one another. When cohesiveness is high, then team members like being members of the team. Studies have shown that teams with high cohesiveness tend to produce more than do teams with low cohesiveness.

Another important quality of teams is the team's relative openness. An open team is one in which there is a high degree of sharing information (facts and feelings). A team can be closed, open, or somewhere in between these two extremes. When the degree of team openness is studied, one finds that open teams tend to produce more and tend to be more cohesive. Openness also directly contributes to a sense of autonomy and personal empowerment (Goldman, 1990).

The Conditions of Productive Teamwork

What Is a Team?   A team is a group of people who share a common purpose or goal. A team is a group of people who coordinate their efforts to achieve a goal they perceive to be important to the members of the team.

What Are the Tasks of Teams?   Driekurs (1957) postulated that every individual has to deal with five life tasks to feel a sense of productivity in life: work, friendship, love, self-esteem, and meaning. In a similar vein, it appears that a team must deal with a series of "life tasks" in order to fulfill its potential.

If a group is to become effective, it must master process and task. As a coach, you need to acquire the competence—skills, knowledge, and attitudes—that enable you to influence the learning process in others. Creating a process for learning will help you develop an effective work team. Some of these tasks are referred to in the literature as task phases in group development. We refer to these tasks as *norms*.

The Norms of Effective Teamwork.   It is possible to define a general set of norms that seem to characterize more effective teams, distinguishing them from ineffective teams. These norms are

1. *The Norm of Trust.*   Trust occupies a central role in many theories of development. Erik Erikson maintained that the first task of human development is to learn how to trust. Alfred Adler speculated that all human action is motivated by our needs to overcome feelings of inferiority and superiority and to learn how to trust ourselves to be the master of our lives with the "courage to be imperfect" (Driekurs, 1957).

2. *The Norm of Acceptance of Individual Differences.*   Everyone is unique in some manner. Each person brings her uniqueness to the team. The team provides an atmosphere in which it is OK to be yourself or in which being authentic leads to some form of rejection. Effective teams learn to create a behavioral expectation that it is OK to be yourself and that uniqueness is seen as a strength and not as a liability.

3. *The Norm of Feedback.*   When people work together, they do things that both facilitate and hinder relationships. Feedback is communicating to others how their behavior affects you.

4. *The Norm of Problem Solving.*   Feedback enables team members to discover problems, but feedback alone does not solve problems. Effective teams develop as a norm effective processes for using feedback to solve problems.

5. *The Norm of Focusing on the Present.*   As a team works to achieve long- and short-term goals, there will be times when it succeeds and times when it fails. There is a tendency to allow the pain of failure and the pleasure of success to distract the team from what is important today because the team gets caught up in the emotions associated with the experience of failure or success. Effective teams develop an openness that enables members to cycle through a period of letting go of past events, especially failure. Teams are slow to move on to new tasks if the completion or failure to complete old tasks is not celebrated or mourned.

Compliance or Acceptance

Definitions and Distinctions. *Conformity* is a word that often connotes something negative. Yet sometimes it is clearly productive to conform. Thus, it is effective to create conditions that encourage members to conform to the norms of effective teamwork.

Conformity is the process of changing your behavior in response to another's influence, real or imagined. However, when people conform, is the change in their behavior permanent or temporary? Social psychologists make some useful distinctions regarding conformity and change. Compliance is the process of conforming to group rules because of external pressures. Remove the pressure and the change vanishes.

On the other hand, *acceptance* is conformity based on internal pressures. It is the outcome of a process by which an individual comes to own the change. During this process, people come to identify with the change and to accept the consequences of the change. They become willing to live within the limits imposed by the change and to accept the responsibilities associated with it. As a coach, your goal is to help people become self-motivated. When associates accept and own their behavior and the goals of the team, then they are capable of becoming truly empowered.

How Do You Gain Someone's or Your Own Acceptance of the Need to Change? As a leader of the team, you will occasionally want to influence your team members to change their behavior to align with the task or purpose to be accomplished. Change occurs when people recognize a difference between where they are now and where they want to be. You and the person want the change to be permanent and internalized. So it is important for both of you to know how to make such changes.

Again, social psychology offers clues about how you can gain this acceptance. For example, if you give yourself and others the opportunity to publicly endorse a given norm, you and those others are more likely to act in accordance with this public commitment. Or, if people act as if they believe the norm is valid, their attitudes tend to change in the direction of their behavior.

Another more powerful means of gaining acceptance is to allow the team to participate in the development of norms. This could take the form of a group meeting in which team members discuss how to work together and then develop a list of core group values. The outcome of such an effort is that team members develop a sense of ownership of the norms they have created.

C H A P T E R 5

Laying the Foundation for the High-Performance Environment

PURPOSE

People need to feel confident in their ability to succeed. This confidence is fostered by consistent successes obtained by combining their abilities and skill with effort equal to the task. When you and your associates have a supportive work environment, autonomy, resources, and competence to succeed—and expect that you will succeed—you have a sense of mastery. When you have met the *can/want/ try* criteria, you feel free to manage yourself and your actions. This awareness of your personal power is called *empowerment*.

How do good coaches help create this sense of empowerment in their associates? They don't. Rather, good coaches create an environment and the conditions under which their associates can empower themselves. The solution to this puzzle of empowerment lies in our understanding of the conditions under which people develop self-esteem and a sense of mastery in a given role or life space. One of these conditions is the development of a sense of personal power. People feel their power when they have the competence, the desire, the tools, and the opportunity to achieve valued goals—when every element of an assigned work role can be influenced by their ability and assigned responsibility to plan, do, check (evaluate), and act. Acting includes any modification deemed necessary to improve results.

We use the word *agency* to describe the state of being empowered or in charge of your own life space (roles). Individuals have agency or *efficacy* (personal power to produce a desired effect) to the extent that they believe they have the skill and energy—power to produce the results they wish to produce—and also believe in their own abilities to produce results. This is an internal state—very private and personal—and is reflected in competent performance. If people don't have agency or self-efficacy, they do not produce at the level at which they are capable. As a coach, one of your primary responsibilities is to create the conditions under which associates can find successful pathways toward autonomy, self-mastery, internal control orientation, and self-efficacy—empowerment.

A key challenge for you as a coach is to establish a clear focus for you and your associates. Focus involves mutually setting goals and finding ways to achieve partnership in the accomplishment of those goals. This chapter discusses some processes by which you and your team members can come to an agreement about the goals for accomplishment, the standards of excellence, and the methods to measure and correct variations in performance. With respect to this latter point, we suggest evaluating performance by applying an empowerment model. Empowerment provides a psychological underpinning for Deming's Plan, Do, Check, Act (PDCA) problem-solving process that lies at the heart of continuous improvement and learning.

FIGURE 5.1
A PROBLEM-SOLVING MODEL TO GUIDE THE EMPOWERED*

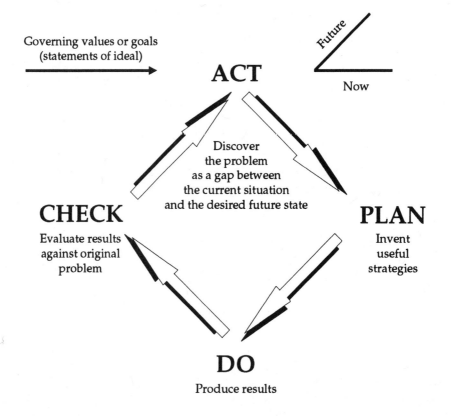

* A measure of whether an individual is self-managed, or a work is self-directed, would be the degree to which the person or team feels free to apply the PDCA model to their work. They would be demonstrating a sense of empowerment.

A focal topic discussed in this chapter is the concept of personal psychological strength. Psychological strength is both the sense of confidence in oneself that comes from having successfully met one's needs, and the belief that if one tries, one can succeed. In other words, psychological strength is both an outcome and a determiner of experience.

LEARNING GOALS

By the end of this chapter, you will be able to:

- Create an effective work environment for associates that enables personal empowerment

- Establish shared goals by mutual consent

- Develop standards of excellence

- Create meaningful expectations

- Identify, mutually evaluate, and correct variations in performance

- Create opportunities that develop and build psychological strength

DEVELOPING A PERFORMANCE EMPOWERMENT PROCESS

Why You Need a Performance Process That Encourages Empowerment

As a member of a team, you share responsibility for achieving performance goals. For the team to succeed, everyone on it must be able to work as a unit; they must be able to teach one another and to learn from one another. You as an individual have little direct control over the total effort required to achieve those goals. This responsibility is shared by each team member.

In a productive climate, each person takes responsibility for succeeding and works hard to produce the expected results. When everyone is working well together and all are performing competently, everyone succeeds. However, working well together is not enough. People also have to work with competence toward shared goals. This is why one of the most important things you can do as a coach is develop a performance process that can serve as an instrument of empowerment. You and your team will succeed only insofar as you and your team members are effective in directing performance toward the accomplishment of long-term goals that foster creative tension both in individuals and in the work team as a whole. This creative tension energizes every member and the whole team. According to Senge (1990), creative tension is the positive energy created by setting and communicating challenging, shared goals that allow people to stretch themselves and push their capacity. A group with a shared vision that is challenging and compelling holds more power than one with a low expectation in which no one is interested (see Senge [1990], chap. 11).

When everyone is aligned and excited about the vision, success is all but assured. The vision must be clear. When people have a clear image of where they need to be, they can self-manage to realize the vision.

Managing the Process of Performance: Self-Management and Constraints

We don't believe that performance evaluation constitutes a way of life in organizations. Most of us do not look at the results produced by our own or another person's performance. We screen actual results. Most performance is automatic. Conscious examination of results seems counter-intuitive. Most results produced automatically by highly skilled individuals are governed by Model I values (Argyris, 1990). These values are

- I'm right, you're wrong

- Maximize winning and minimize losing

- Suppress feelings

If you hold these values, you will act unilaterally.

Poor results are produced because unilateral actions are routine and often outside conscious awareness. When environments change and performance takes an automatic trial-and-error form, errors can easily be produced. When the task is nonroutine, error may be the rule. If the performance produces an unintended error, the associate may not detect it. Many people in organizations perform well below their potential.

When you make judgments about performance, discover which constraints operate against performance, then remove or reduce them. Then ask yourself these key questions:

- Is the performance you observe driven by highly perfected competence?

- Is the performance outside of conscious awareness?

- Can you respond to the observed performance openly?

- Do you have valid information (facts and feelings)?

- Can honest problem solving take place?

- How will you communicate with one another about performance?

- Will others learn and grow from the process, and thus become more competent?

- How do you establish valid criteria?

- Will these criteria include allowances for existing constraints?

- How will you apply the results of performance observations to improved performance?

As you address these issues, reflect on key elements of a successful system for performance improvement.

Learning and the Competence Ladder

As you have no doubt discovered, good coaching is a learning process. As such, it can be very challenging. Many alternative learning models and approaches have spawned a semantic wonderland of terminology, as well as enough conceptual input to satisfy the most thirsty of computer data banks. To make matters even more challenging, areas in the psychology of learning, such as motivation, cognition, memory, and language, seldom receive treatment in relationship to each other; they are most often investigated as discrete areas. We've attempted to build an applied model—can/want/try—and place it in a context or environment to encourage holistic thinking on your part. We focus on sharing principles of learning, motivation, adult development, and related phenomena like self-efficacy, locus of control, expectancy, self-esteem, and **single-** and **double-loop learning** or Model I and **Model II learning** as discussed by Argyris (1990) and Senge (1990) (under the topic of new mental models). The glossary defines these terms, which are critical to our view of good coaching.

This model of acquiring competence recognizes the existence of the unconscious and its role in performance. We have defined a competence as including skill, knowledge, and attitude. Competence and the observable performance from which it is inferred may be repeated again and again. Many jobs have an established method, and workers become machinelike in performing these jobs. When the person can perform at the expected level or standard without thinking about the method (that is, a good free throw, tennis serve, swimming stroke; or soldering the same spots on circuitry or setting correct torque on head bolts), we say that person operates at the level of *unconscious competence*.

On any new competency, however, most of us begin at the level of *unconscious incompetence*. When challenged to perform, we become aware of our incompetence. We are then **consciously incompetent**. With intensive coaching and practice, we can and do acquire the competence. When we are conscious of our actions while performing competently, we operate at the stage of **conscious competence**. Most performance errors occur outside of conscious awareness—unconscious incompetence—and are unintended.

FIGURE 5.2
COMPETENCE LADDER

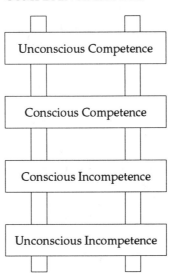

KEY ELEMENTS IN THE PROCESS OF IMPROVING PERFORMANCE AND ENCOURAGING A SENSE OF EMPOWERMENT

The goal of any process designed to encourage empowerment is to give people the opportunity to accomplish their goals. Any process has interlocking and interdependent parts. Remember the nine windows for observation discussed in Chapter 4 of this book. A process that focuses team efforts and creates a climate for empowerment depends on having specific goals. In addition, one must track the degree to which accomplishments match original goals. Emphasis must be placed on continuous learning.

The elements of a performance improvement process that may enhance empowerment include:

- *Consensus Commitment to the Vision and Mission of the Team.* Success depends on everyone committing to the concept of high performance.

- *Shared Goals and Standards of Excellence.* The team as a unit must agree about what the goals are. Empowerment means, among other things, people having opportunities to participate in establishing the goals, levels of expected performance, and processes for continuous learning and improvement.

- *Clarification of Roles.* Each person's role in relation to goal accomplishment is defined. These expectations are translated into specific performance goals and specific results to be achieved by a specific time.

- *Competence in Analyzing and Understanding the Causes of Performance That Don't Meet the Agreed-on Standards.* Team members must know how to think about variations from standards and the possible causes. In order to determine how well performance matches goals and both internal and external customer expectations, data are collected and evaluated.

- *A Continuing Process.* Obtaining valid information must be seen as an ongoing process. There is a continuum of interaction, with major goal-setting events taking place as needed. Between these points are numerous small interactions during which analysis of performance occurs. Performance is continuously evaluated, and judgments are made about the results being produced. When goals are achieved, team members celebrate their achievements; when performance falls below expectations, the team goes into problem solving to reexamine goals, strategies, and areas for improvement.

- *Problem-Solving Skill.* To succeed, the team must know how to discover solutions to problems, and they must feel and be empowered to implement solutions.

- *Renewal and Refocusing.* Goals are renewed or new ones set, and the process continues through similar cycles.

Taken together, these seven elements define the performance empowerment process. Without such a process, it is hard for the team to achieve its goals. Such systems point behavior in a specific direction, provide feedback along the way, reward excellence, and correct poor performance. If any one of these key elements is absent, the whole system eventually drifts off course and falters. Now, let's examine the empowerment process.

TWO ASPECTS OF THE PERFORMANCE EMPOWERMENT PROCESS

The empowerment process has two distinct aspects: the mechanical and the interpersonal.

The mechanical aspect includes

1. Defining job responsibilities

2. Setting goals

3. Gathering information

4. Assessing performance

The interpersonal aspect includes

1. Evaluating performance

2. Problem solving

3. Deciding on a course of action

4. Coaching for performance improvement

The mechanical features of the system are relatively straightforward. However, the interpersonal aspects are most often cited as reasons for difficulty in implementation.

DESIGNING AN EMPOWERING WORKSCAPE: AN APPROACH

As coach, you have a great impact on creating a climate of productivity. Here are six conditions you can create to help your associates feel empowered:

1. Ensure that each person meets the level of can (skills), want (motivation), and try (will) required to accomplish the job.

2. Define all jobs and responsibilities in terms of both processes and outcomes.

3. Enable each team member to use her skills autonomously.

4. Allow each person to express her uniqueness through her work.

5. Entitle each person to design the specifics of her job as it unfolds.

6. Create identification (that is, establish the relationship between an individual's needs and successful job performance) with the job.

Let's explore each of these in detail.

The Right Person

A productive climate is made up of individuals, each of whom makes a significant contribution to the efforts of the whole team. If individuals are out of place, if they do not experience being in control in the environment, then an empowering environment does not exist. Ultimately, you cannot force anyone to do what she is not inclined to do. You can only provide opportunities that encourage a person with the desire to achieve. You can provide opportunity and meaning by sharing and interpreting vision, mission, goals, tasks, or purposes.

There are two attributes you want to ensure: (1) you want people who are willing to work hard, and (2) you want people who identify with their jobs.

Three qualities (apart from ability) enable a person to become a productive member of a team:

Mastery. The individual's desire to master the job is quite natural to the person. People seek ways to be competent in their environments. This human need is called competence—mastery motivation. Those who achieve the most in life have the greatest desire to master their environments. They aren't driven to win so much as they are driven to be the best at what they are doing.

Energy.   The pursuit of excellence is signified by a willingness to go beyond what is considered normal. Achievers always seem to be willing to work hard to prepare themselves for whatever task they want to accomplish. As a coach, you should strive to assemble people with a willingness to work hard—to do whatever it takes.

Capacity.   Self-management or empowerment becomes more probable when team members identify with the team, share a common purpose, and share the work they are expected to perform.

Team identification must be mutual. On the one hand, each individual has a value system that organizes her personality—including attitudes—and guides her behavior. On the other hand, as trust and knowledge of each other develops, the team will develop a shared value system. If individuals are to be successful in sharing the team's work efforts, their value systems and the team's shared values must overlap to the extent that shared values can be agreed on.

A good coach seeks ways to enable individuals to identify with the team, as well as to enable the development of shared values. The former is done by knowing the individual's values and relating the meaning of the job to the individual's values. Coaches contribute to their associates' understanding of the purpose of a job and the appropriate performance by developing trust with the associates.

Through your capacity to inspire trust in others and your capacity to empathize with associates, you can develop a meaningful shared purpose with your associates. According to Bennis (1989), the capacity to position yourself by managing trust has several dimensions, including:

- *Constancy.*   Constancy is the degree to which you stay on course and maintain personal integrity.

- *Congruity.*   If you wish to inspire confidence in your leadership, you cannot say one thing and do another. What you say and what you enact must be the same.

- *Reliability.*   You must be there when it counts. Associates must be able to count on you under every condition, not just when things are going well.

- *Integrity.*   You must do what you have agreed to do.

As a coach, it is important that you spend time helping individual team members assess the degree of match between their value systems and their performance, and the value system of the team. It is equally important that you enable people to participate in shaping the values that define the team's identity and its working climate.

Defining Job Responsibilities in Terms of Process and Outcomes

Empowerment is not an abstraction. People empower themselves only in relation to goals or results to be accomplished. One of the great inducements to self-management can be achieved by helping team members define each member's job or role in terms of both work process and some specific set of outcomes. One of the first tasks in developing a self-management system, therefore, is an accurate description of job responsibilities or activities, work processes, and outcomes. There are often two types of outcomes.

The first type of outcome is management expectations from the view of someone higher in the organization. These expectations are imposed on the work unit, team, or person. Work and task accomplishment comprise the second type, the results and feedback necessary for each individual to achieve and receive. By so doing, both the person and the team develop more capacity for doing the job, for testing performance, and ultimately improving performance. Empowered environments exhibit a high degree of congruence between results achieved and process improvement activities. That is, they exhibit the qualities of the learning environment.

To determine the primary responsibilities of jobs within your team, you and your team members should be able to answer the following questions:

1. What does it take to perform this job successfully?

2. If the job were to be eliminated suddenly, what would be missing?

3. What is the primary output of this job?

Once responsibilities have been defined, the team's attention should focus on specific performance goals. There are four key processes in developing goals for jobs: framing, setting, documenting, and reviewing.

Framing Goals. Goals express what should be achieved during a set period of time. As such, they are future-oriented and form a common point for a developmental plan. However, although a goal generally specifies an end point to be achieved, it is often necessary to spell out the process by which a goal is to be achieved. This might be called the frame within which accomplishment is expected to take place.

For example, even though it may be possible to achieve a certain level of production, if this is done at the expense of wearing out the team, this may not be a good goal. A better way to frame the goal might be to specify both a certain level of production and a certain degree of team satisfaction. This approach makes it clear that both result and method are important aspects of job success. When framing goals, then, it is helpful to develop a matrix in which both results and methods are specified, as shown in the following example:

Goal Matrix

Goal Areas	Results	Method	Measured by	When
Quantity				
1.				
2.				
3.				
Quality				
1.				
2.				
3.				
Interpersonal				
1.				
2.				
3.				

Such a matrix would be completed for each team member and for each specific responsibility. The team would complete the matrices through discussion and negotiation.

Setting Goals. The key to successful goal setting is to get everyone to accept, or own, the goals. You get people to own team goals by encouraging them to participate actively in goal development. Some steps that facilitate the development of truly motivating goals include:

- Ask each person to set goals for her own area of responsibility.

- As a team, discuss each team member's goals and determine the degree of fit with the goals of the team and the broader goals of the organization.

- Resolve any differences or inconsistencies between individual and team, and team and organizational goals.

- Modify team and individual goals as indicated from the course of the discussion.

- Discuss and establish methods for reaching goals.

- Develop ways to monitor process.

- Identify ways to measure achievement and establish time lines for reviewing accomplishment.

- Check for understanding of the goals.

- As a group, establish times at which performance will be reviewed.

- Review process measures as often as required.

When setting goals, it is important that the goals meet the following criteria of acceptability:

- *Realistic.* Goals should be achievable.

- *Clear.* Goals should be clearly defined.

- *Controllable.* Goals should be under the associate's control.

- *Consistent.* Goals should be consistent with team goals.

- *Challenging.* Goals should stretch the associate.

- *Efficacious.* Goals should make a difference in the quality of the services and of the products delivered to the customer.

Documenting Performance-Related Goals. Part of your role as a coach is to encourage record keeping that can be used as information for improving performance. The team needs to document what is happening in order to identify what is going well and what is not going so well. The basic tools of Total Quality Management may help. For example, **Pareto charts** could be used to establish team and individual priorities by identifying the high-payoff activities—that 20 percent of work that provides 80 percent of the payoff for the work unit. Pareto charts can be used to spot problems to be solved and to determine priorities for solutions. They typically take the form of a bar graph.

The challenge of documentation is to use methods of measuring performance that are reliable and valid. A *reliable method* yields consistent data over time; a *valid method* measures what it is supposed to measure. The best way to achieve these two goals is to seek multiple sources of data for each key result area. Some helpful hints about documentation include:

- *Representativeness.* Sample aspects of the job that are typical of the work.

- *Variety.* Observe a variety of job situations—morning versus afternoon, low versus high pressure, and so on.

- *Direct Observation.* Schedule time to observe the work directly. Create your own fishbone diagrams to get a more complete view of the team's work situation.

- *Records.* Keep records of critical incidents. Keep statistical control charts.

- *Regularity.* Make your observations frequently and regularly.

- *Recurrent Data.* For all goals that are clearly measurable, keep records of performance over time. Establish and use good existing baseline data.

You document performance by sampling behavior. A sample is a unit of observation. For example, you sample a team member's behavior when you observe that person work in the morning, when you examine a machine the person just assembled, when you examine an order that has just been entered, when you look at the number of products sold in a given time period.

Sampling is not easy, however, because:

- During the course of a day, you may not see each person often enough.

- You may be biased against behaviors you don't approve of.

- You may misinterpret the behaviors.

- Not all behaviors have an equal chance of being observed.

To overcome these difficulties, consider doing the following:

- Observe aspects of behavior that are typical of the job.

- Schedule your observations to cover a wide variety of important job situations.

- Directly observe the behavior. Ask for and encourage clear statements of fact and feelings from the person about her own or the team's performance and about constraints on performance.

- Work side by side with the person when the project merits.

- Encourage everyone to keep process improvement records and goal attainment records in ways that processes or goals can be measured.

- Keep records of behavior that clearly relate to success or failure (for example, a critical incident card or observed deviations that might reflect common or special causes).

Reviewing Goals.   For each important individual and team goal, a target date should be established at which time performance will be reviewed. Goal review should be an ongoing process in which everyone is involved and for which everyone is responsible. This ongoing review gives team members, as well as the team as a whole, opportunities to gauge the development and success of the team and its members.

Encouraging Others to Analyze and Understand Variations in Performance

At any moment in time, a gap will probably exist between actual and hoped for performance. This gap can be viewed as variation. One of the ways people empower themselves is to learn how to analyze and understand the causes of such variation; then they need to feel free to develop ways of reducing the variation. When the team or an individual discovers variation between expected and actual performance—either process or outcomes—the situation must be understood and corrected.

There are two categories of variation: common and special. For example, perhaps team performance declines over time. When they look for potential reasons for this decline, the work team establishes that the new air conditioning system is too noisy for good conversation. This variation is common because it affects all members of the team and reduces meaningful communication.

Take another example. Team performance declines for three weeks in succession. Reflecting on the causes of this decline, the team discovers that the new person has not yet gotten up to speed under the typical conditions of the team's performance responsibilities. This variation is special because the decrease in performance is a unique event. It is due to a specific and temporary lack of skill in one associate.

To understand the causes of variation, the team must evolve processes for documenting both individual and team performance. They must have the skill to identify, analyze, and solve performance problems—process and outcome. They also need to become skilled at using selected tools of Total Quality Management, such as Statistical Process Control (SPC).

Encouraging Self-Management

We believe that individuals need to be free to act autonomously—to make free and informed choices. A job's potential to motivate is a function of the extent to which it enables the person to act in an autonomous manner. People are more creative and productive when the situation allows a high degree of autonomy. The more the organization exemplifies values reflected in the Open Organization Model introduced in Chapter 3, the more autonomy people develop. The heart of continuous improvement centers on valuing valid information (both facts and feelings), free and informed choice, and internalized commitment to the process of continuous improvement.

The message is clear: In an open, empowering, supportive environment, people become more autonomous. Effective leaders create the conditions through which shared vision can emerge and flourish; where team learning is a norm. Ideally, all of your associates work because that is what they choose to do.

So how do you increase self-management or autonomy in the workplace? The list below provides some suggestions.

- Provide a role model of personal openness.

- Respond fully to associates' needs and requests.

- Allow each individual to take an active role in determining how to perform the tasks for which she is responsible.

- Enable the team itself to define job responsibilities.

- Allow your associate to solve problems that affect her performance.

- Help your associate understand how her job contributes to the whole. Help your associate see and understand that her job is vital to the success of the team.

- Give your associate leeway in determining the goals for her job. Emphasize learning and problem solving.

- Be a facilitator of problem solving, not the problem solver. Listen to the problems your associates are experiencing with empathy and concern, and let them be responsible for the solution.

- Communicate high expectations and make sure everyone has the opportunity and the resources to succeed.

- Encourage experimentation.

- Make every aspect of a person's job/role open to discussion and support the expression of true feelings that relate to personal, team, or organizational functioning.

- Keep the picture of desired performance clear to all.

- Trust in the process of self-management.

Once clear goals are agreed on, each person will attempt to self-regulate toward goal completion. Each person will seek to be competent—to master the environment—and each one will work to achieve the goal.

Encouraging People to Express Their Uniqueness

Work provides many opportunities for an individual to develop self-esteem. In fact, work is a major source of (or detriment to) self-esteem because of the many opportunities for real achievement. Self-managed people can develop self-esteem through work (and thus be self-empowered) to the extent that their jobs allow them to be themselves—express their uniqueness through their work.

Some people believe it is easier to control people, and thus their performance, by strictly prescribing what they should be doing. However, the bulk of the studies of performance show just the opposite: People perform better when they identify with a goal and are allowed to achieve it in their own unique manner.

How can you as coach encourage people to express their uniqueness? One of the major ways that you facilitate development of a sense of uniqueness is through how you communicate with others. One of the goals of communication is to enable the development of a sense of self-esteem through work. People build self-esteem by recognizing and accepting themselves as individuals, by verbally acknowledging their uniqueness, and by otherwise encouraging self-expression. Another way you can encourage a person's sense of uniqueness is by listening with acceptance and understanding. And finally, you may enhance the individual's sense of uniqueness by freeing her to learn and solve problems—innovate on the job.

Supporting Identification with the Job

There are different levels of commitment. A person can accept a job. She can choose a job when given a choice between two or more jobs. Or she can be identified with the job. When a person is identified with a job, the job in a sense has become an extension of her personality—the person meets personal needs through her work. The job may become a crucial part of a person's self-concept, of how she thinks of herself.

When a person identifies with a job, her priority system changes, leading her to structure time so that she can be involved in the activities typical of the job. In other words, the person invests more of herself in those things with which she is identified. She is more productive in those areas, too. She sees a direct relationship between her own needs and the job.

The person who identifies with her job is not just passing time there. Instead, this individual is adding value to time. Mastering the job, improving herself, learning, and growing are prime motives in her life.

Empowerment occurs when a person truly identifies with what she is doing and manages her own work efforts. A person who is empowered acts out of her own value system. Actions are not scripted or prescribed. They don't need to be forced, because working at a job with which the person identifies is what she has chosen.

The process by which people develop an identification with their jobs can be dissected. One of the most important avenues for building job commitment and identification is getting people involved in making decisions about their jobs. When people are so involved, they develop a sense of ownership for their jobs.

But ownership is not enough. People identify with their jobs when they are able to do them well. There is a saying: "First you get the habit of success, and then the habit gets you." When you succeed at something, you *become* that something. So it is important personally to ensure that other team members are equipped to do what is expected of them and to do it well.

People tend to identify with what enhances their feelings of worth. When a self-empowered individual contributes to her work in her own unique manner, that individual feels good about herself. She feels good about the work that she is doing.

People tend to identify with the job when they feel a sense of connectedness to the job and the work environment in general. When they are surrounded by others who value their work and each other, they develop a relationship to the team and the job that becomes important to them. Healthy people feel appreciated and loved, and in turn they express love and appreciation for others.

People need to believe that what they do is meaningful. When they perceive their work as meaningful, it is more satisfying to them; work becomes a more significant aspect of their personal identity. To enhance identification with the job, link it to a broader view or to the vision of the organization. Show them that they are the source of causation—that they are the creators of personal, as well as organizational, success. Also, when your associates can focus on clear goals and have the freedom to pursue those goals without rigid prescriptions, you will see more role or job identification.

PROVIDING LEADERSHIP THAT FOCUSES ON SELF-MASTERY

Ultimately, your effectiveness as a coach is determined by your ability to lead. Effective leaders typically share these common themes:

1. *Having a Guiding Vision and Sharing It.* Your effectiveness as a coach depends on your ability to create a shared vision with your team. This is different from the concept of managing. When you manage, you strive to control events so that they match a predetermined target. When you lead, you strive to release the potential of your team. Leading is the process of creation, while management is the process of maintenance. Leaders seem to share a number of qualities:

   - A guiding vision

   - Passion

   - Integrity (knowledge, candor, maturity)

   - Trustworthiness (setting examples)

   - Curiosity and daring

2. *Understanding Themselves.* It has been said that most of us are once born, while effective leaders are twice born. What this means is most people tend to live their lives as if life were happening to them. They react to the events of life. A leader, on the other hand, creates her life by getting free of the past and allowing what is most true about her to come to the fore. If you hope to encourage others to overcome their limitations, you must overcome your own.

3. *Knowing the Environment.* Not only do leaders know themselves, they also know the environment or context in which they work. This knowing has a lot to do with how people learn. Most of us learn because of shock—a crisis happens and we adapt. This is not what effective leaders do. They learn by anticipating, reflecting on their experiences, getting free of constraints, and taking risks. They reach out through the future.

4. *Trusting Themselves.* Effective leaders have an overall sense of purpose. They understand their vision—they feel it, they think it, they experience it. To be effective as a coach, you must trust and operate from your intuitions.

5. *Acting Their Vision.* The key to effective leadership is overcoming fear. We do this by developing our capacity for self-reflection and resolution (letting go). To be a leader, you must know what you are doing. And, you can do so only when you make the process conscious. Leaders learn how to lead by leading. When you can deal with uncertainties and ambiguity without grasping for the pat solution or taking rash action, then you are capable of leadership.

Desire + Mastery + Strategic Thinking + Work Capacity*
+ Self-Expression + Synthesis = Leadership

6. *Getting People on Their Side.* Leadership is ultimately only possible when people trust the vision. There are four ingredients to this trust:

- *Constancy of Purpose (Intentions).* I am the same yesterday, today, and tomorrow.

- *Disclosure Experienced by Others.* I am open in my sharing of data—facts and feelings.

- *Competence.* I am experienced as competent.

- *Contractual Experience by Others (Integrity).* I keep my word.

You can't make people work for you; you can only elicit from them the desire to do so. You lead through voice and through inspiring trust and empathy.

7. *Coaching for the Future.* The ability to create the future can be broken down into several components:

- Managing the dream

  - Creating a guiding vision

  - Communicating the vision

  - Recruiting

  - Rewarding

  - Retraining

  - Reorganizing

- Recognizing and accepting error

- Encouraging reflective dialogue

- Encouraging dissent

- Possessing optimism, faith, and hope

- Understanding the power of positive thinking

- Knowing where the culture is going to be

- Seeing the long view

---

*Work capacity is the number of minutes, hours, days, weeks, months, and years that a person will pursue a single task when experiencing empowerment to use her own discretion. Eliott Jacques, a noted British psychiatrist, has developed this concept over the last thirty-five or so years. In recent times, Jacques's thinking has influenced other authorities on leadership, for example, Marshall Sashkin.

WRAP-UP: SOME TRAPS TO AVOID

The performance development and empowerment process also presents opportunities for hooking associates and yourself into some very unproductive behaviors. Thus, it is helpful to review some of the potential traps:

1. Publicly criticizing your associate or your associate's behavior in a way that creates fears

2. Blaming the team's performance problems on any one associate

3. Discounting or failing to value the positive contributions an associate has made

4. Overgeneralizing from one failure, and assuming that everything an associate does is wrong

5. Being superior and not letting the associate get involved in helping herself get better

Remember, the performance empowerment process can make a real difference *if you make a total commitment to making it work.*

ACTIVITIES FOR DISCOVERY AND GROWTH

The activities in this section can help you create the performance leadership tools you need to create an empowered environment.

Activity 1
Criteria for Evaluating the Empowerment Process

Purpose

This activity can help you think about the kinds of problems you might encounter as you evaluate performance in an empowered environment.

Directions

Complete each part as indicated.

Part 1

List the criteria you currently use to evaluate yourself and your associates.

1.

2.

3.

4.

5.

6.

7.

8.

9.

10.

Part 2

Identify problems that exist with performance appraisal as you currently practice it. Is the practice consistent with the concept of empowerment?

1.

2.

3.

4.

5.

6.

7.

8.

9.

10.

Part 3

Identify barriers to success, how your performance review system might fail. In groups, brainstorm ways to make this system a viable aspect of team and organization success. How can you develop a performance appraisal system that is truly collaborative? Is it founded on the values of valid information (data and feelings), free and informed choice, and involved, committed associates?

Activity 2

Assumptions about Associates

Purpose

This activity helps people examine the kinds of assumptions they make about others and how they evaluate their performance. Often, assumptions may be contrary to the concept of a self-directed individual carrying out her work in a supportive environment.

Directions

1. Complete this instrument by checking the degree to which the following phrases describe your associates.

2. Score your responses by circling the correct number on the scoring form below, and then totalling your scores.

Assumptions about Associates: Scoring Form

	Never	Sometimes	Usually	Always
Enjoy their work	0	1	2	3
Are committed	0	1	2	3
Waste time	3	2	1	0
Work hard	0	1	2	3
Strive for excellence	0	1	2	3
Are competent	0	1	2	3
Lack initiative	3	2	1	0
Ask questions	0	1	2	3
Are creative	0	1	2	3
Know their jobs	0	1	2	3
Resist change	3	2	1	0
Take risks	0	1	2	3
Complain a lot	3	2	1	0
Care about the job	0	1	2	3
Want to do well	0	1	2	3

Value the company	0	1	2	3
Understand the goals	0	1	2	3
Are open	0	1	2	3
			TOTAL: _____	

If you score above 45 on this instrument, you probably believe people are capable of self-directed activity. If you score less than 30, you may need to change some of your assumptions before you will succeed at creating an empowering environment.

Activity 3
Creating an Empowering Environment

Purpose

This activity can help you systematically create an environment in which high performance is encouraged.

Directions

Complete each of the steps below.

Step 1: Defining Job Responsibilities. Have your associates record in priority order what they believe to be their top five to ten job responsibilities. Do the same yourself for each of these jobs. Then, compare your answers to those of your associates and discuss any discrepancies until a consensus is reached.

Primary Responsibilities of Jobs under My Supervision

Job _____
Primary Responsibilities

1.
2.
3.
4.
5.
6.
7.

Repeat this step for each job.

Step 2: Setting Goals.   For each job, complete a Goal Matrix.

Goal Matrix

Goal Areas	Results	Method	Measured by	When
Quantity				
1.				
2.				
3.				
Quality				
1.				
2.				
3.				
Interpersonal				
1.				
2.				
3.				

Step 3: Documenting Performance. For each job you are responsible for evaluating, identify sources of data that will enable you to make a valid evaluation.

Job	Success Criteria	Data Sources
1.		
2.		
3.		
4.		

Step 4: Discovering Rating Problems. Examine typical jobs that you currently supervise. Identify problems you have or expect to have in validly rating these jobs. Then, for each problem, together with your colleagues, identify ways to overcome these rating problems.

Jobs	Problems	Solutions

ON PSYCHOLOGICAL STRENGTH: THE OUTCOME OF DEVELOPING SELF-ESTEEM

What Is Psychological Strength?

One of the outcomes of coaching is the development of strong employees. We use the word strong to describe a person who always seems to get the job done no matter what the circumstance. All of us have fervently wished for such team members when nothing seems to be going right. In this section, we discuss this concept of strength so that you can create conditions that empower the development of strong associates.

Let's start with an example. Some time ago one of us was at a track meet watching the 1600-meter relay. The race was very tight between several teams, and the exchange zone was very crowded. As the athletes were passing the baton to the anchor in this race, one of the runners was knocked down, and it looked as if that team was out of the race. The anchor did not hold this view, for he got up and ran an incredible 400 meters, and won the race and the team championship. This young man could have lain there on the track lamenting his bad fortune; instead he got up and began to run like he had never run in his life.

This act represents what we mean by psychological strength. It is the inner attitude or belief that, whatever the situation, you can still prevail if you have the will to try.

> Psychological strength is the belief that you can succeed through your deliberate, focused effort.

Let's examine some dimensions of this definition.

One ingredient is belief. Strength is a belief that you can succeed. Everyone fails. It is how that failure is handled that separates people. Strong people predict that they will succeed, even when their most recent experiences have been failures. Other people predict they will fail, even when their most recent experiences have been successes.

Strength thus has a lot to do with having the faith and courage to continue what you believe to be the right thing to do, even when external events are not what they are supposed to be. When you fail, you get discouraged because there is a good chance that if you try again, you will also fail again. This discouragement leads you to feel anxious about your ability to succeed.

So, oftentimes when you fail, you stop yourself from trying again because you are afraid of failing again. Also, when you are excessively anxious, it is more likely you will fail because that excessive anxiety interferes with your performance. Most of us come to understand this relationship, at least subconsciously. So, strength is in part the ability to bind or overcome anxiety or to control its intensity. To accomplish this level of self-control, you have to hold a firm belief in your ability and in the impact of personal effort on achieving a goal.

Where does this belief come from? It is formed by having numerous successful experiences and from having the opportunity to learn that it is OK to fail. Effective coaches give their associates many opportunities to succeed and to learn through failure. W. E. Deming (1982) says, "Drive out fear!" We believe that fear inhibits both learning and problem solving. Obviously, we see hope as critical to pursuing vision.

People who get into the habit of succeeding develop a perceptual framework in which they identify themselves as winners. They expect to succeed. They act in a manner consistent with this mindset. On the other hand, people who get into the habit of failing develop a framework in which they expect to fail. They tend to act in a manner that fulfills the failure expectancy.

Psychological strength consists in the *courage to act*. When you act, you never know exactly what the outcome will be; even when you make good decisions and exhibit true competence, sometimes failure still occurs. Thus, when the most recent actions have resulted in failure, it takes courage to act again.

Many American business leaders know when things are wrong, but they fail to act because they lack courage. Most of us are so used to acting within a framework in which we are relatively comfortable that, when we go outside this framework, we feel discomfort if only because we are in an unfamiliar place. Courage is the willingness to go beyond that place of comfort. It is the willingness to operate within a zone of discomfort in order to accomplish an important goal or to realize a value you hold dear. It is the willingness to try and try again.

Yet why is it that some people try, while others just stay put, secure in their illusion of safety? It has a great deal to do with how much we trust ourselves and with our sense of self-efficacy—the feeling that we can cause positive action as a result of our competence. If you tend to do what you set out to do over time, then you come to trust yourself; further, if you tend to do what you set out to do in a competent manner, then you develop a sense of efficacy—the belief that you have the power to produce the outcome you intended to produce. At the critical point before action is taken, the person acts on the hope of succeeding. She will fail to act out of the fear of failing.

Again, coaches can greatly influence their associates by helping them develop a sense of efficacy, or personal power. This is done by providing opportunities for learning, doing, and accomplishing. As a coach, you do not take the place of a player (although there have been player/coaches), but rather provide direction and support from the sidelines to facilitate the person's succeeding.

Another dimension of our definition of psychological strength is *effort*. How hard are you willing to work to attain what you believe to be important? It has always amazed us that the really great people, besides having such great skill, also have an extraordinary commitment to hard work. According to their own testimony, they realize that to be the best they can be, they have to hone their talents. It is not enough to have talent when you want to be the best. You have to work hard also.

What Are the Requirements for Developing Inner Psychological Strength?

Studies of the development of self-esteem increase our understanding of the requirements for developing inner strength. People act to meet their needs. Four expecially important basic needs underlie the development of self-esteem:

1. *Connectedness.* To develop self-esteem, people need a sense of belonging or connectedness to themselves and to the larger world in which they live and work.

2. *Competence.* People need to feel that they are the masters of their own ships, that they have the power to produce positive outcomes through their own efforts. To feel powerful you must be competent.

3. *Uniqueness.* The development of a sense of uniqueness is also critical to the development of self-esteem. People have a need to feel special and unique.

4. *Sense of Purpose.* Finally, to feel worthwhile and good about themselves, people need to develop a sense of purpose. This sense refers to the development of frameworks that enable them to create meaning in their lives, to solve the problems confronting them, to make choices, and to plan for the future.

Under What Conditions Do People Develop This Core of Inner Psychological Strength?

There are four conditions you can create to encourage individuals to develop feelings of worth and self-esteem. First, you can ensure that every team member feels accepted and valued by the team. Second, you can ensure that each person's uniqueness is respected and allowed expression. Third, you can ensure that each team member has the skills she needs to succeed and provide opportunities for accomplishment. And fourth, you can help team members discover the meaning and purpose underlying their actions in the team.

P A R T 3

Tools for Coaching

How adults learn and the specific skills required for effective coaching are the focus of this section. As a coach you probably already have a theory about how people learn. You may not have articulated this theory explicitly, but nevertheless it is revealed in your approach to the many coaching opportunities you encounter every day. It is our belief that, while your theory may be sound, you will increase your effectiveness by clarifying the assumptions you make about how to facilitate learning in associates.

Chapter 6, Understanding How People Learn and Grow, develops some general ideas about the process of learning with the intent of increasing your understanding of how adults learn.

Chapter 7, Coaching for High-Performance, examines the specific kinds of skills that are involved in effective coaching. Coaching is a process of enabling, supporting, and encouraging another person to go beyond current limits. It is a way of facilitating learning.

CHAPTER 6

Understanding How People Learn and Grow

PURPOSE

As a leader/coach, you probably have a theory about how people learn. You may not have articulated this theory explicitly, but it is nevertheless revealed in your approach to the many coaching opportunities that you have daily. However, although your theory may be sound, you can increase your effectiveness by clarifying your assumptions about how to facilitate learning.

This chapter introduces a range of ideas about why and how adults learn and grow. These ideas are based on current research and theory about adult learning and provide a sound basis for understanding how to facilitate learning more effectively.

LEARNING GOALS

The goals of this chapter are to have you

- Understand the principles underlying adult learning
- Understand the gradual developmental nature of learning
- Understand how a person's expectations influence her learning
- Understand how your own expectations affect the learning process

LEARNING IN TODAY'S ORGANIZATIONS

Supporting learning is an important leadership task in an organization striving to achieve high levels of performance. Each manager must ensure that the people she supervises know how to perform at the highest possible levels. Ultimately, the future of the organization is determined by the effectiveness of its members. Again, the key coaching role is to stimulate learning as an essential component of performance.

However, changes in technology, the marketplace, and people are so rapid that your and your associates' competence must continuously improve. Every person must be equipped to deal with the many demands for change placed on the organization: technology changes, customer demand for more and better service, the competition, and new products emerging at an increasing rate. All of these demands, and myriads of others, make it imperative that you as well as the other members of your organization keep learning. To do so regularly requires peer support. You must know how to coach.

To induce ongoing learning in individuals, the various work groups, and the organization, coaching becomes an important and vital task. Because each person learns differently, your coaching success depends on your ability to adapt your methods to the unique learning characteristics of your associates. Coaching competencies often are not the same as those required to perform your specific duties within the organization. Therefore, in order to coach, you must learn a new set of competencies.

PREREQUISITES FOR EFFECTIVE COACHING OF LEARNING

To be an effective coach, you must master four sets of concepts:

1. Factors affecting adult learning

2. The learning process

3. How to design instruction

4. How to coach

PARADIGMS AND THEIR EFFECTS, OR WHY YOU NEED TO EXAMINE YOUR THEORY

Your knowledge, attitudes, skills, and values—*and* those of your associates—affect the outcomes of learning, problem solving, and coaching. Let's examine some of the relationships between competence and values and learn how to use this knowledge to increase your chances of success as a coach.

How Your Knowledge, Skills, and Attitudes Affect Your Associates' Success

As a coach, you have great influence over your associates. Your positive results in coaching are determined by three *success factors*, namely:

1. Your competence as a coach

2. Your expectations about your associates

3. Your expertise relative to the content of the coaching

Success Factor 1: Your Competence as a Coach. Among the most important determinants of your success as a coach is your personal effectiveness in facilitating learning in others. To what extent are you capable of facilitating learning in others?

Research about what qualities are ideal for facilitating learning has revealed that the most effective facilitators are people who convey patience, friendly persuasion, acceptance of others, and unfeigned love. This doesn't mean that the coaching relationship is always characterized by camaraderie and the absence of conflict. In fact, the coaching relationship will often be problematic and stressful.

The ideal coach holds associate autonomy in high regard. When agreeing on learning goals and making plans for learning, the best coaches respect the essential independence and freedom of their associates. They do not attempt to impose their goals or plans on their associates.

Good coaches enter into the coaching relationship as a dialogue between equals. Coaching is a relationship built on mutuality and collaboration. Both participants work together to achieve agreed-on goals. The best coaches are open to change. Openness refers to the coach's understanding that reality is contingent on one's perspective. If the data seem to warrant such a change, good coaches explore and alter their perspective.

Table 6.1 summarizes some of the qualities associated with effective coaching and facilitating:

**TABLE 6.1
QUALITIES OF EFFECTIVE COACHING
AND FACILITATION OF LEARNING**

- Knowledge of the specific content area

- Genuine interest in people

- Ability to communicate clearly

- Patience with the learning process

- Empathy or understanding of others

- Tolerance for mistakes during learning

- Sense of humor

- Ability to treat each person as unique

- Uncompromising respect for people

Success Factor 2: Your Expectations about Your Associate. Another competence of good coaching involves managing your own expectations of another person's performance. Effective coaching depends on your assumptions and attitudes about your associate's ability to learn from you. How do your assumptions about others and your attitudes toward an associate's learning affect the outcomes of coaching?

Numerous studies have shown that a coach's expectations have a profound influence on the performance of others. For example, if you believe that people are able to learn, that they enjoy learning, and that they will take responsibility for learning, then they will typically learn more, and learn more rapidly, than if you held a contrary point of view. This has been referred to as the **Pygmalion effect**: You get what you expect to get.

A sociologist, Robert K. Merton (1948), while at Columbia University, first observed the phenomenon that the expectation of an event could be a self-fulfilling prophecy. For example, during the depression years of the 1930s, many banks—quite solvent by banking standards—experienced a run on their funds that caused them to fail. The withdrawal of funds was modest at first and then grew finally to staggering proportions. The expectation of an event (failure) leads quickly to its actual occurrence.

A social psychologist at Harvard University, Robert Rosenthal (1974), and associates conducted over three hundred studies of this phenomenon in a wide variety of learning situations. Their findings clearly support the notion that expectations of significant others can definitely influence performance. More important, if a person promoting learning in another person had positive expectations of the other, the person holding those expectations behaved differently toward the learned by (1) creating a supportive psychological climate, (2) giving more feedback, (3) providing more information, and (4) encouraging and receiving more output, including additional assignments.

Keeping the effects of expectations on performance in mind, let's review the most effective setting for facilitating learning and growth. Brookfield (1986) describes six additional qualities of learning-promoting relationships among adults.

1. More learning takes place if learning is seen as a voluntary, self-initiated activity. People learn best what they want to learn because they are naturally motivated to learn.

2. More learning takes place in a climate of mutual respect. People must feel psychologically safe and be receptive to having their assumptions challenged. It also helps if you enable them to challenge you.

3. The best learning takes place in an environment characterized by a spirit of collaboration.

4. Learning involves a balance between action and self-reflection. The best coaches encourage associates to investigate new ways of being, to experiment with new behavior, and then to reflect on their experience.

5. Effective coaching involves facilitation of critical reflection. The coach and the associate together reflect on the usefulness of current assumptions and perspectives, explore alternatives, and discover more useful frameworks for guiding action.

6. People learn best when their learning is self-directed. The learner plays an important role in setting the goals for learning and in establishing the criteria by which learning is to be evaluated.

In light of what is known about the effects of expectations on associates' performance, it is useful to think about your own assumptions and attitudes about learning. What are your basic assumptions about learning and about learners? Activity 2 at the end of this chapter will help you answer these questions.

Table 6.2 compares two approaches to teaching: **pedagogy** and **andragogy**. Remember, the assumptions you embrace have a profound effect on your success as a coach.

TABLE 6.2
LEARNING ASSUMPTIONS

Pedagogy	Andragogy
1. The learner	
A dependent person	An independent person
2. Role of experience	
Instructor is major source of experience	Adults bring much useful experience
3. Readiness to learn	
Instructor initiates readiness to learn	Readiness is generated by the learner in the context of the need to learn
4. Orientation to learning	
Learners deal with subjects	Learners deal with their needs to know in the context of a job to do
5. Motivation	
External motivators are usually required	The strongest motivator comes from within the person

Success Factor 3: Your Expertise Relative to the Content of Coaching. Coaching effectiveness depends on your understanding and mastery of the competencies you wish to coach. You must understand what you are expected to produce and how to go about producing it to effectively coach others to produce. Evered and Selman (1989) state that one of the characteristics of the most famous coaches in sports and other walks of life was an undying commitment to preparation. These coaches knew their trade inside out, and their knowledge of the game enabled them to be so effective.

Having clarified your own expectations and assumptions about learning and having explored your competence to facilitate learning, let's examine learning from the perspective of others.

How Learners' Attitudes Affect Their Success: Motivation

Effective coaching begins with the learner's needs. Good coaches always start with an understanding of what the learner wants to know and why she wants to learn it. Then the coach applies her knowledge of the learning process to facilitate learning. We therefore examine some of the principles underlying the motivations for adult learning.

What motivates people? There are many different aspects to this intriguing question. First, we can look at motivation from the point of view of what people need—drive reduction theory. People learn what they need to learn. Brandeis University psychologist Abraham Maslow developed a model he called the *hierarchy of needs*, shown in Figure 6.1.

FIGURE 6.1
MASLOW'S HIERARCHY OF NEEDS

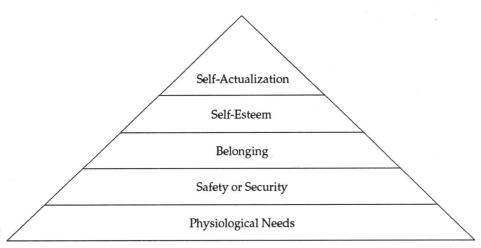

Maslow theorized that needs are hierarchical and occur in an order of prepotency. Lower-level needs—for instance, physiological needs for food and water—come before safety or security needs. It is possible to identify what people need. Maslow's hierarchy of needs remains a viable theory of motivation and personality.

The lower-level needs are more powerful than the higher-level needs and must be satisfied before the higher-level needs can be fully met. The needs can, therefore, be arranged as a pyramid. To be effective as a coach, you must first understand what people need and then provide an environment in which they are able to meet their needs.

Studies of associate satisfaction have shown that when an environment enables people to meet their needs for safety, security, and belonging they are neither dissatisfied nor satisfied. They feel neutral about that environment. However, when an environment enables people to meet their needs for esteem (competence, power, purpose, uniqueness) and growth (actualization through creative accomplishment), people become connected to that environment.

A need is a specific absence of something—a deficit in the person. Thirst created by a lack of fluid in the body cells is a physiological need. By contrast, self-actualization needs are created by a person holding a value like honesty and needing to work in an environment where that value can be experienced or realized. Felt needs at any level in the hierarchy cause the learner to increase her activity level. A goal becomes anything which, when accomplished, fulfills the need. A *motive* connects the *need* and the *goal*. The increased energy state is called *drive*. Progress to the goal is marked by feedback, and obstacles to the goal often cause frustration and anger in the learner. Organizational constraints, such as the lack of a necessary tool, represent barriers to learning and performance.

FIGURE 6.2
A MODEL OF NEED SATISFACTION

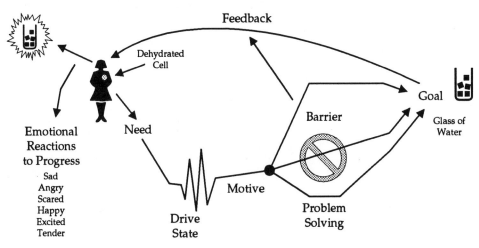

Need activates desire; desire activates goal-directed behavioral experimentation. When the behavior leads to a valued incentive, it is repeated. If this leads to a relatively permanent change in behavior, learning has taken place.

Given that people learn best when learning meets their specific needs, it is possible to identify some general principles that provide a foundation for adult learning.

1. Learning in adults is lifelong and continues outside any formal class setting.

2. Learning is based on the intentions and desires of the learner to meet a specific need or to grow because of curiosity or in search of mastery—for the sake of growing.

3. Adults learn best when their learning is problem-centered—a job to do: Their learning helps them deal more effectively with their personal lives and life at work.

4. Learning is enhanced when it is meaningful in relation to the adult's life-style.

5. Learning is enhanced when the outcome of the learning process is immediately applicable to the learner's life.

6. The learner's past experiences play a crucial role in determining whether learning takes place. Past learning can either facilitate or inhibit present learning. The learner's expectations of success or failure are critical to expectations and beliefs about the learning experience.

7. Adults prefer the outcome of learning to increase their sense of independence and autonomy. All learning should lead to autonomy and empowerment.

8. Learning is enhanced when it taps the experiences of the learner. One critical role of the coach is to encourage the learner to explore her current outlook on life and to encourage the learner to challenge the assumptions on which that outlook is built.

How Learners' Expectations Influence Their Success

Another reason people learn considers not only their needs, but their beliefs and expectations. This area is called **expectancy theory**. Stated simply, people learn only when they believe they can learn and when that learning helps them obtain an incentive they value.

This is the general manner in which the expectancy theory explains human action:

- Beliefs about the learning situation influence thoughts.

- Thoughts influence feelings.

- Feelings influence actions.

- Actions influence outcomes.
- Outcomes generally corroborate beliefs.
- Negative beliefs produce negative outcomes.
- Positive beliefs produce positive outcomes.

If learners have a history of failing they will most likely fail to learn even when they are fully able to learn. Why? Because they expect to fail in the long run, even if they are currently succeeding. People do not learn, even when they are able, if they believe that learning will not get them a desired reward. There are several important implications to this theory:

1. Make sure that you help the learner understand how learning relates to what she wants to learn. Help the learner see how learning new skills will help get what she wants.

2. Find out about the learner's learning history. If it is characterized by failure, then show the learner how to gain control of the environment by planning and producing successful experiences.

3. Make sure that the incentive the learner expects to receive is available yet contingent on successful learning.

THE LEARNING PROCESS

Learning is a process by which a person's behavior changes as a result of experience. Effective coaches understand this and use it to facilitate learning.

Types of Learning

There are two basic types of learning. The first is **maintenance learning**. This is learning in which you acquire new knowledge and skills to adapt better to an existing situation. For example, you may choose to learn a new set of skills to stay current in your present position.

A second type of learning is **innovative learning**. It involves the process of critically reflecting on the assumptions that underlie your thoughts, feelings, and actions, and of becoming open to discovering and experimenting with new modes of experiencing the world.

In the role of coach, you must facilitate both maintenance learning and innovative learning. Which methods are most appropriate for the two types of learning?

In our view, the two types of learning require different methods. In maintenance or skill-acquisition learning, the most appropriate methods focus on task analysis, breaking down competencies into core skill areas, practicing skills with ongoing corrective feedback, and repetition. The method most appropriate to innovative learning involves critical reflection on values and assumptions, feelings and intuitions, and thoughts and actions. It involves a process of self-discovery and empowerment in which the coach's role is one of a mirror and challenger. This method is more of a dialogue than an activity, and it is more collaborative and participative than didactic.

To be an effective coach you must be prepared to teach as well as to reflect and challenge the associate's self-limiting assumptions.

Principles for Facilitating Maintenance Learning

Understanding the developmental nature of learning and strengthening your ability to apply the principles of learning will make you a more effective coach. Remember these key points about learning:

- *Repetition.* Provide repetition because this allows for continued practice of the new skills.

- *Motivation.* Motivate the learner by frequent reinforcement.

- *Results.* Break the learning down into manageable steps so that the learner can master the new skills in small steps and obtain positive feedback in the process.

- *Pace.* Pace the learning so as not to fatigue the learner.

- *Individualization.* Treat each learner as an individual who learns at her own pace.

- *Involvement.* Get involved with the learner. It is easier to instruct if the learner trusts you.

- *Memory.* Show the learner the task several times because memory depends, in part, on repetition.

- *Problem Solving.* Having the learner think through a problem helps her master the problem.

- *Performance.* Learning by doing is the best way to help someone quickly master a new skill.

- *Modeling.* Learners learn by watching you do the job well.

Principles for Facilitating Innovative Learning

Innovative learning involves going beyond the known and creating new models and strategies. Because innovation always involves an element of risk, your effectiveness as a coach depends on your ability to help the associate/learner manage the level or risk. Some general principles for helping your associate feel confident are:

- *Listening.* Your ability to facilitate change is determined by your ability to understand your associate.

- *Caring.* Ultimately, learning is determined by what the other person needs and wants. Your ability to understand what these needs are and to act in a manner consistent with these needs determines the fruitfulness of your coaching relationship.

- *Openness.* Your effectiveness is determined, in part, by the degree to which you allow yourself to enter into a partnership with your associate based on mutual sharing.

- *Awareness.* To mirror successfully another person's frame of reference, you have to allow yourself to concentrate on the other person. You must become aware of the person's values and how her actions relate to those values. Through this awareness you can help your associate examine the values and assumptions upon which her choices are based and transcend these limitations.

- *Challenge.* Often you must confront and challenge other people's limiting assumptions. It is up to you to mirror this reality to your associates.

- *Honesty.* Honesty is your willingness to share what you see without the need to protect your associate or yourself. Growth sometimes involves considerable pain. You are honest when you choose to deal directly with this pain.

Putting It All Together: Can/Want/Try

Learning takes place through interactions between the learner and the environment. From the learner's point of view, there are three essentials: *can* (knowledge, attitude, skill); *want* (motive); and *try* (belief). From the coach's point of view, environmental requisites of the learning processes include *opportunity, feedback* (data), and *value* (purpose).

When the learner has opportunities to try new behaviors, when the learner gets feedback about results, and when the learner sees the meaning of her actions, the learner learns and grows.

ACTIVITIES FOR DISCOVERY AND GROWTH

These two activities can help you think about the kinds of opportunities for coaching you now enjoy and the effects of your assumptions on the coaching process.

Activity 1
Identifying Coaching Opportunities

Purpose

This activity helps you to identify coaching opportunities in your environment.

Directions

Among your current associates, what coaching opportunities now exist? List each individual associate's name and describe the opportunities. What learning needs are there? Diagnose the opportunities. Are they skill or attitude problems?

Associate	Behavior Exhibited	Type of Problem, Skill, or Attitude
1.		
2.		
3.		
4.		
5.		
6.		
7.		
8.		
9.		

Activity 2
Assumptions about Learning and Learners

Purpose

This exercise develops increased understanding of your assumptions about learning and how these assumptions affect your coaching.

Directions

Respond to each of the following statements by circling the number that most accurately explains your assumptions about learning and the learner. Use the following scale to describe your specific beliefs:

1	2	3	4	5	6	7	8	9
Never		Occasionally		Frequently		Often		Always

1 2 3 4 5 6 7 8 9	1. I believe all learners are different.
1 2 3 4 5 6 7 8 9	2. I believe that given enough time and proper instruction, learners can learn anything.
1 2 3 4 5 6 7 8 9	3. I give my learners opportunities for frequent practice.
1 2 3 4 5 6 7 8 9	4. I break instruction down into reasonable steps.
1 2 3 4 5 6 7 8 9	5. When I coach, I give clear instructions.
1 2 3 4 5 6 7 8 9	6. The pace of learning is determined by the learner.
1 2 3 4 5 6 7 8 9	7. The learner progresses to new material when she has mastered a particular step.
1 2 3 4 5 6 7 8 9	8. I explain carefully how the associate's job fits into the rest of the organization.
1 2 3 4 5 6 7 8 9	9. I provide many incentives for learning.
1 2 3 4 5 6 7 8 9	10. I influence the learning environment.
1 2 3 4 5 6 7 8 9	11. I make the learning experience enjoyable.
1 2 3 4 5 6 7 8 9	12. I get to know the learner.
1 2 3 4 5 6 7 8 9	13. I enjoy coaching.
1 2 3 4 5 6 7 8 9	14. I enjoy people.
1 2 3 4 5 6 7 8 9	15. I believe people like to learn.

The ideal response for each of these statements would have been a "9". You may recognize this to be true but may have honestly and appropriately rated yourself lower on many of the statements. If that is the case, then rewrite the statements so that you could honestly respond with a nine. What are your assumptions about learning and the learner?

ON ATTRIBUTION—HOW PEOPLE EXPLAIN BEHAVIOR

Attribution is a topic usually reserved for texts in social psychology; however, we feel that an understanding of how people make judgments of themselves and others is an important element in the tool kit of the successful coach. We approach the concept of attribution in the context of its relevance to coaching.

We all have a need to make sense of our world, to explain why things are as they are. This need arises from our deeper need to perceive our world as orderly and predictable.

Attribution is the process of explaining the causes of events in our lives. For example, from your perspective as a coach, you observe that an associate has failed to achieve an important goal. Your immediate response might be to explain why this failure has occurred. Is it because of incompetence, or is it because of unpredictable obstacles in the way of achievement?

If you explain the failure in terms of competence, then you have made a **dispositional attribution**: you have attributed failure to an internal characteristic of the individual. If you explain the failure in terms of environmental barriers, then you have made a **situational attribution**: you have attributed failure to circumstances.

The implications of a dispositional versus a situational attribution are vast for both the associate and you. If you believe an associate is incompetent, then you tend to act consistently with that expectation. If you believe that failure is due to unfortunate circumstances, then you will act in a manner consistent with that belief.

Your perceptions of an associate are determined by your expectations and by the information you possess about that specific person. You tend to base your initial attributions on several factors:

1. Your perception of the person's abilities

2. Your perceptions of the person's motivations or intentions

3. The perceived degree of difficulty of the act

4. The perceived level of choice in the situation

For example, you may observe that a capable associate is not performing well (intentions) even though the task is easy. You infer from this evidence that he is lazy.

Once you begin to make attributions regarding another's behavior, these attributions form your implicit theory of personality for that person and bias your decisions. This bias is called the **halo effect**. Once you develop a theory, you tend to see only what conforms to your model. In short, unless you are conscious of the bias, you don't see the person at all; you see only your perception of that person.

Other factors also affect whether we make a dispositional or situational attribution: distinctiveness, consensus, and consistency. The *distinctiveness* of behavior is the extent to which the behavior stands out from the norm or the extent to which the behavior is unusual. Distinctive behavior tends to elicit dispositional attributions. *Consensus* is the degree of unanimity regarding the cause of behavior. A behavior that conforms to a consensus expectation is usually labeled as situationally determined. *Consistency* is the extent to which a behavior is consistent with other behaviors exhibited by the individual. Finally, the *stability* of the environment affects the type of attribution people make to explain what they observe. All these factors explain a given performance.

We explain behavior by the distinctiveness, consistency, and consensus, as well as by ability, intentions, task difficulty, and freedom of choice.

The Fundamental Attribution Error

Coaches often use one set of criteria to evaluate their own behavior and another set to evaluate their associates' behavior. For example, people typically tend to explain their own successes in dispositional terms, but they explain their associates' successes in terms of situational factors. The reverse is true for failures. This fundamental attribution error increases the gulf between coaches and associates.

Consequences of Attributions

People alter their behavior on the basis of the attributions they make about others and about themselves. This is the *Pygmalion effect* at work. We tend to perceive what we expect to perceive. When we make attributions concerning others, we are often using a certain perceptual set, seeing what we expect to see. If you expect someone to be competent, you are more likely to give that person the opportunity to demonstrate her competence and to interpret successful performance as being due to that competence. If you think someone is lazy you may explain her failures as due to her lack of effort, or you may not provide that person sufficient opportunity to complete the task.

Our attributions about our own performance also have important implications. Is our performance caused by external or internal factors? People who believe that their performance is due to their own skills and efforts are said to have an *internal locus of control*, and those who believe that performance is controlled by luck or powerful others are said to have an *external locus of control*. These positions become beliefs.

Two major effects of locus of control are relevant to us as coaches. One is the immediate effect. People who are externally focused do not work as hard to learn new skills as those who are internally focused. A long-term effect of this orientation is that externally motivated people come to expect that there is nothing they can do to help themselves, and, in effect, they lose the capacity to see that their own set of assumptions is limiting their ability to succeed.

Many of those whom you coach have assumptions that are essentially self-limiting. In your role as a coach, you must help people explore their assumptions and encourage them to experiment with and reflect on new sets of assumptions. To do this effectively, you must explore, understand, and perhaps, change your own assumptions. As a coach, a critical factor for success is your own ability to engage in **double-loop learning,** where you challenge your own assumptions.

C H A P T E R 7

Coaching for High Performance

PURPOSE

Chapter 6 shares some general ideas about the process of adult learning by explaining how adults learn and what they want and prefer regarding the learning environment. In this chapter, we examine the specific kinds of skills that go into effective coaching, the process of enabling, supporting, and encouraging other people to go beyond their current limits. Because coaching is a process that facilitates learning, we focus especially on the general steps of the coaching process.

LEARNING GOALS

The learning goals for this chapter are to help you

- Be aware of the many coaching opportunities that may exist
- Increase your information regarding the role of leadership in coaching
- Understand the steps of coaching
- Become a more effective coach

COACHING AND LEADERSHIP

Coaching is leadership in action. Effective leadership skills are not necessarily related to your personality traits or to your style of leadership. Rather, leadership effectiveness is related to how mature and well developed you are as a person. The most effective leaders are fully developed as individuals and have the personal capacity to think ahead, visualize, and develop alternative futures.

Integrated or well-developed individuals seem to have a number of qualities in common. Fundamental to their well-being is a sense of guiding vision. These people know what is important to them and what they want to accomplish. They also know how to communicate their visions with other people in ways that enable others to share their dreams.

A second quality of integrated people is their self-knowledge. Effective leaders know themselves. They understand the various factors that have influenced their development. Although they have learned from the past, they are not bound by the past. Rather, they have let go of the past and have learned how to be themselves. They have learned how to shape the world in terms consistent with their own guiding visions. They are self-organizing and self-managing.

A quality related to self-knowledge is knowing the world. Effective people have a deep understanding of the world and how the world affects them. In more practical terms, the best coaches know their associates well. Eric Fromm (1947, pp. 54ff.) contended that mature relatedness depends on an in-depth knowledge of the other person, a responsibility to that person's unique needs and values, and the self-discipline to work within the framework of those needs. Coaching is done within the context of a productive (as opposed to destructive) relationship between people who are equals in the most vital aspects of life—personal worth, value, and unique contribution. Carl Rogers (1961, pp. 420ff.) used the phrase *unconditional positive regard* to express the worth and value of every human being. He saw the act of accepting the worth of another human being as the quintessential step in inviting that person to become a "fully functioning person."

Self-knowledge coupled with knowledge of the world gives rise to a sense of trust and confidence in yourself and your intuitions. Effective leaders, effective individuals, and effective coaches believe in what they are doing and have the inner confidence to trust their instincts and intuitions. Sometimes as a coach you must play your hunches and go with your instincts in order to support another person's growth. Human beings flower as a result of enhancing experiences and supportive climates. Karen Horney (1945, p. 19) said, "My own belief is that man has the capacity as well as the desire to develop his potentialities and become a decent human being, and that these deteriorate if his relationship to others and hence to himself is, and continues to be, disturbed. I believe that man can change and keep on changing as long as he lives."

Effective leaders have a well-developed perspective on life and a point of view consistent with this perspective. This means that the best coaches have a well-developed philosophy of life, and they live in a manner consistent with this point of view. They live in a manner consistent with what they believe to be true.

Another quality typical of the best coaches as well as the best leaders is the ability to get people on their side. You cannot demand trust, you must earn it. Effective coaches have the ability to earn the trust of others. How do they do this? For one thing, they are reliable. They do what they say they are going to do. Second, they are constant. They act the same every day. They live according to their values every day. Third, they have the capacity for empathy, the ability to place themselves in the other's perspective and appreciate and understand what that person is experiencing (Rogers, 1961, p. 420).

Finally, effective coaches lead by acting. They are willing to take risks and embrace errors, and they thrive on adversity. They do not need scripts or guarantees of success. Instead, they have ideas or visions of what is possible, and they are willing to work hard to create the full expression of these visions, even in the face of uncertainty.

THE MANY MODES OF COACHING

Coaching takes place in a variety of ways, using a variety of methods. We identify four modes of coaching:

1. Modeling

2. Instructing (teaching/facilitating)

3. Mirroring

4. Counseling

FIGURE 7.1
MODES OF COACHING

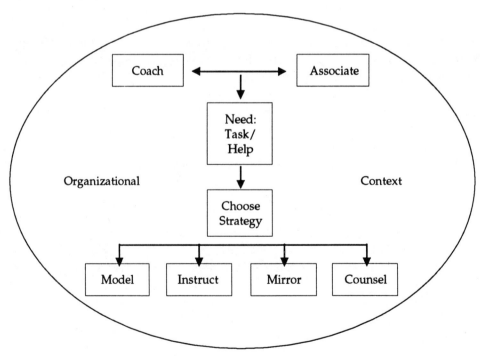

Modeling is coaching by example. You are coaching when you live by the values that you tell others are important to you. When you coach by example or emulation, you create conditions of empowerment. Effective coaches often enable others through their own example. Your power as a model is enhanced by several qualities:

1. Competency

2. Credibility

3. Trustworthiness

4. Intentions

To be an effective coach, it is necessary for you to live by the values that you hope will be an inspiration for change in your associates.

Coaches are often teachers, actively instructing their associates to help them learn new skills. To be effective in this mode, you have to know how to instruct and how to create opportunities for learning and growth.

Mirroring is what you do when you help a person reflect on her past experience and, in the process of reflecting, enable that person to transcend old concepts and values that limit her potential.

A final mode of coaching is counseling. This is similar to mirroring in that you act as the other's eyes and ears, but it goes beyond mere reflection to efforts to enable your associate to consciously make changes in her behavior.

The remainder of this chapter discusses the instructing mode in depth.

THE COACH AS INSTRUCTOR/TEACHER

Success in the role of coach as instructor involves knowing

- How to enable learning

- How to prepare for and deliver effective instruction

A Four-Step Strategy for Coaching

Effective coaches tend to follow a specific strategy when they teach new skills. There are four steps to this teaching process:

1. *Telling.* Tell the associate what the task is, how it fits into the broader context of the team and organization, how it is done, when it is done, and how well it is to be done.

2. *Showing.* Show the associate how to perform the skills and explain the relevance of each task as you demonstrate.

3. *Doing.* Allow the associate to perform the task, and as she does this, ask her to explain why she is doing each task and step along the way. This might involve having the associate instruct the coach in the process, telling and showing what, how, when, and so on.

4. *Correcting.* Correct the associate's performance by providing feedback. When a coach provides feedback that allows the associate to correct mistakes and reinforces accomplishments, the associate builds competence and self-confidence.

Preparing for Coaching

A good coach, like a good teacher, prepares ahead of time. It is not enough to know how to do the job. Even the best practitioners often forget key points during training. Thus, it is essential to make a plan. There are several steps to developing a learning plan.

Step 1: Defining Learning Goals. The first step toward effective coaching is defining the goals you wish to accomplish. When coaches deal with adults, the development of goals evolves out of a collaboration between the coach and the associate. Goals are mutually agreed on.

Goals are based on need. There are two origins for learning goals. When the associate reflects on a gap between her dreams or aspirations and the current situation, the associate is experiencing a felt or recognized desire or want. On the other hand, when the associate observes a gap between the current situation and her life requirements, then the associate is experiencing a felt or recognized need.

Whether the goal is based on a felt want or a felt need, it seems clear that most coaching situations are initiated by the associate and not by the coach. When the associate enjoys an open relationship with the coach, the coach is likely to understand that individual's wants and needs and to be in a position to provide coaching. In such an open relationship coaching is most likely to succeed.

Often the associate you coach wants to acquire a new competency. Maybe technology affecting her job has changed. Maybe your associate has transferred to a new role. Maybe your associate simply wants to develop new skills. Whatever the reason for wanting to learn, it is helpful to think of the task of helping an associate acquire a new competency at three levels. First, every competency involves acquisition of a specific set of facts or knowledge. This is called the *cognitive component* of a competency. Second, each competency has a value component. This is called the *affective component* of a competency. Third, most competencies involve acquiring a set of behavioral skills if they are to be implemented successfully. This is known as the *behavioral component* of a competency.

Thus, when you and your associate set goals for coaching, establish objectives at all three levels: the cognitive, the affective (or conative), and the behavioral. Table 7.1 displays the hierarchy of learning objectives at each domain.

TABLE 7.1
TYPES OF LEARNING OBJECTIVES

Type of Objective	Example
Knowledge (Cognitive)	By the end of this session you will be able to explain the four functions of the molding machine to your peers.
Attitudes (Affective)	By the end of training you will successfully stop your work process to solve problems anytime you observe that any motor mount produced exceeds the established control limits.
Skill (Behavioral)	By the end of training you will successfully produce motor mounts within established cost and quality standards.

Step 2: Analyzing a Competency. Each competency you share usually consists of a number of specific skills, that is, specific steps necessary to execute the competency. In turn, each step can be divided into a number of key points. A Competency Analysis tells you and your associate, in detail, what the associate must do to execute the competency. Engage your associate(s) in the process of competency analysis. Thus, you engage the other person in the process so that the associate will become self-directed at acquiring new competencies. This encourages learning how to learn or metalearning on the part of the associate.

To analyze a competency:

- Define the skills that constitute the competency.

- Create a skill list for the various competencies required by associate(s) on the job(s).

- Record the steps required to perform each key skill.

- For each key skill, develop a list of the key points to address during coaching.

- Develop a coaching worksheet for the competency to be coached. (See Activity 1 at end of this chapter.)

Step 3: Developing Learning Activities. An analysis of the actions of the best coaches shows that they are expert at creating situations in which learning can occur and at getting associates actively involved in the learning process. A learning activity simulates a work experience so that an associate may practice using the competencies she needs for her job. For example, if you were teaching your associate to program a computer using Pascal, you would set up problems that relate to the job she is expected to solve using Pascal.

Some general principles for designing or choosing learning activities include:

- Activities should provide opportunities to use the competencies that form the basis for the learning goals.

- Activities should be as similar as possible to the real-life situation in which they are to be used.

- Activities should yield information that can provide feedback about performance.

- The learner needs to see the relationship between the job to be done and the competency(ies) to be acquired.

Step 4: Creating a Coaching Schedule. There are several reasons why you should create a training schedule: It helps you work within an established timeframe; it helps you break down instructions into manageable parts; and it helps you teach the skills in the proper order. Generally, the schedule should show

- The skills to be taught

- The order in which they are to be taught

- The resources needed to teach the skills

- Any remarks about progress

- The results of evaluating the learning experience

Step 5: Getting Ready for Coaching. By planning your coaching, you should be able to reduce the time required to teach a new competency. This means you should have everything (the learning environment, equipment, and so on) you need in place and ready to use. Planning makes coaching easier for both you and the learner.

Delivering Coaching

The first requirement for learning is readiness and willingness to invest personal time and energy. Being ready and willing to learn varies from person to person. However, good delivery can help increase the learner's readiness for learning.

Learner readiness is transitional and problematic. It is also absolutely required for high-performance coaching and a peak learning experience on the part of the learner. Determining learner readiness presents the coach and associate with a complex challenge. On the simplest level, readiness can be created by a clear objective and a recognition on the learner's part that she is not competent to achieve that objective. The complexities of learner readiness are depicted in seminal research completed and reported by D. W. Combs and D. Snugg (1959, p. 366). These components appear to be established by prior experience, life stage, expectancies (self and others) and existential state at the time of learning. Basically, the challenge becomes one of meeting the learner where she is. In systems theory, we say, "Start where the system is!" Humans are complex, open systems and require at least equal treatment with mechanical and other nonhuman systems. Gordon Lippitt (1979), one of the founders of Human Resource Development (HRD) and Organization Renewal, believed that the periods of life transition create challenges, stress, anxiety, coping needs and the search process for meaningful answers and new learnings— competence. See also D. Levinson (1978).

Delivery of instruction can be broken down into five discrete steps that make it easier for you to be an effective teacher.

Step 1: Preparing for Learning.   First, develop readiness for learning. Learning is facilitated when you build a positive relationship with the learner. However, there is more to preparation than readiness. A person's expectations also affect what will be learned. It is important that both coach and associate clarify what is to be learned and why. What are the goals we are trying to reach? Why? How will this learning be beneficial?

Step 2: Presenting the Competency to Be Learned.   Next, describe the competency to be learned, the specific results to be obtained, and the procedures by which the goals are to be achieved. Remember, people differ in the amount of material they can learn at any one time and differ at the rate by which they can learn it. Remember that people can only learn a few steps at a time. So present no more than a person can learn in a given time. Here are some general guidelines to follow:

- Describe the competency to be learned.

- Show the learner how the competency fits into the broader context of team and organizational goals.

- Describe how the learning will benefit your associate and you.

- Demonstrate the competency.

The following sequence is an effective way to demonstrate compentency:

1. *Tell* the associate what she is supposed to do.

    • Make your explanations clear.

    • Go at an appropriate pace.

    • Ask questions.

    • Be clear in your use of terms.

    • Repeat explanations, if necessary.

2. *Show* your associate how it is to be done.

    • Demonstrate each task step by step.

    • Show what you tell the associate.

    • Explain the work as you go along.

    • Point out spots where mistakes occur.

    • Allow for questions at any time.

    • If needed, repeat the demonstration.

3. *Illustrate* the work using media. Use

    • Charts

    • Sketches

    • Films, Video

    • Interactive Software, Models

    • Whatever it takes

4. *Stress* key points.

    • What would happen if . . . ?

    • Why would you do . . . ?

    • Does it matter if you . . . ?

    • Is it OK if you . . . ?

Step 3: Providing Opportunities for Practice.   The goal of this step is to give your associate experience in performing the skills that define the competency. Learning is an active process by which the associate gains new knowledge, skills, and values by doing and reflecting. Without the doing and reflecting steps, there can be no real learning.

- Have the associate do the job.

- Point out what the associate does well and correct errors as they occur.

- While completing the job, have the associate explain each key point.

- Continue until the associate has proven that she knows how to perform.

- Give the associate feedback about errors and successes.

- Continue until you know the associate knows.

Step 4: Providing Corrective Feedback.   Without meaningful, accurate feedback, an important source of learning is lost. The goal of feedback is to create an environment in which you and the learner can discuss openly and supportively how to increase the learner's chances of success. People who succeed also focus on pathways (how) to success as well as the goal.

Most people believe that feedback is either positive—what the learner is doing right—or negative—what the learner is doing wrong. It is actually both. The challenge is to provide feedback that is both relevant and useful in terms of enhancing learning and performance.

Here are some general guidelines that may help you make your feedback more effective:

- Give feedback frequently. Have the learner take an active role in pointing out what she is doing well.

- Make sure the feedback describes what the person is doing. Make sure the learner describes the reasons for her successes. As people grow in the ability to do this, they will come to believe in their ability to win.

- Make sure the feedback is immediate and that it is given as close to the event as possible.

- Make sure the feedback provides the associate with alternative behaviors.

- Make sure the associate wants and needs the feedback. Work with her mistakes from the perspective that positive alternatives are available.

- Make sure the feedback is presented on the activity and not as critical of the person.

- Make sure you give feedback frequently in the early stages of learning.

- Whenever possible, provide corrective information before errors occur—feed forward.

Step 5: Following Up. Follow-up begins when your associates begin to operate on their own. It is not the end of the coaching period, nor the end of the coach's responsibility. It is the beginning. Some competencies are acquired slowly. People often need encouragement to deal with the setbacks and failures they typically experience. For example, an associate cannot initially hope to keep pace with a more experienced colleague; yet she may expect to do so. When people realize they cannot keep pace, they may get discouraged. It is important that you provide support and encouragement at these critical times in the learning process. It is important to evaluate routinely what your associate is doing, so that mistakes can be corrected and skills refined. The importance of follow-up cannot be overestimated. Here are some keys to effective follow-up:

- Put your associates on their own as soon as you believe they have developed a good grasp of the competency.

- Encourage them to value teamwork and collaboration.

- Invite your associates to feel free to come to you whenever they experience a problem.

- Initiate and maintain frequent contact with your associates.

- Be available to check your associates' work regularly.

- Emphasize constant improvement by teaching your associates the fine points of the job and pointing out possible shortcuts.

- Emphasize the availability of such useful resources as particular people, handbooks, and other support.

ACTIVITIES FOR DISCOVERY AND GROWTH

The activities in this section can help you increase your competency as a coach by emphasizing the role of preparation in being an effective coach.

Activity 1
Getting Ready for Training

Purpose

This activity provides a general framework to help you in preparing for coaching. It is really a mental model for successful preparation.

Directions

Complete each part of this activity as described.

Part 1: Analyzing a Coaching Opportunity (Position)

Choose a position in your department. Record the position title and list the jobs involved in that position. Then list the tasks required to perform those jobs.

Position title: _____

Job 1.

Tasks within Job	Steps
1.	
2.	
3.	
4.	

Part 2: Developing the Job Training Worksheet

Develop for each key task a list of the steps required to complete the job and the key points to stress in coaching when demonstrating how a task is to be completed.

Job 1.

Task 1:_____

Steps	Key Points
1.	
2.	
3.	
4.	

Part 3: Developing a Schedule

Next develop a schedule for the training events.

Title: Job:

Tasks	Date to Begin
1.	
2.	
3.	
4.	

Remarks

Evaluation

Part 4: Getting Everything Ready

Think about the tools and materials (resources) you need to complete a training session. List them in the order you need them.

Task	Resources Required
1.	
2.	
3.	

Activity 2
Putting the Learner at Ease

Purpose

This activity provides a tool for evaluating how effectively you are creating a learning environment.

Directions

Use the following checklist to find your current skill level for putting the learner at ease. Every "No" answer represents an area in which you need to develop alternative behaviors.

Do you

1. Act with warmth?	Yes	No
2. Use personal pronouns like "I" and "me"?	Yes	No
3. Make good eye contact?	Yes	No
4. Smile?	Yes	No
5. Use humor?	Yes	No
6. Focus on the learner without getting distracted?	Yes	No
7. Do what you say you will do?	Yes	No
8. Get to know things about the learner?	Yes	No

Activity 3
Judging Your Effectiveness during Performance Tryout

Purpose

This checklist can be used to judge your effectiveness in creating for the learner a meaningful opportunity to practice.

Directions

Use the following checklist to assess how well you conduct a performance tryout. Every "No" answer indicates an area in which you need to develop alternative behaviors.

Do you

1.	Stress success, but correct errors immediately?	Yes	No
2.	Ask questions that call for an explanation, not just a yes or no?	Yes	No
3.	Emphasize doing something rather than stopping something?	Yes	No
4.	Have the learner explain what she is doing?	Yes	No
5.	Provide support for the learner after the instruction?	Yes	No
6.	Model correct behavior for the learner?	Yes	No
7.	Demonstrate that skill and effort lead to success?	Yes	No
8.	Stop the learner when she is not following instructions?	Yes	No
9.	Walk the learner through each step of the instruction?	Yes	No

Activity 4
Examining Your Skills for Following Up

Purpose

This checklist helps you look at how effectively you follow up on your associates' performance.

Directions

The following actions define how to effectively follow up. Items for which you answer "No" suggest the areas in which you need to improve.

Do you

1.	Routinely check with the learner to see if work is being done?	Yes	No
2.	Meet with the learner at a set date for a progress report?	Yes	No
3.	Ask the learner to review the order of the work process?	Yes	No

4. Stress the importance of effort?	Yes	No
5. Stress the need for skills?	Yes	No
6. Correct mistakes as soon as you detect them?	Yes	No
7. Recognize exemplary performance as soon as possible?	Yes	No
8. Expand the learner's duties as she demonstrates her competence?	Yes	No
9. Teach the learner when mistakes are detected rather than punish the learner for those mistakes?	Yes	No
10. Review the training itself to determine its effectiveness?	Yes	No

ON COMMUNICATIONS—A TOOL FOR SUSTAINING HIGH PERFORMANCE

Every person develops a concept of herself, a *self-concept*. This concept of self consists of habitual patterns of beliefs, attitudes, preferences, thoughts, concepts, feelings, and actions. It is organized by personal values. Individuals who sense themselves as competent and capable of learning and growth tend to act in a competent manner. Those who sense themselves as incompetent and believe they have reached the height of their potential may be reluctant to try learning anything new.

The self-concept is both a product and a determiner of experience. As a coach you must deal with the reality of your associate's self-concept; especially when a person's self-concept acts as an inhibitor of learning. It is thus important for you to develop the ability to communicate well with your associates. In effect, you must ask yourself how you relate to your associates, and strive to relate so as to help them see that learning and growth are possible.

Communicating as a Tool for Enhancing Self-Esteem

The way you communicate with associates can profoundly affect your ability to facilitate learning and growth. How you communicate expresses what is important to you. It conveys how much you respect others, signifies the extent to which you care about others, and symbolizes your compassion and concern for others.

Words have great power to enhance or destroy self-confidence and self-esteem. A coach's words should encourage, challenge, and enhance others. Three goals should underlie all of your communications with associates. Your words should

1. Enhance, not destroy, your associates' self-esteem

2. Enable you to deepen your connectedness with your associates

3. Empower your associates to be more competent and more self-directed

Acknowledging Your Associates' Efforts

Let's look at each of these goals more closely. How do you use communications to enhance self-esteem? A basic human need is for connectedness. Each of us needs to feel we are accepted and to sense that we belong somewhere. You can help your associates meet this basic need when you use the skills of acknowledgment and recognition. When you acknowledge and recognize another person, you are saying she is a unique individual. When you acknowledge and recognize an associate's actions, you are telling that individual that she is a valuable person.

It is easy for us to take people for granted and to forget they need simple acknowledgment. Indeed, their very behavior may suggest strongly they don't need recognition. However, this behavior may be a defense against the pain associated with not being recognized.

Using Empathy and Understanding

People have a need to be accepted for whom they are. When they feel unaccepted, they often strive to prove themselves acceptable. However, such behavior is not authentic; it is chosen to be acceptable to others, not to express truly one's authenticity.

As one who desires to be an effective coach, you must understand this universal need for self-acceptance, and you must communicate so as to help create self-acceptance. How do you do this? You learn to demonstrate to others your understanding of and empathy for their thoughts, opinions, and feelings.

Empathy is the foundation skill for understanding another person. Through empathy, you come to know the other person's frame of reference, and through this understanding you empower yourself to become an effective coach.

Empowering Your Associates

To develop a sense of personal mastery and self-direction, people need to learn how to think through (reflect on) and solve their own problems. As a coach, you can facilitate this personal empowering process. When you help others see their problems, when you create conditions where others can investigate new options, when you allow others to experiment with new behaviors, you are empowering them. Be careful not to diminish your associates by taking responsibility for their problems and solving them yourself.

How do you design communications that encourage self-esteem? By understanding your associate's frame of reference, by facilitating the associate's evaluation of her own choices based on that frame of reference, by challenging the validity of assumptions your associate seems to be making, and by honestly reacting to her behavior, you can do a great deal to encourage development of self-esteem.

Coaching

Coaching in its essence is excellent communication. We have coined an acronym from the word *coach* that conveys the central role of communications in the process of coaching:

C = Caring. Caring for another is hard work. It involves knowing and supporting what the other needs and wants. It necessitates self-discipline and self-control so as not to impose your own needs and requirements on the other.

O = Openness. To be in a relationship that enhances another person, you must be open both in the sense that you are able to listen and that you are able to share.

A = Awareness. To facilitate growth, to nurture another, you must understand the uniqueness of the person's needs and requirements.

C = Commitment. Coaching is not a one-time encounter; it is a relationship built on commitment and feeling.

H = Honesty. You cannot be helpful if you cannot be truthful. Many times you will observe that your associate's behavior is not helpful, and when you do, you must be willing to say so.

Coaching is caring with openness, awareness, commitment, and honesty.

PART 4

When Coaching Is Not Enough: Enabling People to Deal with Motivational Problems

Your associates' performance limitations may often relate more to their beliefs and expectations than to their skills. Even people who have outstanding abilities are limited to the degree that they have confidence and a fundamental belief that success is possible. One of your important roles as a coach is to help your associates see beyond their current frameworks to envision situations where new levels of achievement are possible.

The two chapters in this section explain how you as a coach may help your associates learn a new set of beliefs about what is possible and attainable. In this respect, you may be acting much as a counselor might act. Coaches empower individuals to confront their own behaviors, and in the process they open the door to transcend their current performance.

Chapter 8, Coaching as Renewal, explains how to encourage your associates to challenge their current paradigms and to help them go beyond their current limitations.

Chapter 9, Coping with Failure, continues this discussion by examining the process of failure, and describing how to transform this process into an opening for renewal and growth.

C H A P T E R 8

Coaching as Renewal

INTRODUCTION

The role of a coach is complex. Not only do you spend a great deal of time teaching, but you also spend a great deal of time confronting a learner's self-limiting attitudes and beliefs. This latter role is the focus of this chapter. We explore how the learner's attitudes can become self-limiting, and we discuss the cycle of success and failure. We then develop a practical approach for dealing with performance problems that come from self-limiting attitudes and beliefs.

GOALS

The goals of this chapter are to help you

- Appreciate and understand the cycle of failure and success

- Encourage individual learners to evaluate and confront their own behavior

- Work with an individual to develop and implement a performance improvement plan

- Build the learner's commitment to trying new behaviors

- Become more effective in using communication to encourage, correct, and support change in the learner

WHEN CURRENT BEHAVIOR DOESN'T WORK

It's a Question of Belief

Sometimes individuals fail to reach their potential, and so fail. This is very frustrating for both the associate and the coach. From the individual's point of view, failure represents a loss of self-esteem. From the coach's point of view, failure reflects not only on your coaching skills, but also affects the performance of your team. Since failure costs time and money to hire and/or retrain employees, failure represents a lost opportunity for the organization.

Failures are often due to the *try* dimension as opposed to skill deficits. Many studies indicate that people with competence to do a job often do not try to do that job because they expect to fail. If you, as their coach, master basic counseling skills, many of these individuals can transcend their negative beliefs about themselves.

Why You Need to Learn Counseling Skills

One critical aspect of the coaching role is the ability to counsel. There are many occasions when you must confront an associate who performs below potential, not because she is incompetent, but because she has a motivational problem. A *motivational problem* is unproductive behavior exhibited by an associate who can perform but who is currently performing below her potential.

When a problem is due to a self-limiting attitude, the coach must act like a counselor by helping the individual think about and change the assumptions she makes about self, reality, value, and opportunity. This role is not just one of teaching; it is also one of helping the learner see herself clearly, evaluate the assumptions underlying her actions, and change assumptions that are not valid.

PROVIDING COUNSELING

What Is Providing Counseling?

Providing counseling is a special aspect of the coaching role in which you enable your associate to overcome motivational problems affecting performance. By helping your associate evaluate and confront ineffective behavior and by helping her develop an improvement plan, you help the associate become more productive for herself, as well as for the team. The quality of this counseling has a direct impact on individual and team success. *Providing counseling* describes the process by which you help individuals evaluate their current, ineffective behaviors and discover and learn more productive behavior patterns.

How Is Providing Counseling Done?

Providing counseling involves influencing or leading your associates to examine and evaluate their current assumptions and behaviors, to accept full responsibility for their behaviors that produce the consequences they are experiencing, and to make a commitment to learn new, more effective assumptions and behaviors. You help them confront their ineffective behaviors and guide them in the acquisition of more positive, productive behaviors. This counseling process is part of facilitating behavioral change.

Because counseling is not typically a well-defined role, you may find it helpful to examine the Counseling Skills Checklist in the activities section at the end of this chapter. This checklist allows you to assess your current ability in this area by evaluating yourself in terms of the competencies exhibited by effective counselors.

CRITICAL REFLECTION: A MODEL OF EMPOWERMENT

To understand the empowerment process, think about what you are actually doing when you empower an associate: You are facilitating critical reflection. The learner comes to see the world through a different set of lenses, to reframe the problem from alternative points of view. You can teach some key aspects of critical reflection by challenging assumptions and beliefs and creating a climate that encourages reflection. **Critical reflection** is the process of recognizing the assumptions underlying our beliefs and behaviors, judging their appropriateness to objective reality, and choosing to act more effectively. Figure 8.1 depicts this model of critical reflection.

FIGURE 8.1
THE CYCLE OF SUCCESS IS THE RESULT OF LEARNING TO VALIDATE YOUR ASSUMPTIONS

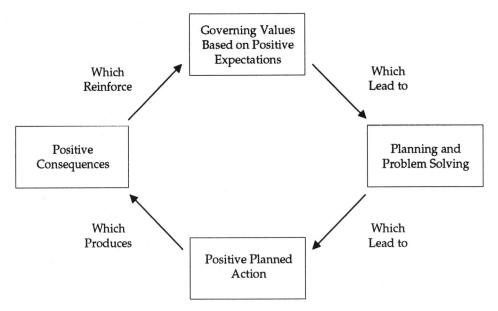

The cycle of success is the result of learning to validate your assumptions.

Empowerment is actively reflecting on the assumptions one makes and the relationships among the assumptions, the actions flowing from these assumptions, and the consequences produced by the actions.

However, this process of critical reflection is often inhibited. For example, it is inhibited in organizations that display hostility to associates who question assumptions. When the process is inhibited, the individual is stuck in the cycle of failure. This cycle is illustrated in Figure 8.2.

FIGURE 8.2
THE CYCLE OF FAILURE IS THE RESULT OF A LACK OF CRITICAL REFLECTION

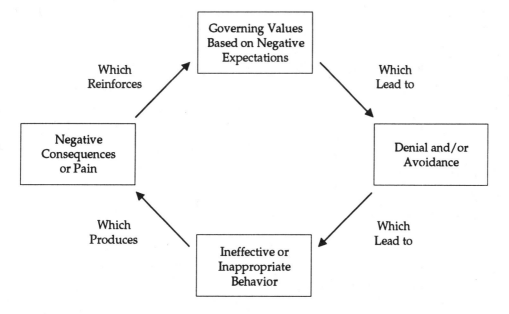

The cycle of failure is the result of a lack of critical reflection.

The main feature of the cycle of failure is the absence of critical reflection about assumption, action, and consequence. This leads to situations in which invalid or destructive assumptions result in ineffective behaviors that are repeated, perpetuating a cycle of failure.

When the cycle of failure comes to characterize an individual's actions with respect to a given goal, then she does the same ineffective thing over and over, even though the action is clearly not working—in fact, it may be producing much frustration. When someone gets stuck in this process, the part of her that is stuck is identified with failure. The individual sees herself as a failure in that area of life, and her self-concept is that she is a failure.

As a coach, your role is to help the individual look at the relationships among assumption, action, and consequence. However, people are not usually inclined to do this. Why? Because the process of self-reflection is often painful. It requires that the individual examine and perhaps let go of long-held assumptions.

To understand how painful this is, imagine that you awaken one day and find that the services you have been providing your customers, which took a great deal of time to develop, fail to even meet their expectations—that you don't even know who your customers are anymore! Your whole world seems to be crumbling around you. This is the level of pain that is often involved in looking carefully at the relationship between assumption and action.

THE EMPOWERMENT PROCESS

Performance Empowerment: A Tool for Enabling High Performance

Empowerment is facilitating the growth of those associates who have yet to reach their potential because of fear or self-doubt, a process of challenging invalid or inaccurate assumptions that produce fear and doubt; the relationship between you and your associate through which problem solving can occur. There are three distinct aspects to this counseling process:

1. Creating the empowering relationship

2. Facilitating critical reflection

3. Empowering improved performance

These processes are inextricably interwoven. Your success depends on your ability to help the associate see that options exist and to provide the tools to experiment with these new ways of being.

The goals of performance empowerment are to help your associates succeed by developing the capacities of

1. *Being Responsible.*   Help associates accept responsibility for their actions and the consequences that follow.

2. *Believing in Themselves.*   Have associates control the important consequences in their work lives.

3. *Becoming Committed.*   Motivate associates to persist in their efforts to become more effective.

4. *Developing Positive Self-Discipline.*   Encourage associates to engage in behaviors that they know build strength.

To achieve these goals, **performance empowerment** breaks down the process into nine discrete behavioral steps:

1. Get involved.

2. Find out about current behavior.

3. Explore the consequences of current behavior.

4. Become clear about values.

5. Develop an improvement plan.

6. Obtain a commitment to the plan.

7. Follow up on the plan.

8. Allow for natural consequences.

9. Keep working. Don't give up.

Each of these steps is discussed in depth.

THE STEPS OF THE EMPOWERMENT PROCESS

Step 1: Getting Involved

Your success as a counselor is a function of your ability to establish a positive helping relationship with your associate. The most important outcome of this step is having the associate trust you. Trust is the confident belief that it is okay to be open and honest, and that the environment is safe.

Trust is a crucial ingredient in the change process. When trust is high in a relationship, people feel free to open up and confront reality, as opposed to getting caught up in a game of pretense. Confrontation with reality is the first step in realizing what is real and learning how to deal with it.

How to Build Positive Involvement. Each person develops relationships in different ways. It is possible, however, to identify some common aspects of creating positive involvement with associates. Here is a list of some of the things that work:

1. Engage in small talk. Spend time with the person.

2. Find out what interests your associates.

3. Let your associates know what interests you.

4. Arrange to do things with your associates.

5. Ask questions about other aspects of your associates' lives outside of work. What are their hobbies? Do they have families? What do they read? Community service?

6. Ask your associates for suggestions about what the team might do to work smarter.

7. Seek your associates' opinions about work-related issues.

8. Discuss problems that arise with work.

9. Keep your word.

10. Use your associates' suggestions when they are feasible.

11. Recognize each person by name every day.

12. Recognize your associates' accomplishments.

Each of these strategies involves communicating with your associates. Talk with your associates about what they are doing and about what is going on in their lives. Talk about yourself. It is through this process of becoming involved that you build the level of trust and confidence necessary for your associates to become willing to confront and change their ineffective behaviors.

These involvement strategies all contribute to your associates' self-esteem. By building a person's sense of connectedness to you, you enable that individual to listen and to learn.

Step 2: What's Happening? Finding Out about Current Behavior

Performance limitations for the person stuck because of self-doubt are always revealed in that person's current behavior. To help such individuals see what is going on, you must enable them to explore and evaluate the effects of their current behaviors.

If your associate's behavior were effective, there would be no need to help her. However, to help your associate improve performance when behavior is not effective, you must help the associate understand what she is doing and how this behavior produces negative results.

How to Facilitate Exploration of Current Behavior.   How do you enable an associate to discover how her behavior is producing negative results? You must understand what that person is doing and how her actions produce the negative consequences observed. You must be honest with your associate. You must be willing to share what you are observing, to tell the person what assumptions she appears to be making. If you cannot do this, then you probably cannot coach.

There is a direct relationship between your own personal empowerment and your ability to be an empowering helper to an associate. You must be a good model. Good models are

- *Clear.* Good coaches exhibit behavior that others find easy to understand.

- *Consistent.* Good coaches act in a consistent manner.

- *Open.* Good coaches are perceived as honest and respectful of the integrity of others.

- *Communicative.* Good coaches are able to state their points of view clearly; to use illustrations, examples, and metaphors; and to state their ideas and observations clearly.

- *Specific.* A good coach behaves in such a way that an observer can recognize, understand, and try out the behaviors the coach exhibits.

- *Accessible.* Good coaches are not seen as threatening; rather, they are accessible. They are personal and they are avialble.

There are two primary things you can do to enable your associates to understand that current outcomes are a product of their behaviors. By questioning and active listening you help associates explore what, when, where, how often, with whom, and how their behavioral choices produce the pain they experience (for instance, they are in trouble at work, they are anxious about losing their jobs, they are failing in important aspects of their lives).

Through this process one unravels an associate's use of time so that she can discover that her pain is a consequence of how she has structured her time. For example, suppose an associate is consistently late to team meetings. First explore how this situation arises by finding out what the associate is doing before the meeting, how she plans her work load for that day, and so on.

By leading your associate to this point you have helped her see that what she is doing relates directly to the ineffectiveness of her performance. Once an associate can see this, then she can also see that, because she chooses ineffective performance, then she can also choose success. Your goal is to help your associate become aware of her current behavior and to understand she really has other better choices.

Step 3: What's the Payoff? Exploring the Consequences of Current Behavior

Once you have helped the associate become aware of her current behavior, then you must help her look at the consequences of her behavior. For example, if the associate is late every day, what are the potential consequences for her, for the team, and for the company? Your goal is to help your associate discover that her behavior is producing the negative consequences she now experiences, and that this pain can be avoided if she elects to choose new behaviors. You use your questioning skills to encourage your associate to answer the basic question, What is happening as a result of your behavior?

As you confront your associates with the consequences of their behaviors, they will most likely resist accepting responsibility for their ineffectiveness. They will want to tell you why things cannot work, but they will resist admitting that they have created their situation. In turn, their denial will tempt you to agree with them on how hopeless the situation is. To avoid this tendency, acknowledge your associates' feelings but then lead them back to consider *what* they are doing, not *why* they are doing it.

Step 4: Is That What You Want? Getting Clear about Values

The reason to explore current behavior is to set the stage for helping your associate evaluate the assumptions underlying that individual's actions. The goal of this step is to help the associate to evaluate her actions and the consequences which follow, and to challenge the assumptions on which the associate's actions are founded. You have established what your associate is doing, now the challenge is to get that associate to answer these questions:

- What are the consequences of my actions?

- What will happen if I continue doing this?

- Is this what I want?

- What kinds of assumptions am I making about myself and the situation?

- What are the effects of these assumptions?

By getting an associate to judge her own behavior, you help her assume personal responsibility for her actions and the effects of those actions. You also provide her with options for change.

Step 5: Developing an Improvement Plan

Once your associate understands what will probably happen if she continues along the current path and understands that there are positive alternatives, it is time to encourage her to change her behavior. You do this by helping your associate create and implement an improvement plan. An improvement plan is a blueprint that helps the individual make choices about what to do on a day-by-day or, if need be, an hour-by-hour basis.

FIGURE 8.3
CONSEQUENCES AND BEHAVIORAL CHOICES

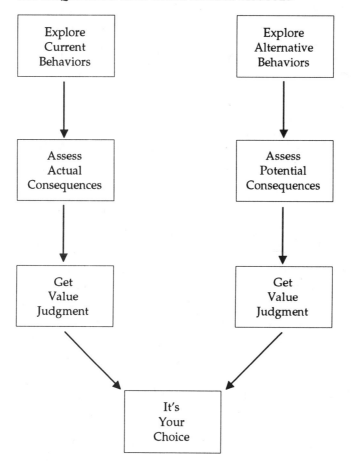

Why would you be so presumptuous as to think you should help your associate develop an improvement plan? This dynamic could quickly degenerate to one of control and telling. The reason to help an associate develop a plan is simple—a plan is a way to verbalize and clarify one's intentions. It provides an alternative positive structure to replace the current structures that support ineffective behaviors. By developing a plan, the associate makes a commitment to use her time in a more productive manner. By developing such a plan with your associate, you tell that individual you are available in a supporting role.

To what degree should you guide the development of the plan? How much you direct depends on your own and your associate's estimates of how mature the associate is. Maturity is the individual's ability to develop and implement a plan. It refers to how responsible that individual has shown herself to be in the past. Because the associate's current behavior is ineffective, you will probably want to offer a lot of direction in developing the initial plan. However, as the associate demonstrates that she can accept responsibility by carrying out the plan, then you will naturally allow that individual to assume more and more responsibility for developing the improvement plan.

Step 6: Obtaining Commitment to the Plan

What Is Commitment?   A commitment is a psychological contract to act in a certain manner over a period of time. A person commits to a plan to the degree to which she attaches importance to that particular vision of the future, and believes she can succeed at creating the envisioned future.

Because a plan can fail, implementing the improvement involves taking a risk. How can you help your associate stay committed to the plan? Part of the answer to this question lies in the effectiveness of the plan. Is it specific? Does it yield many small wins? Does it allow your associate to experience success feedback along the way?

We all know from experience that even the best plans go awry and, that from time to time, we need a bit of sound advice and firm help to keep a commitment. This is your role as coach. You are the person your associate can turn to when she is having difficulties and feels unable to succeed without support.

How to Develop and Maintain Commitment.   There are two main avenues for building and maintaining commitment to the plan: (1) developing a performance contract; and (2) using communications skills to motivate, correct, and reward.

The Performance Contract.   One of the most useful tools to help an associate develop and maintain commitment to carry out the plan is the *performance contract*. A performance contract is a written agreement that communicates clearly what you expect from the associate and what the associate expects from you. It also specifies the consequences of performance or nonperformance.

A contract is essential to the success of the improvement plan because it clarifies the intentions of both people involved in the process: you and your associate. By specifying in performance terms the mutual expectations regarding the associate's performance, you create the climate in which improvement is possible.

Also crucial to the process of performance contracting is deciding on specific dates when you and your associate will assess progress toward the goals you both have established. By making this commitment to an associate, you demonstrate that you value her.

Step 7: Following Up on the Plan

Following up on the improvement plan is one of the most important components of coaching. During the follow-up meeting, help the associate evaluate progress, congratulate the associate for successes, and/or help the associate make adjustments to the plan so that she can get back on track after failures.

Your main job at this point is to review your associate's performance. When you and your associate successfully diagnose the cause of a performance problem, then you are in a position to rework the action plan and to redirect the associate toward her goals.

The Follow-Up Meeting. Follow-up meetings take place at times specified on the performance improvement plan. It is important to conform to these follow-up dates as closely as possible. By doing this, you let your associate know that the plan is important to you and that you expect it to be important to her also.

During the meeting, review your associate's performance relative to the performance targets specified. Some questions to ask during this meeting include:

1. What have you done that has been effective?

2. What has been difficult for you?

3. Did you get the support you needed from me?

4. What could you (we) have done differently?

5. What do you need to do now in light of this experience?

Giving Effective Feedback. The follow-up meeting is designed to help the associate. Sometimes this process may involve giving the associate specific negative feedback. Sometimes it may involve providing specific positive feedback. Successfully giving either kind of feedback depends on the level of trust in the relationship. Therefore, always focus on the quality of the relationship between you and your associate. In addition, review the characteristics of effective feedback.

Characteristics of Effective Feedback

1. Focuses on behavior over which the person has control

2. Describes that behavior

3. Focuses on providing alternatives to negative behavior, as opposed to solutions

4. Is given when the associate is best able to hear the feedback

5. Focuses on what, not why

6. Is intended to help the associate perform more effectively and reach her goals

Step 8: Allowing for Natural Consequences

If you hope to develop associates who gain in self-efficacy or feel empowered, do not allow the use of punishment to shape an associate's behavior; instead, allow natural consequences to follow performance. In addition, devote energy to analyzing and removing constraints on performance.

A natural consequence is the normal or typical environment reaction to an outcome produced by any action or set of actions. If you drop a rock, it typically falls. If you fail to support a teammate at a crucial moment at work, she will quite likely have less trust in you in future events. Organizations are loaded with opportunities for payoffs—advancement, recognition, compensation, profit and gain sharing, "atta boys," special incentives, friendships, opportunities to influence others, goals to achieve, and all the intrinsic value accrued by people who have the need to achieve, the need to belong, or the need to influence others. A smart coach builds strong people by helping them meet their needs through the application of personal competencies and effort to various tasks. In essence, we teach one another how to master our work environments and how to remove or overcome constraints. Do not tamper with rewards and impose punishment yourself. The outcome of arbitrary treatment is arbitrary performance.

For example, if a runner wins a race, she gets a medal or ribbon. On the other hand, if the runner loses the race, she gets nothing. Receiving a medal or not receiving a medal is the natural consequence of how fast the runner runs and the competition. All other things being equal, the medal is a natural consequence of performance; and performance is a function of an individual's talent, the quality of her physical training, and the degree of effort expended on the task.

For the associate, the diligence with which she pursues the plans she has developed to facilitate growth is equivalent to the training of the athlete. If the associate follows the plan, she will reap the natural consequences of success. If the associate does the wrong things, or does the right things the wrong way, then she will face the natural consequences associated with failure. Again, all of this assumes a constraint-free workscape or environment conducive to high performance.

By allowing for natural consequences to follow behavior, you enable your associate to master her own life; you help that individual become more responsible by seeing the connection between behavior and its consequences. Conversely, if the quality of the associate's behavior has no consequences, then you undermine that individual's development. Remember that an individual ideally should identify her own natural consequences. That is why in previous steps we encouraged you to collaborate with your associate to encourage her to evaluate her own performance. By doing so, the associate becomes the director of her learning.

Step 9: Handling Excuses

The associate you can work with is willing to take a risk. She is risking failure with (you hope) the confident expectation that the risk will pay off in terms of performance improvement. When an individual takes a risk, she exposes herself to the possibility of failure.

There can be no long-term learning or growth without some failure. Because failure is a possible outcome, the coach must serve as a buffer for the associate—not in the sense of shielding that person from failure, but in the sense of helping her learn from failure.

Helping an associate learn from mistakes is crucial to your success as a coach. You can do this primarily by maintaining your own confidence in the success of that associate. Don't give up on the individual, but keep working with the person. Frequently communicate your encouragement to that associate. Let her know that you expect her to succeed in the long run, and help her keep her perspective when things seem to be going badly.

Learn how to embrace error yourself. The best coaches have learned how to thrive on adversity, to learn from failure, and to risk. They model these values through their actions, through their communications, and through the way they respond to the failures of others.

How to Communicate Positive Expectations of Success. Three special communication skills can help you communicate to an associate your positive expectations of future success:

- *Acknowledgment.* Acknowledging an associate means paying attention to what that person is doing and letting her know that you have noticed. This is the most basic of the communications skills. It involves spending time with your associate and taking note of what she is doing.

- *Understanding or Active Listening.* Understanding is the ability to put yourself in the associate's frame of reference and to sense her meanings, problems, and victories. This skill involves two kinds of subskills: (1) identifying the associate's feelings, and (2) reflecting these back to her in a relevant manner (for example, "You are discouraged because you are having trouble with the course in technical writing, and you don't quite know what to do."). Through communicating understanding, you let your associate know that you will work with her in resolving her struggles. You build trust when you can accept the associate's victories and defeats without being critical of her.

- *Selective Approval.* Selectively praise the associate's behavior. Praise behavior that is worthy of praise, and ignore behavior that is adequate but not worthy of praise. This skill requires that you know what the other person is doing. That is one of the reasons it is a powerful motivational tool. To know what a person is doing you have to spend time with her and develop a relationship. Through the manner in which you communicate, you become a true support for your associate.

Implicit in this discussion is the belief that you should avoid criticizing. Instead, become a positive force in your associate's development by using selective approval and providing corrective feedback when that individual's behavior is ineffective. Corrective feedback involves supplying the person with another option for behaving. Corrective feedback is not self-limiting in that it does not merely say that behavior is ineffective. Corrective feedback would add, "and an option that you might consider in this circumstance is . . ., What do you think?"

Dealing with Excuses. It is often hard to know if and/or when to intervene in the events that are natural consequences that accompany failure. Failure is often due to circumstances outside the associate's control. So, the question of how to deal with excuses becomes important. When is an excuse legitimate?

To answer this question it is useful to have a set of guidelines. The following model can help you decide whether to deliver natural consequences or to keep trying:

1. Did your associate fail? If you answer no, congratulate your associate for her success. If you answer yes, go to next step.

2. Was your associate's failure due to a lack of attempting to carry out the steps in the plan? If you answer yes, find out what your associate wants and recommit to the plan. If you answer no, go to next step.

3. Was your associate's failure because the plan was too difficult? If you answer yes, simplify the plan by reworking the steps in the plan. If you answer no, go to next step.

4. Be careful to discriminate clearly between circumstances that are clearly beyond a person's control and those that are not. Was your associate's failure due to circumstances beyond her control? If you answer yes, redesign the plan. If you answer no, go to next step.

5. Was your associate's failure due to inability to perform? If you answer yes, teach the individual. If you answer no, allow the natural consequence to take place.

In this chapter, we discuss high-performance counseling. This is the process by which you counsel the associate by helping her alter assumptions that produce poor results. To change results, she must develop new assumptions. You become effective at the process to the extent that you develop a helping relationship with the associate. A helping relationship enables you to tell the truth about behavior that is central to failure.

ACTIVITIES FOR DISCOVERY AND GROWTH

The activities in this section have been chosen to help you practice what we believe are the core skills to providing counseling.

Activity 1
Attitude Problems That Need Resolving

Purpose

This activity gives you the opportunity to think through any attitudinal or motivational problems that need resolving.

Directions

List any recurring problems that result from the associate's attitudes. Describe each problem as specifically as possible, its consequences, how you have attempted to handle it, and how effective your efforts have been.

Recurring Problems	Consequences of Problems	What Actions I Have Taken	Results of My Actions

Activity 2
The Counseling Checklist

Purpose

The following checklist provides an opportunity to evaluate and enhance your effectiveness in using the kinds of skills exhibited by effective counselors.

Directions

The middle column lists behavioral competencies exhibited by effective counselors. For each of these competencies, use the right-hand column to describe how you have used the competency. In the left-hand column, rate the degree to which you are effective in performing that competence by circling the most appropriate number. Use the following scale.

1	2	3	4	5	6	7	8	9
Not at All Effective				Moderately Effective				Very Effective

The Counseling Checklist

Skill Level	Competency	How I've Used It
1 2 3 4 5 6 7 8 9	Developing trust	
1 2 3 4 5 6 7 8 9	Communicating acceptance	
1 2 3 4 5 6 7 8 9	Acknowledging associate	
1 2 3 4 5 6 7 8 9	Exhibiting warmth	
1 2 3 4 5 6 7 8 9	Exhibiting genuineness	
1 2 3 4 5 6 7 8 9	Demonstrating concern	
1 2 3 4 5 6 7 8 9	Demonstrating caring	
1 2 3 4 5 6 7 8 9	Being responsive	
1 2 3 4 5 6 7 8 9	Being open and honest	
1 2 3 4 5 6 7 8 9	Observing performance	
1 2 3 4 5 6 7 8 9	Recognizing success	
1 2 3 4 5 6 7 8 9	Giving feedback	
1 2 3 4 5 6 7 8 9	Receiving feedback	

1 2 3 4 5 6 7 8 9   Expressing feelings

1 2 3 4 5 6 7 8 9   Expressing needs

1 2 3 4 5 6 7 8 9   Diagnosing problems

1 2 3 4 5 6 7 8 9   Developing plans

1 2 3 4 5 6 7 8 9   Creating contracts

1 2 3 4 5 6 7 8 9   Following up

1 2 3 4 5 6 7 8 9   Allowing natural consequences

Processing—Diagnosing Your Skills

As you look over your responses, answer the following questions:

1. To what extent are you satisfied with your current competency levels?

2. What are your strengths?

3. Which competencies are underdeveloped?

4. In what areas would improvement make you a more effective coach?

5. What kinds of support and resources would you need to develop these skills?

Activity 3
Practice in Building Positive Involvement

Purpose

Positive involvement is crucial to the success of your efforts to help another change her assumptions and learn new attitudes and behaviors. This activity helps you think through how you can improve the level of trust and involvement in your coaching relationships.

Directions

List behaviors in section A that you might normally use if you were developing a friendship with another person. Then in section B, review the behaviors you listed in section A and select those you could use in the work environment to build positive involvement with associates.

A. Behaviors I use in building friendships:

1. Spend time together doing activities of common interest.

2.

3.

4.

5.

6.

7.

8.

B. Behaviors I will use in the work environment to build positive involvement with my associates:

1.

2.

3.

4.

5.

6.

7.

8.

Activity 4
Developing the Performance Contract

Purpose

The contract is a useful tool for reinforcing commitment to change. This activity illustrates one way to develop a mutual contract between the coach and the associate.

Directions

Complete the following form after the Performance Improvement Plan has been developed.

The Contract Form

The performance I expect from you is:

The performance you expect from me is:

What I am willing to do is:

What I am not willing to do is:

ON STRESS AND CHANGE, OR HOW PEOPLE COPE WITH STRESS

People with problems are under stress. To deal with stress, it helps to have a general understanding of what stress is and how people choose to cope with it. Stress is defined in several different ways. For us, the most useful definition is *an individual's psychophysical response to any event that is believed to pose a threat to her sense of well-being.*

Stress is the outcome or end product of a process through which the individual perceives a threat in her environment that is intense, frequent, or long enough to require a coping response. The choice of the response rests on how the individual answers the following questions:

1. Is this a threat to my values?

2. Am I competent enough to deal successfully with this event?

Coping describes actions taken to reduce the intensity of a threat. Three different kinds of actions are possible:

- Flee

- Accept

- Confront

These three choices fit into one of two broad categories of coping strategies:

- Problem-oriented strategies

- Emotion-oriented strategies

Problem-oriented strategies focus on removing the perceived threat, or on learning more about the threat. There are several varieties of problem-oriented strategies:

- Problem solving

- Planning

- Seeking information

- Restraining any response at all

Emotion-oriented strategies focus on reducing the emotional elements of the stress response. There are several variations of emotion-oriented strategies:

- Denial

- Mental and behavioral disengagement

- Seeking emotional support

- Reinterpretation of the event

Not all coping strategies are equally effective in helping people deal with stressors. The term *adaptiveness* describes the overall effectiveness of a strategy that promotes an individual's health and well-being.

Adaptive strategies promote the individual's long- and short-term well-being. They help the individual deal positively with the stress trigger. Strategies that do not contribute to the individual's long- and short-term well-being are maladaptive. These strategies seek to avoid the stress trigger rather than remove it.

Research has shown that problem-oriented strategies are more adaptive than emotion-oriented strategies. When people perceive a threat, their first appraisals concern whether they have any control over the situation. When people feel they have some degree of control over the situation, they generally choose a problem-oriented strategy. However, when people believe they have no control over the situation, they choose an emotion-oriented strategy, especially people who rely on denial and disengagement. Moreover, the more important the situation is, the more likely people will use denial and disengagement as a strategy.

Why do people choose a particular strategy? There are three possible reasons. First, individuals tend to choose a particular option when threatened. This is the trait viewpoint. Second, in a given situation, the choice is determined by the characteristics of the situation. This is the behavioral point of view. Third, the choice reflects an interaction between the person and the situation.

All three possibilities are partially true. People do choose the same strategy across a wide range of situations; they also assess the situation and choose according to the demands of the situation. For example, when a problem-oriented strategy is not immediately applicable, people tend to adapt a dispositional strategy, using a habitual emotion-oriented response. Strangely, the more competent the individual, the more denial she may use when an "I can't cope" appraisal is made. It is extremely threatening for a person who realistically expects to succeed when she encounters a situation in which she doesn't have an appropriate response.

People make situational responses to what triggers stress when they already have the capacity to respond. When people learn how to solve problems during development, they learn a number of things. They learn certain rules for analyzing problems, rules for testing hunches about how to solve problems, skills for making choices among a set of competing hunches, skills for implementing their behavioral choices, and skills for controlling their emotions and other competing response tendencies. They thereby develop mental models of themselves as problem solvers.

Once people develop these mental models, they are not bound by lack of skills; therefore, they can turn their attention toward each situation and adapt their coping strategies to the demands present in those situations.

The third choice—reflected in the core assumptions of this book—is that behavior is based on interaction between the person and the environment.

When people perceive threats in their environments (primary appraisal), they appraise their ability to control the situation using available strategies (secondary appraisal). This secondary appraisal then leads to coping behavior, which is either problem- or emotion-oriented. The former tends to be more adaptive than the latter. Figure 8.4 depicts how coping relates to person-environment interaction.

FIGURE 8.4
COPING STRATEGIES FLOWCHART

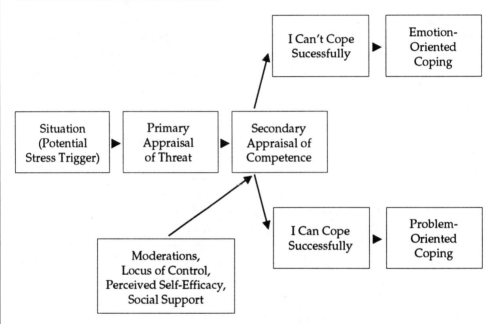

When we believe we can control situations through our own efforts, then we choose to rely on problem-oriented strategies like planning, time management, decision making, and problem solving. When, however, we believe we are unable to control situations, we choose emotion-oriented strategies like acting out, denial, and withdrawal.

Many factors moderate the choice of coping strategy. Among these moderating factors are locus of control, self-efficacy, and the availability of social support. Locus of control refers to the belief that we can control the outcomes in our lives. People with an internal locus of control believe they can control outcomes, and thus they act to do so. People with an external locus of control believe that they are victims of circumstances, and thus they act accordingly.

Perceived self-efficacy is similar to locus of control but includes our perceptions of our own competence. People with high self-efficacy believe they are able to master their environments through their skills, and they act on this belief. Action leads to successful stress management. Low perceived self-efficacy leads to inaction and typically to failure. A result of this failure is that people react to stress emotionally rather than with problem-oriented coping.

Finally, the level of social support can affect the success with which people cope with stress. Once coping strategies are learned, they become self-fulfilling and people react consistently across a range of stressful situations. Support can be appropriate or inappropriate. It is appropriate when it provides a temporary haven in which individuals can sort through the stress and decide what to do. It is inappropriate when it abets denial or when it promotes procrastination or avoidance.

As a coach, you play an important role in empowering your associates to deal with stress. Through the coach's role as teacher, you can build an associate's sense of self-efficacy. Through the coach's role as counselor, you can help an associate understand how she creates stress and how she can create more positive outcomes. Finally, through the coach's role as a support person, you can provide the hospitality your associate needs to gain the strength and courage she needs to cope.

C H A P T E R 9

Coping with Failure

INTRODUCTION

For the person who risks, failure is inevitable. Failure often represents a loss of self-esteem especially when someone does not achieve a desired goal. As a coach, you are in a position to help such a person deal with failure positively. Your contribution can make learning occur and help the person deal successfully with an occasional failure.

Failure is not the issue. What matters is how the person chooses to deal with these failures. As a coach, you are well positioned to help your associates put failure in proper perspective.

This chapter discusses the various ways people deal with failure and shows how you can become a positive factor in helping your associates deal with it.

GOALS

The goals of this chapter are to help you

- Understand the effects of failure
- Be sensitive to and understand the process by which individuals deal with failure
- Create an environment in which healing is possible
- Be effective in helping people deal with their failures

THE EFFECTS OF FAILURE

Self-improvement plans can go awry. Sometimes they simply don't work. We sometimes fail to achieve the goals we set for ourselves. We take a risk when we change some procedures in our work environment only to find that the organization does not support the risk. These and countless other experiences represent failures in our lives.

Failure is the state of being that is found wanting. We've missed success, or we are deficient or inadequate. Failure is also defined as the lack or absence of something that is expected. These definitions tell us clearly that failure is the loss of something that we value.

When we fail, we lose a part of our self-esteem. Most of us try to maintain a consistent image of ourselves as competent, self-directed people. When we fail, this tendency is increased—that is, we strive to reduce the mental anguish aroused by the experience of failure. One way to reduce this dissonance is by externalizing the failure—by blaming it on luck, chance, fate, social deficiencies, or powerful other people. If we believe that any of the above are beyond our control, they will be. Another way of reducing this discomfort is to minimize the importance we attribute to the goal we wanted to accomplish. This in turn minimizes the effects of the failure. Yet another way to reduce this mental discomfort is to discount ourselves, to feel guilty and unworthy. We thereby create an incompetent self-image. We can't succeed anyway, so what's the use of getting upset about a failure?

Unfortunately, each of these schemes for dealing with failure is unproductive in that each diminishes our capacity to learn from experience. If, on the other hand, we learn to embrace error as a way of learning and expanding, we learn to thrive on adversity.

One caution, however. If we allow failure to become a habit, we can literally become failures. When we begin to see ourselves as failures, we also cease our efforts to grow—we become helpless. To reinforce our self-image as a failure, we may also subconsciously seek situations in which we can ensure failure.

Failure is a paradox because only through the process of failing do we learn and grow. The experience of failure does not diminish us; it is the belief that we are powerless to overcome failure that is so dangerous. Therefore, it is important for coaches to help associates learn how to put failure in proper perspective. To be effective in this regard, you should understand

- Your own reactions to and beliefs about failure

- The process of grieving and letting go

- How to facilitate letting go

WHY DO PEOPLE FAIL?

There are four basic reasons for failure. First, people sometimes fail because they lack the skills they need to succeed. Perhaps the training they received was inadequate or perhaps they are trying to do things for which they are ill equipped. Whatever the reason for the lack of skill, when a person does not have the skills she needs, then failure is usually the outcome. However, lack of skill is probably not the main cause of failure.

Second, people often fail because they are reluctant to act. They fail because of omission and not because of commission. Failure by omission takes many forms. It is a subtle enemy. Seemingly capable people often fail, not because they lack the skill to succeed, but because they lack the will to prepare. For example, you may have known associates who would not prepare for a major challenge at work.

Another form of failure by omission is the unwillingness to risk. For example, people are often afraid to risk social rejection. We have seen groups of competent people avoid risk because they were afraid of interpersonal conflict. And we have seen people avoid risks because they were afraid to be found lacking by their peers. Whatever the reason, the unwillingness to risk creates its own failure because risk avoidance leads to inaction. They know, or at least believe, that it is dangerous to take a risk. They therefore fail because they are unwilling to be found lacking by other members of the organization.

A third reason people fail is because they have an expectation of failing. Because they expect to fail, they don't try as hard as they might, or they get so tense about the prospects of failing that they do not concentrate on what they should be doing. This is failure by doubt.

A story about an experiment with the northern pike, an aggressive game fish that loves to feed on perch, is instructive. Hungry pike were placed in an aquarium full of juicy perch. These perch were located on the opposite side of a transparent glass partition. This glass was not something the pike had experienced before or understood, so when they saw the perch moving about in the water, they lunged for them and struck their noses on the glass partition. They lunged again with the same result—pain. Finally, they quit lunging. At this point, the experimenter removed the glass partition separating the pike from the perch. The pike remained immobile and did nothing to satisfy their hunger and, in the end, died. The pike did not die from a lack of the things they needed to ensure survival. They died from the belief that there was nothing they could do to control the important outcomes in their lives, so they gave up trying. And they therefore created the reality they expected.

A great deal of research supports the belief that people get what they expect to get. This idea of the self-fulfilling prophecy is known as the **Pygmalion effect**. Once people start on the cycle of failure, then failure becomes a self-fulfilling expectation.

Finally, people fail because the organizations in which they work are inhospitable to success. These organizations either do not provide the opportunity for success, or actively inhibit the pursuit of success by creating barriers that make success impossible.

PATTERNS OF COPING WITH FAILURE

When people are confronted with failure, they experience stress. Stress is an individual's response to any event that threatens her sense of self-identity. A failure threatens the sense of self because it produces an image inconsistent with the belief that one is competent and intelligent.

When people perceive a threat to their sense of self, they begin to cope. Coping describes strategies to reduce stress and return to feeling comfortable. It is possible to identify two broad strategies by which people attempt to deal with failure: problem-oriented and emotionally oriented strategies.

Problem-oriented strategies are chosen to remove the threat or to learn more about it. These strategies are open, flexible, and adaptive. Examples of these strategies include:

- Problem solving

- Planning

- Seeking information

- Restraining any response at all

- Accepting defeat and letting go

Emotionally oriented strategies are favored by people who deal with failure by distorting the experience in some manner. The goal of emotionally oriented strategies is to remove the threat as quickly as possible. Because these strategies are not chosen for the purpose of learning more about the threat and reducing it, these strategies tend to be closed, inflexible, and maladaptive. One way of distorting the experience is to deny the experience of failure. In denying their failure people create a situation in which it is almost impossible to learn from failure. Some examples of emotionally oriented strategies include:

- Denial

- Mental and behavioral disengagement

- Seeking out emotional support

- Reinterpreting the event

The coping strategy chosen largely dictates how the individual will attempt to work through a failure experience and how successful the process of working through it will be.

As a coach, your task is to help the associate put failure in proper perspective and to deal with it in a positive, problem-oriented manner. In order to do this, you must

- Accept failure as an inevitable component of learning and growing

- Help people let go of failure

- Mutually explore new alternatives for learning and growing

THE HEALING PROCESS: TYPICAL REACTIONS TO THE EXPERIENCE OF FAILURE

Some people go though a predictable series of emotional reactions as they deal with the experience of failure. This is the natural process of healing. The success with which people go through this cycle is critical to learning how to deal with failure in a productive manner. The reactions to failure are similar to those of loss of any person or role (a job).

In the healing process, the first reaction is often shock. Failure leads to a feeling of disorientation. This sudden disorientation is experienced as shock in that the person feels lost and powerless. This feeling of powerlessness is at the heart of the shock reaction. The feelings of shock, disorientation, powerlessness, and impotence are followed by anger and rage. After the shock recedes, the person feels anger because of the frustration of her goals and values. At the heart of this anger, the feelings are still powerlessness and fear. Where there is perceived threat, the recognition that the person does not have the wherewithal to change the situation invites a fear response.

As the feeling of impotence sets in, so do the feelings of rejection and depression. This is the third phase of the grieving/healing process. There is no one to be angry at, there is no one to hurt, or there is no one from whom to seek a satisfying vengeance. Therefore, the individual succumbs to depression, which is often caused by the loss of self-esteem.

As the grieving/healing process proceeds, a person learns to accept the failure or loss. At this point, people are finally able to look at the failure critically and to reflect on its causes and perhaps its solution. They are able to examine their values and assumptions and test those values and assumptions. Argyris (1990) called this process of examining values and assumptions and then revising them in light of experience **Double-loop learning (Model II)**. Double-loop learning (or Model II) is possible only when people are able to forgive themselves or others for the failures they have experienced, and from this perspective to examine the influence of the values, goals, or variables that led to the assumptions and subsequent events that have brought them to the present state of affairs.

Finally, acceptance and disidentification with the failure experience open the way for rebirth and renewal. As people learn to accept their failures, they also learn how to let go of failure and to forget. In the process of forgetting, they are empowered to look to the future and to the opportunities for learning and growth that the future holds.

Not all people will let this natural process of healing take place; instead, they cling to the failure as if it were a core element of their self-identity. According to stage theory, when a person becomes stuck at an early stage of development, the developmental process is arrested, and the individual's ability to learn and grow is thereby diminished.

WHAT HAPPENS WHEN PEOPLE FAIL TO LET GO

People often do not let go of the past. Instead they choose to become its victims. They develop patterns that doom them to boring repetition of the same failures. We have all met people who have had the same experiences for twelve years, as opposed to having had twelve years of experience.

A common assumption made in many psychological theories is that our actions are determined by our pasts. Many of us live our lives as if we were trying to prove ourselves to someone else. We act as if we have taken others' prescriptions for us as definitions of our self-worth, and we spend the rest of our lives trying to live up to these expectations. Of course, we doom ourselves to failure. We can never be acceptable to those critics against whose yardsticks we have chosen to measure our worth. Furthermore, living up to another's standards is not authentic. It may become a pathway to self-destruction.

The antidote to this striving to prove ourselves worthy is to recognize that we must live out of our own value system. Some of us forget this. To recreate ourselves, we must consciously choose our own values.

In the same way that people get trapped in the manacles of their past learning, people also get trapped in their resentments and inability to forgive themselves. They allow their failures to become the central theme in their lives and, being unable to accept that they failed, they cannot forgive themselves and refocus their energies on future goals and objectives. When this happens, these individuals are no longer capable of self-renewal. At these times, they need your support.

WHAT ARE THE CHARACTERISTICS OF
THE SELF-RENEWING PERSON?

On the other end of the spectrum are those people who demonstrate lifelong self-renewal. What is it about these people that is unique? What have they learned that enables them to find life full of wonder and opportunity for self-expression and growth?

Erik Erikson (1979) viewed life as a journey of lifelong development. Along the way all people encounter periods of crisis, challenges with which they must contend if they hope to fulfill themselves. When people are successful, they develop virtue—the inherent strength that comes with having successfully met the challenges life poses. Erikson identified eight such crises or challenges and eight possible virtues resulting from the successful resolution of these crises. Although Erikson's theory is largely speculative, his ideas appear essentially correct when it comes to the requirements for self-renewal, for people who self-renew have the virtues that Erikson postulated as outcomes of successful living.

The first virtue is *hope*, the confident expectation that one can succeed in life. Hope is built on the basis of trust in oneself and is the foundation of faith—a belief that does not require proof. Hope is strengthened in people who see alternatives, have friends, have zest or energy and enthusiasm.

The second virtue is *autonomy*, the experience of freedom, of personal responsibility for one's own destiny. Its opposite is the experience of doubt and shame, of dependence on others.

The third virtue is *purpose.* Self-renewing people have a sense of purpose in life. They have a guiding vision and are free of the guilt that comes from the struggle between initiative and guilt.

The fourth virtue is *competence.* Self-renewing people feel competent and powerful. And, in their feelings of efficacy, they find the courage to experiment with new things, to be curious, and to be full of wonder.

Hope, autonomy, purpose, and competence create the context for the development of identity—a full realization of who we are. The fifth virtue that comes from the development of identity is *integrity*, the state or quality of being complete and whole. Self-renewing people are true to themselves. They act from their sense of who they are.

People do not live in isolation. They are part of a larger community. Self-renewing people have the sixth virtue of *empathy*. They have learned how to be separate and yet to be a part of something larger than themselves.

The seventh virtue of self-renewal is that of *maturity*. Self-renewing people have learned to share of themselves generously. The opposite of generosity is selfishness.

Finally, self-renewing people have acquired the eighth virtue of *wisdom*. This is the virtue of perspective—of seeing things as they really are. Wisdom is the capacity to understand that perspective is everything, and that sometimes you have to look at things differently in order to transform those things.

The effective coach is a self-renewing person. And it is in your own self-renewal that you become an agent for helping your associates deal with their own failures and develop strategies for self-renewal.

THE ROLE OF FORGIVENESS

The Japanese have a ceremony of harmony to reconcile the sinner and the victim. If a person makes a serious mistake, that person formally apologizes to the other members of the organization, and they, in turn, formally accept the apology as a means of forgiving the person and of restoring harmony in the organization. They symbolically erase the ledger in which the sin has been recorded and, in doing so, they enable everyone, including the sinner, to refocus on the present and the future, while having learned something valuable from the past.

This ceremony clearly underscores the meaning of the concept of forgiveness. Forgiveness is a process of admitting to one's mistake, apologizing to those who have been affected by the mistake, asking for their forgiveness, accepting their grace (unmerited divine assistance given for one's regeneration and renewal), and then letting go and moving on to new opportunities for learning and growth.

This same notion was earlier discussed by Carl Jung (1979). In his view, each of us has a basic drive toward self-realization and self-actualization. However, to achieve self-realization and fulfillment and to open the door for self-renewal and learning, it is first necessary for us to confess our current inadequacies, confront our current behaviors, forgive ourselves for our failures, and then let go of the past.

These discussions suggest and experience seems to validate that, for learning to take place, people have to be able to accept the truth about themselves, to see themselves as they are, and then to transcend these limitations. Warren Bennis, in *Becoming a Leader*, says that all leaders must measure the difference between what they need and want and what they are able to do, and between what drives them and what satisfies them. They must then have the courage to transcend the gulf between want and ability, and between motivation and meaning. Truly effective people have learned how to create themselves by bringing together want with ability and motivation with desire.

As a coach, you play a vital role in helping your associates forgive themselves in times of failure. You can help create the situation where your associates feel free to be themselves. How? You promote healing and forgiveness by:

- Having a supportive relationship
- Modeling forgiveness of yourself and others
- Enabling people to talk openly of feelings about failure
- Helping them explore their underlying values and assumptions
- Helping them discover new alternatives for learning

- Making an uncompromising commitment to personal integrity—telling the truth or being honest

- Sharing your enthusiasm for life—*zest!*

You can also make truth the norm in your situation.

TO TELL THE TRUTH

Truth is often the most potent healer. In his book, *The Abilene Paradox and Other Meditation on Management* (1988), Jerry Harvey tells several stories in which the truth liberated people and paved the way for them to act with integrity and honor. The most powerful of these stories comes from the action of the Danes who refused to identify the Jewish people among them and all wore the yellow arm band with the Star of David.

When people fail, they experience anxiety. This anxiety is painful. Most of us try to avoid this feeling of uncertainty. This avoidance often results in our weaving stories by which we can explain away our failures. Through these mental preoccupations, we create myths by which we can maintain a consistent image of ourselves. We often create our own failures through our constant preoccupation with them.

These preoccupations are lies because they have nothing to do with reality. A coach must be committed to telling the truth. In our view, this basic honesty, this willingness to tell the truth, is one of the most central qualities of coaching. The coach may not be the associate's equal in terms of ability or accomplishment, but the coach can often see further and more clearly. Therefore, the coach must be willing to share what she sees, even if it means destroying the myth an associate has constructed in order to justify her shortcomings.

One of the strongest contributions of tennis great Ivan Lendl's coach was that he was able to help Lendl understand that his lack of concentration following a questionable line call caused him to lose. He helped Lendl see the truth of this by confronting him with his own shortcomings. And, in the process, Lendl became one of the great tennis champions.

CREATING THE ENVIRONMENT FOR GROWTH

When the environment makes it difficult for people to acknowledge mistakes and to forgive and be forgiven, then that environment is antithetical to learning and growth. What is needed is a hospitable environment.

Henri Nouwen writes about the concept of hospitality in his book, *Reaching Out* (1986). He says that hospitality is the creation of a space where one can be free to be oneself and to discover grace. In a hospitable environment, there is no imposition of doctrine on one another; there is only a forgiving acceptance of, and caring for, who one is. In such an environment, people are free to think about where they have gone in their lives, and they are enabled to admit that it has been they who brought themselves to wherever they happen to be.

> Hospitality means the creation of a free space where the [person] can enter and become a friend instead of an enemy. Hospitality is not to change people, but to offer them space where change can take place. It is not to bring men and women over to our side, but to offer freedom not disturbed by dividing lines. It is not to lead [the other] into a corner where there are no alternatives left, but to open a wide spectrum of options for choice and commitment. It is not an educated intimidation with good books, good stories, and good works, but the liberation of fearful hearts so that words can find roots and bear ample fruit. It is not a method of making our way into the criteria of happiness, but an opening of an opportunity for others to find their own way. The paradox of hospitality is that it wants to create emptiness, not a fearful emptiness, but a friendly emptiness where the person can discover themselves as created free; free to sing their own songs, speak their own languages, dance their own dances; free also to leave and follow their own vocations. Hospitality is not a subtle invitation to adopt the life style of the host, but the gift of a chance for the guest to find his [sic] own. (Nouwen, 1986, pp. 70–71)

As beautiful as this sentiment is, when we fail, what we often crave is a sense of being occupied, not freedom. However, it is this craving for "busyness" that makes it so hard for most of us to deal with the root causes of the failures of life. In fact, when we are not busy, we often become anxious and fearful. The act of staying occupied protects us from the reality we so badly want to avoid and deny. Our worries and concerns are the indicators that it is almost impossible for us to leave unanswered the many questions that surround our failed efforts. The anxiety that attends failure causes us to seek solutions to our problems without having understood their causes. We become so preoccupied with finding a solution that we close ourselves to having new experiences that might solve the problems we are trying to escape. The preoccupations of our minds continually recreate the world we wish to change. If we would stop telling ourselves that the world is such a place, then it will cease to be so for us.

If we would be open to healing and renewal we must first find a place where we can be free to recreate ourselves. To help others deal with the failures of life, we must create a place where people can be free to be themselves. This is a place that is hospitable.

HOW A COACH CAN HELP OTHERS COPE WITH FAILURE

In this section, we explore some of the strategies by which you as a coach can empower your associates to deal with failure in a positive manner.

Create a Hospitable Environment

One of the main things you can do as a coach to make it easier for associates to deal with failure is to create an environment in which it is safe to risk and possibly fail. In our view, people actually thrive on risking and failing, but only if they can do so in a place that tells them it is OK to fail as long as they learn from their failures.

To create a hospitable environment, the coach must embrace error as a way of life. But the coach must also embrace the learning that is inevitably embedded in the failure. This means that in a hospitable environment it is OK to confess failure and to explore the causes of failure. At the same time, it is an environment in which people typically reflect on the relationships between assumptions, actions, and outcomes, and evaluate the validity of the assumptions that guide those actions.

Model Self-Renewal

One of the most powerful means by which you can help others deal with failure is to model your own self-renewal. As a coach, you will undoubtedly fail. You can either deny this fact, or you can admit to failure and strive to learn from an examination of your failure. Your actions, more than your words, tell others what you really believe and what you value. When you can be seen confessing to failures, when you can be seen examining your assumptions and the actions that flow from them, you are giving others permission to do the same. More than giving permission, you are telling them that the unexamined life is the unfulfilled life, and that you expect nothing less or more than honesty with oneself.

Critically Reflect on Performance

The way you deal with failures largely determines how your associates will deal with failure. If you engage in denial or in some form of group-think, a process in which data that do not fit the current myths are denied or distorted, then this is how your associates will operate. However, if you regularly engage in, and enable others to participate in, a process of critical reflection, when plans are reviewed, performance is compared to expectations, assumptions are tested against reality, and changes are made in light of the resulting analysis you actively demonstrate that failure is not something to hide. Rather, failure becomes something that enables the team and each associate to grow and to become even more productive.

Create a Process for Letting Go of Failures

As a coach you can help your associates ritually let go of failure by providing a space in which people can share their pain and frustrations. One of the best ways to do this is by allowing your associates to talk through their failures. By listening with empathy and understanding, you can help your associates come to see failure in a new light. You can help them put failure in a different perspective and, in doing so, you can help them find new pathways toward goal accomplishment.

Motivate Associates to Take Risks

Associates can learn to deal with failure when you and they create an environment where risk and innovation are valued. You should create an environment in which people have a great deal of autonomy to do things in their own way, where they are encouraged to contribute ideas about how to improve performance, and where their ideas are not criticized. Strive to recognize and reward your associates' efforts to be innovative.

Practice Forgiveness

Performance evaluation should be an ongoing aspect of most work environments. On occasion, you and your associates will fail to meet expectations. At these times, it is important that you demonstrate forgiveness by truthfully examining the causes of the problem, sharing and discussing everyone's reactions to the problem, and exploring ways to solve the problem.

Create a Feeling of Being at Home

Home is the place where people feel they are wanted and where they want to be. A home is characterized by this reciprocal relationship between wanting and being wanted. People describe the places where they feel at home in similar terms: where they feel accepted, and where there is openness. Openness is the willingness to share and the willingness to listen. As a coach, you greatly influence the quality of the work environment. By modeling acceptance and openness, you give others permission to display these same behaviors and, in the process, you enable them to deal with failure.

ACTIVITIES FOR DISCOVERY AND GROWTH

This set of activities will assist you in becoming more effective as an agent of positive change in your associates' lives.

Activity 1
Discovering Prices

Purpose

One way to get a person to begin to let go of a self-defeating pattern is to help that person discover the prices that go along with the behavior. No self-defeating behavior can be maintained without a cost to the person. The purpose of this activity is to acquaint you with a technique to help another person explore the price of her behavior.

Directions

1. Have the individual describe a self-defeating pattern of behavior.

2. Once the person has fully described the pattern, have her explore the price of that behavior. There are several categories of prices:

   - Actual results such as unhappiness, discouragement, depression, ineffectiveness at work, and so on

   - What is missed as a result of the behavioral pattern, such as decreased creativity, lost opportunity, decreased productivity at work, a negative impact on others, and so on

   - Wasted effort in minimizing the price, such as keeping busy in low-value activities, joking about one's behavior, disowning the behavior, and so on

3. Now encourage the person to make a judgment about whether she wants to continue paying this price. Help the person explore behavioral options.

4. Help the individual devise plans to behave in more effective ways.

Activity 2
Using Positive Mental Imagery to Overcome Self-Defeating Behavior

Purpose

Just as mental images are powerful reinforcers of a pattern of failure, they are also powerful tools for assisting a person to overcome a pattern of self-defeating behavior. The purpose of this activity is to show you how to help another person use the power of positive mental imagery.

Directions

1. First, identify problems the person is having difficulty dealing with.

2. Now have the person explore her mental self-image in relation to the problem. What is the image? How does the person feel in the image? What is she doing? What is happening?

3. Once the person has fully explored the mental self-image of coping in relation to her problem, help the person construct a positive mental image of coping with the problem in a highly successful manner. What is the person doing? What is she feeling? What are the results?

Now encourage the person to practice this mental imagery process over and over again until she can see herself successfully cope with the problem with a feeling of confidence and self-efficacy.

Activity 3
Creating Openings

Purpose

One way to get a person to grow is to help that person discover new openings in her life. Openings are simply opportunities for the development of self-esteem and personal growth. The purpose of this activity is to help you assist a person mired in self-defeating attitudes to discover new openings in her life.

Directions

1. There are two kinds of openings: openings in and openings out. Help the individual explore ways to enhance herself (openings in) and ways to enhance her relationships with others (openings out). Make a list of these opportunities.

2. Help the individual prioritize these life choices.

3. Help the individual choose one or more of these choices.

4. Now help the individual create a new opening, a plan for carrying out these choices. What kinds of assistance and coaching does the person require to carry out the choice?

ON COMBATTING LEARNED HELPLESSNESS

In an experiment using college students, Donald Hirota (1975) placed one group of students in conditions where they were subjected to loud noise without the possibility of escape. A second group was subjected to loud noise that they were able to turn off by pushing a button. A third group was subjected to no noise at all. In the second part of the experiment, each group was exposed to loud noise which could be stopped by a movement of the hand. The second and third groups soon learned to turn off the noise, but the first group sat passively and accepted the situation. This study underscores the theory that humans learn to be helpless by encountering situations that they cannot alter by their responses. They learn that responding is futile, and they form the expectation that future responses will also be wasted efforts.

In another experiment, Martin Seligman (1975) used dogs to test the hypothesis that the effects of a single experience of helplessness dissipate with time, but repeated experiences of helplessness produce more permanent behavior changes. The findings of this experiment were identical with those using college students as subjects—the dogs that had no control over their environment soon learned to accept their situations passively, even though the environment was painful and could be escaped by taking action.

The changes associated with learned helplessness can take three forms: (1) the person gives up after having been subject to a crisis which she could not control; (2) a belief that it is useless to act, which interferes with the person's ability to learn; and (3) a failure to act because of depression and/or fear.

Such laboratory research examining the effects of uncontrollable circumstances on people is corroborated by personality research theory, which indicates that a person's belief in her own ability to control outcomes is important to the healthy functioning of the personality. This confirms the validity of Julian Rotter's (1966) locus of control variable as developed in his social learning theory. This variable is expressed on a continuum from total externality (control over payoffs seen by the person to be completely outside her control) to total internality (the person's belief that her behavior can control all payoffs). Therefore, according to Rotter, an "internal" person believes that the outcome of most situations depends on her behavior and personal characteristics; an "external" person attributes the outcome of most situations to outside forces such as fate or the power of others. Rotter hypothesized that the development of a person's locus-of-control orientation depends on her reinforcement history, both the painful and the pleasurable results of past behavior.

All human beings learn to distinguish whether causal relationships exist between their behavior and the outcomes of their behavior. From the overall patterns of their experiences, they build expectations about the degree to which they can control events, and they generalize these expectations to their entire life situations. Repeated failures make people expect to fail at everything, whereas successes at controlling outcomes have the opposite effect.

Other research has verified Rotter's theory, showing that internality results in greater health and personal potency. Internally oriented people have higher self-concepts; they are generally better adjusted, more independent, more successful, more realistic in their aspirations, more open to new learning, more creative, more flexible, and more self-reliant.

The concept of locus of control is important to the realization that so-called lack of motivation in associates may stem from disbelief that they are in control of their own lives. Many people suffer from the learned helplessness profiled by Seligman. These associates have histories of failure in controlling the outcomes of their lives, both in and out of the workplace. They are externally oriented, believing that other people or outside influences—managers, poverty, or the system—control what happens to them no matter how hard they may try to accomplish anything. The tendency to set unrealistic levels of aspiration—too high or too low for their abilities—results in a "Why try?" attitude. They do not see the relationship between the results they produce and the performance appraisals they receive. They do not learn that their own actions control their payoffs.

Learned helplessness must be challenged and overcome in the coaching setting, or wherever it is important for the individual to succeed. How can you help your associates to shift from an external to an internal orientation? Rotter (1966) suggests four conditions necessary for such a behavior change:

1. People must be capable of learning new behavior, or their attempts to change that behavior will be futile. Research on the Pygmalion effect demonstrates that when coaches are convinced of their associates' potential for success and they unconsciously give associates more frequent, specific, and encouraging feedback, their associates get the message that they are expected to succeed, and they perform better as a result.

2. In order to shift from an external to an internal orientation, people need consistent reinforcement for their efforts until the behavior patterns are established, often over a prolonged period of time.

3. The associate must personally value or assign worth to the learning outcomes or she will not make the effort to achieve that outcome.

4. The learner must trust the coach and the work situation in order to learn effectively. A person with a history of failure and an external orientation is likely to expect dishonesty in persons and systems offering services. When the associate does not trust, she will take one of two actions when confronted with failure-producing behavior:

   - Conform verbally to management demands without making a real behavioral change

   - Withdraw from the stress situation. Real change occurs in a helping relationship that combines warm, personal rapport with confrontation about ineffective behavior.

Here are some specific suggestions for combatting learned helplessness in your associates:

1. Be aware that the effects of learned helplessness often dissipate with time, so those returning to new situations may have forgotten typical helpless feelings from youth.

2. Take steps to make the present work environment different from what caused helplessness in the past. You must avoid the look and feel of the past, emphasizing instead that the associate is making a new start. Some evidence suggests that simply starting a new job may be beneficial for victims of helplessness. By providing successful experiences that are the result of genuine

effort by the individual, and taking care to articulate the connection between the efforts and the results, the individual becomes more self-directed and develops the belief that, through their own competence and effort, they can produce good results!

3. Develop personal, supportive relationships with your associates. Convey your concern for them. Disregard their present (negative) patterns of behavior. After you have demonstrated your trust in their ability to succeed, you must develop and state a mutual commitment. The associate must be willing to accept the following standards for her own behavior: (a) honesty and willingness to share all facts that bear on her progress, and (b) responsibility, or the willingness to make commitments and live up to them. However, you should define the terms *honesty* and *responsibility*, otherwise your associates tend to find them threatening and ambiguous. By developing an explicit interpersonal contract with your associate, you lay the groundwork for a helping relationship in which you will be able to help the associate look at and alter her failure-producing behavior.

4. Help your associate select realistic as well as valued work goals, as those individuals with low internality tend to select goals either too demanding for their ability level or far too easy to be challenging.

5. Make clear, once work objectives have been established, what your associates must then do to meet those objectives.

6. Use individual contracts to reinforce your associate's sense of responsibility for achieving the objectives. An individual contract is a tool for making obstacles manageable. It establishes the minimal work objectives and tasks, and allows a degree of individual choice in the methods, the amount of work, and the attainment of objectives. The associate can contract for a desired outcome, and then renegotiate the contract upward or downward in light of her progress during the task. The process of contracting allows the associate to rehearse the steps of successful achievement, and the contract itself serves as a standard whereby coach and associate can evaluate progress together at any time.

7. Confront externally oriented behavior and reward internally oriented behavior, using a variety of helping techniques. First, refuse to accept excuses for failure. Second, confront statements of belief that others are controlling the associate's life. For example, instead of allowing an associate to say, "My wife made me take this job; she wants to buy a house," respond with "What do you want out of this job, and what do you want to do?" Third, praise your associates for making internal statements like "I'll ask my buddy to show me how to do this

job," or "I'm going to take that minicourse to improve my skills." Fourth, help your associates develop behavioral plans that allow them to try new options and gain control in previously helpless situations.

8. Take advantage of peer support and pressure to reinforce self-responsibility, taking care that small groups develop the cohesion necessary to be effective as behavior change agents.

PART 5

Endings and New Beginnings

The final part of this book offers some thoughts and useful ideas about developing what Peter Senge (*The Fifth Discipline*, 1990) termed the learning organization. However we describe organizations that will thrive in the future, surely their major characteristics will include the ability to learn, to adapt, and to generate new ideas and products in a rapidly changing global marketplace. Our goal in this chapter is to share a way of thinking about organizations and how they function, and about the role of coaching in organizations. We also underscore the power of thought to shape reality, both positively and negatively. A good theory enables managers and leaders to be more effective; a poor theory has the opposite effect—it weakens people and their organizations to the point of failure.

C H A P T E R 1 0

Evolution of a New Paradigm

INTRODUCTION

This book provides some tools and resources that will enable you to become a more effective coach. However, the paradigm of the empowered coach is in flux because current views of society in general, and of organizations in particular, are no longer adequate to help us deal with the increasingly complex nature of social reality. More effective views of organizations are required. We thus start at the level of the organization and then conclude with discussion of the role of the manager/leader/coach in these new organizations.

GOALS

The goals of this chapter are to help you

- Develop a model and rationale for the development of the learning organization

- Formulate the role of the manager/leader/coach within this framework

- Identify the kinds of changes that will be required of managers/coaches as they create and work within these environments

THE NECESSITY OF LEARNING

Many writers have speculated about the shape of the organization of the future. What will be its dominant features? What will be its structure? What will be the role of the leader in these organizations? One of the essential ingredients to success in organizations, teams, or individuals is responsiveness. The rate of change is more rapid than ever before. At every level of the organization, people must learn to adapt to frequent change and to do so more rapidly than at any time in our history.

For example, in the past, an automobile manufacturer could introduce new car designs with a cycle time from design to marketing of six to nine years and still expect to remain competitive (assuming the designs were correct in the first place). Now, some manufacturers are able to reduce the cycle from conception to delivery to a mere three to four years. To remain competitive, all auto manufacturers must reduce their development time to such competitive levels, or they will face extinction (cf. *Business Week,* October 12, 1990).

Another example is meeting customer needs and the changing preferences of consumers. It isn't good enough to simply meet the needs of consumers. To remain competitive, businesses must not only meet their needs, but do so on demand and in exemplary ways. To be successful, they must provide products and services with personality, products, and services that fascinate and motivate.

In part, this is because there are more businesses providing goods and services to consumers. Consumers have more and better choices, so naturally they are going to spend their money where they get the best service—service that goes beyond simply meeting their needs.

The organizations that are going to survive and grow in this kind of environment are going to be able to adapt rapidly. Organizations must not only be responsive but capable of developing new and improved responses.

Being responsive involves making the right response at the right time. To make the right response at the right time requires both awareness (openness) and competence. An organization cannot respond if it doesn't have accurate environmental information. Even if it does know, it cannot respond if it lacks the competence to do so. It must acquire new responses by developing new competencies.

In a rapidly changing world, the organization may not have the competence needed to make the right response. But it must have the competence to learn. This involves learning how to learn. How do organizations learn how to learn? We'll answer this question in more detail later. For now, we want to suggest that the role of coaching is central in learning organizations. In our view, learning takes place best where effective coaching is the norm. Those organizations that are, or succeed at becoming, the most responsive are those in which coaches, managers, leaders, and associates are all competent at helping each other learn the new skills and knowledge required to successfully meet the challenges of change. People at the top of the organization can make the responses required to alter the course of the organization. Change is effective only if people in all areas of the organization are competent at understanding what is going on and have the skills and the authority to make the right response at the right time.

BUILDING THE LEARNING ORGANIZATION

The successful organization of the future will be characterized by its ability to learn and to adapt very rapidly to shifts in the local, national, and international environments, and to do so in a way that enables individual members, as well as the organization as a whole, to meet both individual and collective needs. This learning will not only be to adapt to existing situations. Its goal will also be to create new forms and new realities.

There are different types of organizational learning. One type of learning is *adaptive learning*, what members of the organization do to enable themselves to respond to changes in the existing marketplace. This kind of learning is very important as the rate of change in the marketplace is accelerating at an alarming pace.

Another type of learning is *generational* or *creative learning*. This type of learning leads to the development of new products and services that meet the needs of new markets in unique ways. Creative learning is also characteristic of organizations that will survive into the future. This type of learning capacity requires new ways of seeing the world. It requires a new paradigm; therefore, it requires personal and collective change. This type of learning also requires seeing the integrated systems that influence events. Many of us still do not perceive the world as integrated. Some see events as linear and predictable. Yet, contemporary reality is nonlinear and unpredictable.

Despite the glaring need for organizations that are more responsive and more capable of adaptive and generative learning, few organizations attain this shift of paradigm. Why? We lack leaders who understand the large systems' perspective and the roles required to create learning organizations. Effective leaders must be able to build a shared vision of the future, to influence others to challenge their prevailing mental models, and to think systematically.

These are the same skills that are characteristic of the most effective coaches. In the adaptive organization, new roles and skills are required. Leaders have to act as designers, coaches, and stewards. Leaders also have to become adept at building a shared vision, at surfacing and testing current assumptions about reality, and at fostering systems thinking about the organization.

What does it mean to be a learning organization? For some years we, and many others, have emphasized the importance of a guiding vision in the learning process. Learning is not an abstraction, it is a means to an end. Without a dream, there is not much point in learning. Many people in organizations just get by. This is not because they cannot master the skills, but because they do not see the point.

We have also seen these employees, even those who are less able, come alive when they discover a reason for learning. The problem is firing their imaginations as opposed to figuring out how to get them to work. Learning organizations require a sense of purpose and vision as a precursor for learning.

To create a vision is one thing; to make it happen is another. To make a vision happen requires the ability to learn. Learning, in turn, requires valid internal and external data. This ability is called responsiveness. Responsiveness is an informed awareness of what current reality is. For example, what is the competition doing?

How do we compare to our competitors? What is our market? How well are we doing in meeting the needs of our customers? What do our associates think about our efforts to provide quality products and services? What are we able to do? What are we good at? What are our relative strengths and weaknesses? What systems do we have and how well are they working?

But knowledge alone is not enough for learning to take place. Learning indicates that a change in capacity has taken place, that the learner can do more of something, do something better, or do something entirely different than before. Learning requires knowledge and action. This capacity is action mastery. Mastery is the ability to take data from one's internal and external environments and to use it to design structures, create understanding and meaning, and ultimately to achieve a goal. Mastery is integrating many disparate functions and processes in a way that all become focused on achieving the organization's vision.

DEVELOPING THE PRODUCTIVE WORKSCAPE

Anthropology is often very useful in helping us understand organizations. One anthropological concept is *workscape*—the quality of the environmental setting in which work takes place. Workscapes can be either productive or counterproductive. There are three qualities characteristic of productive workscapes. Note that these are the same three qualities of a good coaching relationship discussed in Chapter 2.

First of all, productive workscapes are clearly understandable. Every message conveys a straightforward theme. Everything in the environment is easily understood in terms of the guiding vision. Second, productive workscapes are coherent. Everything fits with and reinforces the core vision and values of the organization. Finally, productive workscapes are open—they value learning and are open to it because they realize that the world is a dynamic place.

Again, we see a convergence of ideas about what it takes to create organizations that will thrive in the future—organizations that have a sustaining, yet flexible vision of the future—organizations that are continuously learning and creating their own destinies. In such organizations, coaching plays a key role because it is through coaching that the fabric of the workscape is woven. As we mentioned in our discussion on developing the high-performance climate, coaches contribute to this development in five ways. First, the coach provides leadership that values and supports learning and growth. In learning organizations, leaders help shape and build commitment to a shared vision and model the core values of the organization.

Second, people in productive workscapes spend a lot of time getting the right people into the organization. Two qualities are especially important—the capacity to identify with the organization and its values, and a preference for hard work.

Third, the coach is a critical player in the process of empowering associates. One of the most prominent features of productive workscapes is the high degree of autonomy enjoyed by associates. Autonomous associates and work groups are best positioned to respond to changes in the environment and to engage in creative learning.

A fourth way the coach contributes to the development of the productive workscape is by making teamwork a norm within the organization. When people work together, synergies of performance are possible. The coach influences the development of teamwork through the example she sets. However, it is not just example that establishes the norm for teamwork. Teamwork is also determined by the extent to which the environment encourages collaboration and discourages harmful competition. In her book, *When Giants Learn to Dance* (1989), Rosabeth Moss-Kanter shows how many organizations defeat themselves by actively reinforcing competition between departments. Competition divides an organization because it emphasizes a part at the expense of the whole. Collaboration shifts the focus to the whole and toward actions that perpetuate and strengthen the whole. Systemic thinking leads to a recognition of the need for collaboration.

Finally, the coach as manager can provide the support for accomplishment that is characteristic of productive workscapes. Coaches support accomplishment by ensuring that their associates have the resources they need. Perhaps the best support coaches can provide their associates is to remove obstacles or constraints on good performance. The key to improved performance is to look at how jobs are accomplished and to enable people to remove identified constraints.

NEW COACHING ROLES

To develop a learning organization, the coach must view her role in a new way. Senge identifies three themes that characterize the design of learning organizations. First of all, in learning organizations, the coach helps design the structure of the work team by determining the governing purpose and core values. Second, the coach builds into the organization policies, strategies, and structures that translate the vision into concrete business decisions and actions. Third, the coach creates effective learning processes that allow policies and strategies to be continuously improved.

At the heart of this role is the coach's ability to create and/or articulate the vision, and then create an environment that frees others to learn and grow with this vision in mind. One of the most important aspects of coaching is the coach's ability to help her associates see things in a new way. By being a clarifier of the vision, by helping others see the pathway to create the vision, and by helping others see how their assumptions act as constraints on performance, the coach frees her associates to become contributors and producers.

A second role of the leader/coach in the learning organization is that of teacher. The main task of the teacher is to help people gain more insightful views of reality. Much human activity is based on assumptions that, for the most part, have gone untested. These assumptions are generally tacit and hidden, which make them dangerous. When people function in habitual ways without examining their assumptions, no learning and growth take place. There is only repetition of the past. Transformation is possible only when people examine the assumptions underlying their decisions and construct new realities based on new assumptions.

A final role of the coach in the learning organization is that of steward. The coach is steward of the organization's larger purpose; she is steward of the dream. The coach must ensure that each person is enabled to participate to her fullest ability in the creation of this vision or dream.

NEW COACHING SKILLS

New roles require new skills and new tools. Senge identifies three skills that he believes will be required to build the learning organization. Among the most important coaching skills is that of building a shared vision. When every member of a talented team shares the same vision, the outcome is a unity and elegance of performance that is difficult to destroy.

Shared vision does not simply mean some verbal endorsement of the team's creed or motto. Shared vision happens when each team member internalizes the vision and senses its value to her. Each individual must truly believe in the vision. This is an emotional reaction as well as a cognitive reaction. People experience a passionate concern for the dream. The passion for greatness is different from the desire just to survive. The former is a positive vision of what is attainable; the latter is a negative vision of something to be avoided.

Another coaching skill in the learning organization is critical reflection. Critical reflection is what the coach does when she encourages an associate to examine the assumptions that underlie her actions and to change these assumptions when evidence suggests change is an appropriate course of action. In altering assumptions, one is actually changing reality. This is because assumptions are so important in determining the shape of reality. When assumptions change, creativity and transformation become possible. To illustrate this concept, think for a moment about the issue of quality. For years, quality was defined in terms of zero defects. This became the assumption under which many companies operated. They attempted to produce products with zero defects. However, what are the underlying assumptions of this fitness-for-use model? The American car industry provides an example. Many of the Big Three automakers are producing products with better quality than ever before; however, many of the products they produce do not have nuance and personality. Many Japanese and European automakers, on the other hand, are going beyond quality as defined by fitness for use. They are producing cars that delight, that bewitch, that fascinate. They are producing cars that have personality and character. Thus, their market share will continue to increase at the expense of those who work on the assumption that quality is defined as zero defects.

Quality is not zero defects. A state of zero defects is just one step on the way to quality. But, as long as people are caught up in the zero-defects assumption, they cannot learn the limiting nature of the assumption, nor will they see the infinite possibilities beyond this assumption. Similarly, having an environment free of toxins is not the same as having a quality environment. In a quality environment, all species live together in a state of harmony for the enrichment of all their lives. In an organization, the coach is in a favorable position to be a positive influence in helping the associate, as well as the organization, examine assumptions about reality, test these assumptions, and experiment with new ideas.

A final skill is that of holistic or systems thinking. Often, organizations and the people in them get caught up in a narrow view of events. They forget that every event is a component of a much larger process. They see problems only in terms of causes and effects, not as patterns of relationships among interlocking and interdependent parts. The coach can help associates see the interconnectedness that defines all processes in an organization.

NEW COACHING TOOLS

New skills mean that coaches will require new tools as they strive to enable others. One of the new tools to foster systems thinking and critical reflection is *system archetypes* to help understand what is currently happening in a work team or an organization. Some archetypes that are useful in this regard are summarized as follows:

- *Balancing Process with Delay.* People often fail to appreciate the delays involved in striving to reach a goal. They give up prematurely, or they work so hard to overcome insurmountable delays that they are unable to enjoy their accomplishments.

- *Goal Erosion.* People reduce their goals when they experience failure and adversity. Often, people give up on important goals or lower their standards to such low levels that accomplishment brings no sense of satisfaction.

- *Shifting the Burden.* Short-term solutions are sought to correct problems, with seemingly happy immediate results. This avoidance of long-term effective solutions leads to the recurrence of the problem, which is usually even more intense than before.

A second tool Senge discusses is *confronting strategic dilemmas.* Often, in the process of learning and growth, organizations and individuals alike must choose between short-term versus long-term gains. Such choices are looked on as either-or dilemmas. The coach's task is to help the associate see that the dilemma is neither "x" nor "y," but both "x" and "y." As a coach, you can do several things to help your associates confront strategic dilemmas:

1. Help your associates become aware of the dilemma.

2. Enable the associate to map the dilemma by identifying the values implicit in the seeming contradictions and to determine her position within this value map.

3. Help her reframe the values that seem contradictory. Reframing is the process of helping an individual examine each value as part of the context for another value.

4. Help her see that improvement is like a wave. When a change is made in a process or a behavioral pattern, things often get worse before they get better. The challenge is to help your associate or the organization "keep the faith" while the cycle points downward.

For example, a coach may see the need for change in how her associates execute a task. The change itself may cause a deterioration in performance in the short run, but lead to significant improvements in the long run. The dilemma is to get your associates to see the long-term gain.

ACTIVITIES FOR DISCOVERY AND GROWTH

The new paradigm requires new skills and new tools. The activities in this section give you the opportunity to practice these new skills and develop new tools for enabling learning.

Activity 1
Scenario Analysis

Purpose

This activity facilitates a work group's development and analysis of alternative future scenarios. The goals of the activity are to stimulate creative thinking and to promote increased responsiveness to a changing world.

Directions

Think of your current team goals. As you do so, imagine all the possible scenarios that could either facilitate or inhibit goal accomplishment. Describe these scenarios in as much detail as possible. Now, for each scenario, visualize how you can exploit (a positive scenario) or diminish (a negative scenario) this potential future. What specific steps would you need to take to create or avoid each possible scenario of the future?

Activity 2
Value Mapping

Purpose

This activity provides a tool for helping individuals examine the values that govern their behavior and demonstrates a process by which to do this.

Background

All behavior is the outcome of governing values, which are usually unconscious. These values determine behavioral strategy and, ultimately, the results a person achieves. This is illustrated in the following figure:

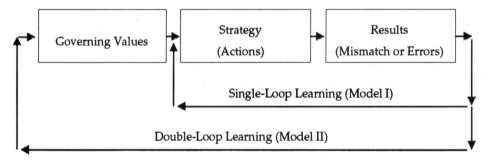

True learning takes place when people learn to reorganize (and change) the governing values that underlie their behavior (Loop II); however, people often get locked into a destructive cycle of failure because they do not examine or map their governing values (Loop I).

Directions

1. Help the individual identify a problem that has persisted over time.

2. Draw a map of the individual's behavior by working backward from results, strategies, and governing values.

3. Help the individual test the values governing her behavior. Are they appropriate?

4. Once an individual has discovered her governing values, help her test some different values. Ask the person to reflect on such questions as, "What would happen if . . . ?"

5. Help the individual make a plan by which she will consistently act on these new governing values.

Activity 3
Surfacing Mental Models

Purpose

This activity promotes creativity and increased adaptiveness in teams by helping them think about the assumptions they make with respect to recurring challenges or problems.

Directions

Think of a recurring problem that your work team is experiencing. Describe this problem in detail. That the problem is recurring implies that it is embedded in assumptions the team is making. Next, describe how you have approached the problem in the past. What happened? Now try to identify the assumptions you have been making. Some of these assumptions have been reinforcing the problem. See if you can build a model of the situation.

For instance, think about a person who is constantly late for regular staff meetings. You might assume that the person is unmotivated, or that the person had little interest in the topics to be discussed, or that the person needed the attention that comes from interrupting a meeting in progress. But if you assume that the person was late because she did not feel a part of the group or she thought she did not have much to contribute, then you could construct the meeting so that there is active participation and the person is a convenor of an agenda topic. Another idea, of course, is merely to ask the person to share with you what her experience of the meetings is, because you have noticed that she seems to be regularly late.

Once you have built a model, try to reframe the situation by making a different set of assumptions. Determine if different kinds of assumptions will produce a totally different set of outcomes.

ON LEARNING AND CHANGE

Three broad types of models seek to predict and explain how change is initiated and, consequently, seek to explain learning. Understanding how learning takes place in an organization may require a new model of the way a system changes.

At any particular moment, an individual's behavior represents an equilibrium between forces that facilitate learning and change, and forces that inhibit learning and change. As long as conditions are fairly constant, these forces define the parameters within which an individual chooses actions. However, when events, either internal or external, force the individual outside these parameters, then that individual may become either disorganized and confused, or may construct a new level of functioning far above her initial state. Such individuals have exhibited learning and transformation. At the point of the change, the individual may organize herself into a more complex, mature, effective individual, or may go into a state of deterioration, stabilizing herself at a lower level of functioning.

The coach plays a significant role in this process. She acts as an agent who helps the individual transform herself into a more complex, whole, effective person. Learning and change, at least transformative change, can be described over time as a series of events: resistance and disequilibrium, symmetry breaking, experimentation, reformulation, equilibrium. The coach plays a crucial role in this transformative process.

Resistance and Disequilibrium. Most of us do not seek out change; in fact, much of the time we resist change. We develop elaborate mechanisms to avoid change and maintain equilibrium. However, the more we resist change, the more unaligned we become, and the less we can rely on our traditional methods of maintaining equilibrium. At some point, our coping systems break down. At this point of disequilibrium we are confronted with a choice: deteriorate or reorganize at a higher level.

Symmetry Breaking. Old behavior is supported by habitual patterns that form a web of functional relationships, each of which contributes to the pattern. The coach often has sufficient influence to enable a person to work through this disequilibrium by confronting these patterns and unfreezing them.

Experimentation. Transformation is a process of experimentation with new methods of action. Within this context, there will be periods of success and periods of failure. The coach can foster experimentation by rewarding both success and failure, and by creating a workscape that values experimentation.

Reformulation.   At some time during the experimentation process, the individual discovers a new identity that feels comfortable or that affords the opportunity to realize her dreams. The coach can foster reformulation by helping the individual experiment with new models and test their effectiveness.

Equilibrium.   When a person discovers a comfortable identity, she strives to live in a manner consistent with this new identity. This is the equilibrium phase. The coach can foster this consolidation by providing the individual the opportunity to identify and make choices.

High-Performance Coaching: A Behavioral Checklist

The checklist assesses the core dimensions of effective coaching behavior:

Dimension 1: Developing Focus with a High-Performance Environment

Communicate Expectations in Action-Oriented Terms. Describe the job—and excellent performance on the job—in terms of the specific, concrete results expected.

Create a High-Performance Environment of Continuous Learning, Open Information, and the Recognition of Excellence. Make problem solving part of everyone's job and assure that the information required for effective problem solving is widely shared. Create an environment that fosters learning, and always be on the lookout for excellence in any aspect of performance.

Dimension 2: Creating Positive Relationships

Develop Positive Interpersonal Relationships. Get to know the associate as a person. Learn as much as possible about how she feels and thinks about her daily work circumstances. Cultivate positive expectations about her capacity to learn and succeed.

Dimension 3: Instructing for High Performance

Evaluate Present Performance against Desired Performance. Gather baseline data on the associate's current level of skill or performance, including information about both the associate's performance and her feelings and thoughts regarding her performance. Look at past performance as well as desired future performance.

Dimension 4: Evaluating Performance and Giving and Receiving Feedback

Give the Associate Feedback on Potential Areas for Performance Improvement.   Ask the associate to look at the difference between her actual performance and the performance required. Focus only on directly observable behavior she can change.

Dimension 5: Developing the Performance Plan

Ensure that the Associate Has Free and Informed Choice Regarding whether to Commit to This Change.   Help the associate develop a commitment to change by allowing her to judge for herself whether the consequences of not changing are acceptable. Give her a sense of what will be involved in making a change.

Dimension 6: Getting a Commitment to the Plan

If She Decides to Do So, Help Her Develop a Performance Plan.   Together, determine general areas that could benefit from improvement and the levels of improvement required.

Determine Learning Tasks and Resources Needed and Time Lines for Completion.   Together, determine specific learning tasks the associate will accomplish, time lines by which she will have accomplished them, and ways in which she will demonstrate mastery.

Dimension 7: Following Up on the Plan

Follow-up.   Help the associate make corrections during implementation of the plan. Use modeling and demonstrations, especially at the beginning of the learning program, to help the associate get a clear idea of what the changes in her management practice should look like.

Dimension 8: Building Responsibility

Building Responsibility.   A strong development plan produces many benefits for the person. Besides being an excellent road map, it encourages development of both self-esteem and self-efficacy through the building of responsibility that comes with fulfilling the contract established in Dimension 5 of this checklist.

Dimension 9: Dealing with Excuses for Failure

Accept Results, Not Excuses. If the performance plan is a good one—specific, behaviorally anchored, and controllable—then don't accept excuses for failure. Keep trying to understand the cause of failure. Especially look for ways in which the coach may be ineffective.

Dimension 10: Allowing for Natural Consequences

Allow Natural Consequences. Don't protect the associate from the natural consequences of her failure if she does not improve after many opportunities and continued coaching. This step and the previous one reflect as clearly as possible the realities of any environment that stresses performance.

This checklist allows you to assess how well you perform in each of these essential aspects of coaching.

Directions

On the following pages are a series of questions for each of the steps of high-performance coaching. These questions assess the core knowledge, attitudes, and skills necessary to be an effective coach. Rate yourself on each of these questions, using the following nine-point scale.

Skill Rating

1	2	3	4	5	6	7	8	9
Very Ineffective				Moderately Effective				Very Effective
		Ineffective				Effective		

1. Rate your current skill level. For each item, think of your current work setting and judge how effectively you execute that behavior. This estimate should be based on the standards of performance you have established for yourself and your team. Record the current level in the column marked I for "is now."

2. Rate your ideal level of effectiveness, that is, where you should be or where you want to be. Record this level in the column marked S for "should be."

3. Subtract the current rating from the ideal rating and enter this number in the column marked D for "discrepancy score."

4. Define your learning needs on the basis of this discrepancy score.

Dimension 1: Developing Focus with a High-Performance Environment

A most important step in the coaching process is creating a context in which excellence is possible. The items in this dimension evaluate your effectiveness in performing the tasks necessary for developing a high-performance environment.

To what extent do you effectively

I S D

__ __ __   1. Facilitate the definition and development of team/department goals?

__ __ __   2. Help establish consensus regarding team goals?

__ __ __   3. Help establish mutually agreed-on performance goals for each person?

__ __ __   4. Help every team member clearly understand the results expected of her?

__ __ __   5. Facilitate the definition of standards of performance for each goal?

__ __ __   6. Develop agreement among associates about what is expected of them?

__ __ __   7. Help the team define and agree on the criteria for assessing performance?

__ __ __   8. Ensure that feedback about performance is readily available to you and to others?

__ __ __   9. Give each person the freedom to organize job tasks according to her personal view of can, want, and try?

__ __ __   10. Help the team learn how to work together to succeed?

__ __ __   11. Facilitate the development of effective means of communication?

__ __ __   12. Ensure that the resources needed to succeed are available?

__ __ __   13. Identify valued performance incentives?

__ __ __   14. Help each team member obtain the skills required to succeed?

__ __ __   15. Facilitate the development of effective relationships?

__ __ __   16. Ensure that performance is regularly evaluated against expectations?

__ __ __   17. Make ongoing performance feedback available to all associates?

__ __ __   18. Identify and solve problems as soon as possible?

— — — 19. Guarantee that each team member has the data and the information she needs to succeed?

— — — 20. Provide associates positive encouragement to perform up to their potential?

— — — 21. Recognize and value excellent performance?

— — — 22. Encourage experimenting with new ways of doing things?

— — — 23. Promote excellence in an ongoing way?

Dimension 2: Creating Positive Relationships

Effective coaching requires a lot of trust and mutual respect. The following set of questions assesses your ability to develop trust.

To what extent do you effectively

I   S   D

— — — 24. Share openly with your associates?

— — — 25. Get involved with your associates in a personal as well as a job-related way?

— — — 26. Spend time with each of your associates on a regular basis?

— — — 27. Listen to your associates' views about the job and the organization?

— — — 28. Keep your commitments?

— — — 29. Develop trust between your associates and yourself?

— — — 30. Communicate acceptance of your associates?

Dimension 3: Instructing for High Performance

One of your goals as a leader is to help others perform at the highest possible levels. This often involves instructing. The following items assess your effectiveness in inviting your associate to accept responsibility for producing quality results.

To what extent do you effectively

I   S   D

Step 1: Preparation Phase

— — — 31. Understand the process of skill acquisition and learning?

— — — 32. Explain the skill acquisition and learning processes to your associates?

— — — 33. Ensure understanding of the tasks to be performed?

— — — 34. Prepare plans for providing systematic instruction?

— — — 35. Ensure that the necessary resources are available?

— — — 36. Jointly establish goals for the learning process?

— — — 37. Design learning activities appropriate to the required performance?

Step 2: Telling

— — — 38. Clearly describe tasks to be performed and results expected from each task as needed?

— — — 39. Clearly show each associate how each job or role fits into the larger team or organizational context?

— — — 40. Tell associates how the tasks are to be performed?

— — — 41. Ask associates to paraphrase your instructions?

Step 3: Showing

— — — 42. Demonstrate or model the correct manner for performing tasks as needed?

— — — 43. Organize in a logical manner the presentation of strategies and tactics to produce results?

— — — 44. Use multimedia and hands-on learning and skill practice?

Step 4: Doing

— — — 45. Assist associates in planning, carrying out, and evaluating their practice?

— — — 46. Observe associates as they perform the expected tasks?

— — — 47. Provide consistent feedback about needed adjustments so that performance produces desired results?

Dimension 4: Evaluating Performance and Giving and Receiving Feedback

The challenge of getting people to change or acquire skills is helping them assess and evaluate the results of their actions. The goal of this step is to help each associate make value judgments about the results of her actions and, when needed, to move the associate toward a commitment to change. The questions that define this dimension can help you determine how effectively you give feedback to others.

To what extent do you effectively

I S D

__ __ __ 48. Get associates involved in assessing their own performance?

__ __ __ 49. Participate with associates in evaluating current behaviors?

__ __ __ 50. Relate discussions of past performance to present performance?

__ __ __ 51. Encourage associates to raise and discuss feelings openly?

__ __ __ 52. Help associates review the way they spend their time?

__ __ __ 53. Encourage associates to describe what they are doing on the job?

__ __ __ 54. Help associates identify the results of their behaviors?

__ __ __ 55. Help associates evaluate the results of their behaviors?

__ __ __ 56. Help associates examine the reasons for performance gaps?

__ __ __ 57. Avoid criticizing or putting down your associates?

__ __ __ 58. Refrain from making value judgments for associates?

__ __ __ 59. Target feedback on behaviors that can be changed?

__ __ __ 60. Help associates examine alternative ways of behaving?

Dimension 5: Developing the Performance Plan

The best way to help your associates improve their performance is to help them develop personal action plans. This is especially true when their performance is below standard. The next set of items helps you assess your effectiveness in this important role.

To what extent do you effectively

I S D

__ __ __ 61. Participate with your associates in jointly developing action plans?

__ __ __ 62. Ensure that their plans are under your associates' control?

__ __ __ 63. Ensure that their plans can be immediately implemented?

__ __ __ 64. Ensure that their plans are simple enough to allow initial success?

__ __ __ 65. Ensure that the outcomes of their plans are stated in performance terms?

__ __ __ 66. Ensure that their plans are focused on what to do (on success) instead of what not to do (on failure)?

— — — 67. See that a method for monitoring success is built into their plans?

— — — 68. Ensure that time lines for important accomplishments are part of the plans?

Dimension 6: *Getting a Commitment to the Plan*

A plan is successful to the extent that the associate and the coach commit to its success. The goal is to get the person to accept responsibility for the success of the plan. The following items help you assess your skills in facilitating commitment.

To what extent do you effectively

I   S   D

— — — 69. Help your associates say what they are willing to do?

— — — 70. Get commitment to specific times to follow up on results?

— — — 71. Get mutual agreement about performance improvement plans?

— — — 72. Help your associates write their contracts in performance terms?

— — — 73. Encourage your associates to set time limits on implementation of their plans?

Dimension 7: *Following Up on the Plan*

A key reason we do not improve our performance is because we do not follow up on the plans we make. The main skills assessed in this dimension are related to following up on a plan.

To what extent do you effectively

I   S   D

— — — 74. Follow up on the plan at agreed-on times?

— — — 75. Jointly review agreed-on results?

— — — 76. Help associates make adjustments to their plans when needed?

— — — 77. Reestablish follow-up dates when needed?

— — — 78. Keep your commitments to follow up on their plans?

Dimension 8: *Building Responsibility*

Often, plans fail because they have not been carried out. When this happens, the goal is to help your associates be responsible for the consequences of their performance and take positive actions to improve performance. The following items will help you evaluate how well you do this.

To what extent do you effectively

I   S   D

___ ___ ___   79. Help your associates assess their own performance?

___ ___ ___   80. Help your associates discover options to the ways they are currently behaving?

___ ___ ___   81. Model responsibility by accepting your own mistakes?

___ ___ ___   82. Allow associates to make their own value judgments?

___ ___ ___   83. Create situations in which your associates can make value judgments?

___ ___ ___   84. Help your associates identify the consequences of their actions?

Dimension 9: Dealing with Excuses for Failure

People who lack needed skills, who don't value the payoffs for performance, or who don't believe rewards will follow success often fail. Often they have excuses to explain away their failures. As a coach it is important for you to listen to their excuses but not to accept them. If you buy into their excuses, you are in effect colluding with your associates to fail. The behaviors listed below allow you to judge your own effectiveness in staying focused on performance.

To what extent do you effectively

I   S   D

___ ___ ___   85. Ensure that the plans were controllable by your associates?

___ ___ ___   86. Find out if your associates had the resources needed to succeed?

___ ___ ___   87. Help your associates determine if their plans were simple enough?

___ ___ ___   88. Help your associates determine if their plans were specific enough?

___ ___ ___   89. Help your associates determine if their original plans were good plans?

___ ___ ___   90. Help your associates judge whether failure was due to events beyond their control?

___ ___ ___   91. Assist your associates in developing new plans?

___ ___ ___   92. Encourage your associates to recommit to their plans?

Dimension 10: Allowing for Natural Consequences

People need incentives (payoffs they value) to perform well. Excellent performance should be followed by rewards that people value. Poor performance should be followed by the absence of valued rewards. The items defining this dimension evaluate your effectiveness in allowing natural consequences to be effective.

To what extent do you effectively

I S D

__ __ __ 93. Work with your associates to identify the consequences of excellent and poor performance?

__ __ __ 94. Discuss the consequences of various results openly?

__ __ __ 95. Discuss the consequences of failure openly?

__ __ __ 96. Develop mutual agreements to allow natural consequences to be contingent on performance?

__ __ __ 97. Engage your associates in the process of creating and discovering multiple opportunities to learn and to succeed?

Unique Applications of High-Performance Coaching

PROBLEMS AND ADVANTAGES OF MANAGING FROM A DISTANCE

Developing and Maintaining Mutual Trust: The Case of Carl and Gene

During his five years as vice-president of manufacturing at the main plant of a large capital goods manufacturer, Carl had proven himself a highly effective leader: an excellent problem solver, a good strategic planner, an exemplary supervisor, coach, and mentor for his associates. When the corporation began to look for a new president, he was the obvious choice. In conjunction with his promotion, Carl and the CEO decided to reorganize the company, decentralizing key operations into six separate, geographically based business units. Each operating unit contained new machine sales, parts sales, service centers, field rebuilds, and final assembly of some products.

During the years that Carl had been vice-president, he had developed a strong rapport with Gene, his plant manager at the same facility. With the reorganization, Carl demonstrated his confidence in Gene by putting him in charge of the San Antonio unit, a thousand miles distant from corporate headquarters near Pittsburgh. Almost immediately, Carl's healthy working relationship with Gene began to deteriorate.

With his added responsibilities, Carl faced serious time constraints that limited his opportunities to visit with Gene, and vice versa. The two kept in contact via letters, telex, and occasional telephone calls, but it soon became clear that Carl—who had been a successful manager on-site, with Gene reporting directly to him and interacting with him on a daily basis—was having difficulty managing this highly competent associate from a distance. Gene's trust and confidence in Carl began to wane because of Carl's persistent—and often inappropriate—demand for more and more detailed information about real and projected new machine sales, accuracy of on-hand parts inventories, and so on. On the other hand, after two or three minor surprises in Gene's operation, Carl began to have doubts about Gene's competence.

Carl's relationship with Gene was just one example of seven or eight relationships in the same kind of trouble. On-site, in direct relationship on a day-to-day and week-to-week basis, Carl was a highly trusted manager who inspired enthusiastic performance on the part of his associates. But when these associates began to manage at the decentralized locations, their high level of trust in Carl plummeted—along with the company's problem-solving capacity and morale—and, eventually, Carl's confidence in himself.

What was the problem?

Not the reorganization itself: The notion of decentralization was quite sound. The six market segments represented by the six decentralized locations each had unique qualities, and the corporation was appropriately following Ashby's law of requisite variety (Ashby, 1956; Conant and Ashby, 1970), which suggests that organizations must be as varied and complex as their environments. In other words, the best way to manage diversity is with diversity.

Nor was it the fitness of Carl's associates: Each of the site managers was quite competent and knowledgeable about the business and able to operate successfully on an independent basis. Their business units were performing very well financially, customer satisfaction was improving, parts sales and service billings were increasing, and sales of new machines and machine rebuilds were also on the rise. The quality of work being done in the decentralized locations was consistently higher than the work in the previous centralized location. And these site managers made a good team as well, working together effectively in their strategic planning sessions and quarterly managers' meetings.

Nor was the problem Carl's competence: He was the ideal business leader for the newly reorganized company. In his new position, Carl revitalized the plants under his supervision and prepared them for future competition in the world marketplace. He pursued companywide innovations in manufacturing—developing and installing computer-integrated manufacturing where appropriate. He also hired consultants to design and implement a manager-centered management development program that kept associates' skills and knowledge in pace with changing technology and fostered improvements in managerial and organizational performance.

Overall, the entire corporation had been strengthened by the new arrangement. But Carl's morale with respect to his relationships with his associates and their morale with respect to their relationships with him had deteriorated badly. Somehow, the variable of geographical separation had introduced new and inexplicable dynamics between Carl and his site managers.

Maintaining mutual trust seems to be the core task in managing from a distance. Often, without his realizing it, the general manager's trust in his site managers shifts off-center. He may lose some measure of confidence in his associates' competence, even when their performance appears quite satisfactory. He may wonder whether his associates are being open, fully disclosing information about the events and issues of concern to him and of importance to the organization. He may begin to question whether his associates can or will keep agreements that they have made with him. And the site managers begin to experience the same lack of confidence, the same doubts, the same subtle damage to their trust in their general manager.

Many aspects of the situation contribute to this mutual deterioration of trust. When the general manager is based at a different location, his site visits (no matter how frequent they might be) are unusual occasions. The site manager and his people prepare for the general manager and—whether they are aware of it or not—perform in his presence. As a result, the general manager is less likely to get the firsthand information he needs to truly grasp the issues and events that impact operations at that site.

Further, his secondary channels of communication are also unreliable. The more the general manager and his site managers must exchange ideas, information, and opinions in writing, on the phone, or via computer, the greater the odds for misunderstanding each other. Lost memos, missed phone calls, computer glitches, and so forth, also increase the likelihood of mistakes. Distance not only affects the quality of communication, it also affects the quality of the information communicated by compounding the problem of getting only what you measure: What usually gets measured are outputs that are easiest to measure, not necessarily those critical to the organization's success. These factors make problems harder to see from a distance and, since help seems far away, the site manager may not ask for any, even when he knows he needs it. The general manager may not know anything is wrong until the whole operation self-destructs.

At a distance, the general manager cannot garner an adequate supply of philosophical impressions—conscious and unconscious—regarding the site manager's style, the nuances of action and interaction that express his personal values and demonstrate the clarity and alignment of his goals. Nor, under such circumstances, can the general manager accurately assess the site manager's performance strengths and weaknesses. In short, the human side of the enterprise cannot be assessed accurately with the quantitative methodologies of the technical side. Technology does not, indeed cannot, accommodate the holistic impressions needed to form and maintain trust, openness, and a sense of safety—dimensions absolutely required in human communication.

For his part, the site manager may feel that no one tells him anything, whether or not that actually is the case. He may have trouble developing and maintaining in his staff a shared sense of purpose with the total organization. If morale at the distant site is low, the general manager may never know it—and if he does, that also is difficult to fix from a distance.

On the other hand, geographical separation of a general manager from his associates doesn't automatically spell disaster. A number of positive effects can accrue from distance as well. For instance, the requirement to send written communications forces the general manager to be more clear in his thinking and directions. In addition, the constraints that distance imposes on his time and attention are likely to force the general manager to delegate tasks he typically would retain—which allows him to focus on larger strategic issues and critical nonroutine dimensions of his leadership role.

For site managers, distance encourages them to take more responsibility and makes them less likely to hide negative information (data and feelings) behind a screen of false confidence. Being removed from the normal sources of supply, advice, ideas, and so on, can foster innovation and result in significant improvements and cost savings at the distant location. Further, geographical separation can foster increased team spirit among personnel working at the site—a sense of uniqueness, cohesion and self-reliance that generates organizational momentum. Finally, and perhaps most important, all of this leads site managers to experience a much greater sense of control over their own destinies—using their skills, abilities, and efforts to produce results.

STRATEGIES FOR SUCCESSFULLY MANAGING FROM A DISTANCE

Assessing and Aligning Values: The Case of Marta

As head of public relations for a large pharmaceutical manufacturing firm, Marta had been put in charge of creating a corporate-wide group of committees—one at each of six plants—for planning and organizing volunteer community service programs. At each site, the director of personnel invited all employees interested in serving on the committee to sign up and appointed a chairperson. To launch the project, Marta traveled to each plant and met with the committee members. She described the principles and purposes underlying the company's interest in community service and encouraged each team to go for it, to make a difference in their communities.

After a year, however, only one committee had come up with a workable—and working—community service program. At the other sites, the committees had accomplished almost nothing. Some members were not interested enough to participate in the committee meetings, and those who did attend had difficulty reaching consensus on what community problems were appropriate for the company to become involved with. When the time came to appoint new committee members, Marta realized she had to handle the committee selection process differently. She visited each plant and invited all employees interested in serving on the local committee to a workshop where a work values instrument was used. New members for the committees were selected from among the participants who gave high importance ratings to work values such as Help Society, Help Others, Work with Others, Creativity, and Community.

This process resulted in the formation of committees in which the members shared common work values directly related to the task they had been brought together to accomplish. Marta met with each committee to clarify the task before them and focus their energy and attention on accomplishing it. Specifically, she spent time discussing with them what success at the task looked like and what the rewards for success would be—for them personally, for the company, and for the community.

All six committees developed and began implementing community volunteer service programs within just four months.

The foundation for a healthy long-distance managerial relationship is trust—and trust is anchored in shared values, shared information, and shared experiences. The general manager and the site manager must come to know each other much more explicitly than would be the case if they worked together on a daily basis. They must mutually explore their respective points of view regarding personal and professional codes, priorities, standards, and practices—in other words, their *values*. In their respective value systems lie the taproots of their personalities (Allport, 1955; Maslow, 1967).

The general manager can assess his site manager's values through both formal instruments and value-focused dialogue. He must develop an understanding of the attitudes/assumptions, thought processes, and emotional responses that inform the site manager's perceptions, interpretations, and decisions. Although for the most part we think of values as underlying behavior, they are also formed from the results of behavior. People develop and express attitudes and value systems to explain and justify their behavior patterns. Values simply give them an interpretive framework with which to determine whether their behavior is acceptable (Maslow, 1967; Rokeach, 1973). Through values assessment, the general manager gathers critical knowledge about how his associate's behavior and values system manifest in two key areas: performance orientation and work style.

Performance Orientation.   Assuming the site manager has a clear understanding of the goals to be achieved (which is addressed in the subsequent section, Planning), he will be a high performer if he (Heider, 1958; Rotter, Chance, and Phares, 1972)

1. believes that *trying* will lead to success

2. believes that success is *rewarded*

3. *values* the reward

Through the values assessment process, the general manager must uncover his associate's opinion about the difficulty of his position, his sense of his own (the associate's) competence to handle the responsibilities of his position, his attitude toward effort, and his level of desire for the personal, professional, and organizational payoffs that could accrue from achieving the objectives and goals set for his area of responsibility.

Of these four variables, the most subtle—and the one over which the general manager has the least influence—is the associate's attitude toward effort, which is a function of his belief about his own ability to produce results, that is, his locus of control (Rotter, Seeman, and Liverant, 1962; Roueche and Mink, 1982). If the site manager believes that he can control the rewards or successes he derives from his environment—which indicates an internal (rather than an external) locus of control—then he is likely to invest greater effort than someone who believes that forces outside his control (the government, the economy, the executive group) determine his success or failure.

The probability of the site manager expending the effort necessary for success is influenced by other factors, in particular the degree to which his identity is invested in his career goals and his personal life. All organization members must strike some sort of balance between their current jobs, their career aspirations, and their personal values and life-styles. This balance is uneasy and ever-changing as situations alter and priorities shift. During values assessment, the general manager must get a sense of how willing (and likely) the site manager is to put organizational needs ahead of his personal life-style preferences—in other words, will he put in the effort necessary to accomplish organizational goals, even if it means giving up time with his family or pursuing his hobbies? The general manager also must determine how well the site manager's individual career goals match the company's needs—in other words, will the site manager's efforts lead to professional rewards that he values within this organization? Finally, the general manager must assess whether his associate is just a professional manager or if he also is interested in creating a better future for the organization.

Work Style. To work together successfully at a distance, both the general manager and the site manager must value—and use—a collaborative work style. True managerial collaboration depends on free and informed choice based on valid information (consisting of both data and feelings). Collaboration leads to increased involvement and, therefore, increased commitment on the part of the associate. At the same time, it leads to increased confidence on the part of the general manager as values are truly shared in open collaborative efforts, problem solving, and planning.

Successful collaboration depends on an open systems approach to management. An *open system* strives to maintain a constant interchange of information among all the organization's internal parts and between the organization and appropriate outside groups. The open systems approach stresses process over structure—interaction over prescription, goal setting and attainment over quota meeting, democracy over autocracy. It assumes that, given sufficient information (sufficient in quality as well as quantity), and both the freedom and the responsibility to act on that information, people will make sound and often creative decisions (Argyris, Putnam, and Smith, 1985; Mink, Schultz, and Mink, 1991).

Collaboration cannot occur when the flow of communication is restricted by either the power of authority or the power of opinion. In the former case, if the general manager imposes his will on his associate, he reduces his associate's willingness to participate and share information. In the latter case, if the general manager thinks he is right, he cannot hear the information (data and feelings) his associate is communicating. These noncollaborative approaches lower trust, and neither learning nor problem solving can occur in low-trust situations.

Planning: The Case of Andrew and the Executive Committee

Andrew was made CEO of a large and successful cable TV company when it was purchased by a media conglomerate. During the fifteen years since its founding, the company had grown from an owner-operated entrepreneurial business to twenty-three operating divisions spread geographically from Hawaii to New York and from Minnesota to Texas.

At the time of the purchase, the company faced diverse challenges from its many different publics throughout the country. At the same time, it faced a highly competitive marketplace and often unpredictable regulatory bodies. The cable industry is very competitive and the rate of change in the technology of the industry is very rapid. Also, the controls on the industry remain in the hands of municipal governments, some of which make absurd demands on their local cable franchise holders. Eventually, its size prompted the company to become genuinely concerned about its ability to respond in a timely and knowledgeable way to its many locales.

Toward this end, Andrew and other members of the Executive Committee initiated a strategic planning agenda. A primary goal was to decentralize operations and to delegate control to the twenty-three resulting decentralized operating units. The question was how to do this while at the same time maintaining and enhancing the owner's investment, paying for the cost of capital, and providing a superior service to the American viewing public.

The Executive Committee began by asking, What are we doing here? and Why? Through developing a corporate vision and mission statement, they established basic principles that would serve as reference points when difficult decisions had to be made. They then identified corporate values and philosophy that articulated how they would act as a company to create their vision. After seven months of sharing, discussing, and aligning, the executives and senior management drafted statements of vision, mission, values, and philosophy (Figure 1). In terms of the bottom line, the company is now one of the two largest cable TV companies in the United States, and it continues to outperform its competitors.

When a general manager and associates work at different locations, planning is especially important in the process of building and maintaining mutual trust. If the general manager and the site manager are equally familiar with and committed to the character and direction of the organization, then they have a shared framework within which to interpret information and make decisions. The key, once again, is collaboration. The site manager must be a fully informed participant in all stages of the planning process.

The planning process begins with the development of a shared *vision* of the organization—a view of the highest purpose the organization wishes to serve, the key values that inform that purpose, and the underlying nobility and feasibility of that purpose. This vision must be translated into a clear written expression of *mission*—a succinct but inclusive statement of the product or service the organization sells and to whom. If that mission is valid, it will naturally fit in as an expression of the organizational vision at the outset of each planning cycle.

The next step is developing a strategic plan. The *strategic plan* describes the largest components implicit in the mission—the major areas for action and the major actions required within those areas. Then the strategic plan must be converted into specific *business plans* for each part or subunit of the organization—the intermediate goals, objectives, strategies, and tactics required to fulfill the strategic plan.

When the general manager and the site manager begin to convert the strategic plan into a business plan for the site manager's area of responsibility, they must explicitly build in guidelines for working together and a structure for communication and decision making. They must identify particular times in the plan—either at regular increments or at specific points when decisions must be made or actions taken at the site—when they will communicate about what has happened or is happening in regard to executing the business plan. Depending on the situation, the general manager may use a "management by exception" approach to particular types of decisions his associate encounters. When certain kinds of nonroutine situations arise, the site manager must consult with the general manager before making a decision or taking action—perhaps even offer to cede authority completely to the general manager in situations that are extremely complex or risky. Together, the general manager and site manager must establish the scope and levels of responsibility the site manager has in all major aspects of his position and, at the same time, remain willing to renegotiate these role responsibilities when circumstances change.

FIGURE 1

Vision

Working together to provide entertainment and information choices.

Mission

We develop, market, deliver, and service in a quality and profitable manner a broad selection of electronic entertainment and information for as many customers as possible in our communities.

Values and Philosophy

We believe in our	*We will operate our business so that*
Heritage—of high performance	In all we do, we strive to be the best.
Customers—the most important part of our business	We provide our customers with quality entertainment and information choices and service at fair prices.
People—our greatest resources	We treat people in all positions with fairness and dignity and we give them room to grow and achieve. Our people are proud of their high standards and are rewarded equitably for high performance and contributions.
Communities—they and we both benefit from our contributions	Our communities benefit from our service and from our individual and company commitments and activities.
Growth—it provides vitality to our enterprise	Our company grows by adding new customers, building new businesses, and serving more communities.
Financial Strength—from efficient and profitable operations	We provide stable and fair returns to our shareholders, stable employment and opportunity for our people, and quality facilities and services to satisfy our customers.
Adaptability—in a competitive and changing world	We test and try new concepts and services. We understand that one of our key strengths is the ability to identify and benefit from change.
Integrity—in all our actions	We treat our customers, people, communities, and suppliers with fairness and honesty.
Teamwork—it enables each of us to be more effective	We communicate openly and with trust in mutually pursuing opportunities and solving problems.

Communicating: The Case of Michael and Brian

Michael and Brian headed up separate units within Carl's corporation. Before their promotions, they had worked together at the same site, where Brian was head of the engineering and design functions and Michael was head of the finance and accounting functions. Although their present locations were different, the two men had to work together on strategic planning, succession planning, general corporate strategy, operating principles, performance standards, and a wide variety of common efforts.

At the same site, Michael and Brian enjoyed a close working relationship. But following their promotions, they experienced a great deal of difficulty communicating with each other over the telephone. The relationship had deteriorated to the point where Michael actually avoided using the telephone, and Brian had more and more reasons to be unavailable to Michael. Yet when they were together, they seemed to communicate very well.

Brian, a creative and innovative engineer who designed large systems, was very right-brained, visual, and tended to approach problems holistically. Michael, on the other hand, had spent years in finance and accounting, and focused on details. Evidence clearly indicated that his representational system was auditory and that he would be most happy dealing with facts and details. When communicating face to face, Michael and Brian picked up nonverbal cues outside of conscious awareness that enabled them to be highly functional in their relationship with each other. However, when they were located at a distance from each other and limited to one means of communication—auditory—then communication broke down. They were trying to represent information *by voice alone* through different representational modalities, and they simply weren't getting through to each other.

Their problems with communication that managing from a distance entails fall into two general categories: those having to do with the flow of information and those having to do with interpersonal communication style.

Information Flow.   Given the natural screening effect that physical separation has on the flow of information, the general manager and the site manager should develop a mutually acceptable structure or framework for ongoing, standardized communication. For instance, the general manager might produce a monthly or semimonthly management letter discussing matters that the site manager would naturally be cognizant of if he worked in the central office—projects that have been in the works, problems that have arisen, issues that have been addressed, trends that have been noted, changes that have occurred, and so on.

Managers and associates should also establish guidelines for determining when a communication can be handled in writing, when it can be handled on the telephone, and when it must be handled in person. For instance, they might choose to adhere to the one-page rule: If an idea or direction can't be explained clearly and thoroughly in a single page, then it should be discussed person to person (either over the phone or on site). A corollary rule might be the half-hour rule: If an idea or direction can't be explained clearly and thoroughly in a half-hour phone call, then it should be discussed face to face.

Interpersonal Communication Style.   The ways people communicate reflect their distinctive representational systems—the way they represent the world to themselves through their perceptions and cognitions. There are three basic representational systems: visual, auditory, and kinesthetic (Bandler and Grinder, 1979).

Some people tend to think visually; in other words, their thought processes tend to occur through pictures and images, and they describe their thoughts using visual language. (For instance, "From where I stand, this problem looks unclear." "How do you picture this situation from your perspective?") People who tend to think auditorially communicate their thoughts using auditory language. (For example, "I get you loud and clear." "The tone of the meeting was off-key.") For those who think kinesthetically, feeling language seems most natural to communicate their thoughts. ("I can't seem to get a firm grasp on this situation." "Last quarter was a rough ride, but I feel like we've gotten things smoothed out now.")

When co-workers have different representational systems—a common situation—they may have difficulty understanding each other. Yet these difficulties are usually manageable because, communicating face to face, they unconsciously pick up nonverbal cues that help them translate what's being said into their own representational language. However, when these co-workers must communicate over the phone, such nonverbal cues are unavailable. Suddenly, mysteriously, their efforts to communicate lead only to confusion, frustration, and a loss of confidence in both themselves and each other.

If the co-workers are a general manager and a site manager, the implications for the organization and for their relationship can be serious. To avoid communication problems, the general manager and his associate must determine their respective representational systems and develop explicit strategies to compensate for any differences. Workable strategies range from deliberately trying to convey information using the other person's representational system (for instance, translating one's kinesthetic thought, "The market is softening, getting squishy, over-saturated," into the other's visual language, "The market is losing definition, getting fuzzy, overexposed") to establishing a policy to meet in person when working on important, subtle, or complex matters.

For instance, the solution to the difficulty between Michael and Brian was simple but effective: Michael asked Brian to describe to him the pictures of what he was seeing in his own mind and drew pictures on paper of what Brian was telling him. Similarly, Brian made notes point by point of what Michael was saying and read them back to Michael to be sure he had caught all the salient points. These strategies significantly improved their relationship and their ability to plan and solve problems almost overnight.

Coaching: The Case of Jerry and Bob

Jerry and Bob, both vice-presidents in Carl's company, work together on a task force that was created to develop and introduce a companywide quality improvement program. Both are talented managers, good at problem solving and goal achievement. Outside of the task force meetings, Jerry and Bob seem to get along quite well, but during the meetings they have frequent misunderstandings.

Jerry is often the idea man of the group, enthusiastically suggesting that the task force try this or that possibility. Generally, his ideas seem sound to the other members of the task force, although they need to be developed and refined and some of the practical details need to be worked out. Bob is usually the first one to question Jerry's ideas on the grounds of practicality. He often states his position in such a blunt way that he causes hard feelings. At this point, Jerry stops talking and lets his ideas simply fade away, without the group addressing them further.

Usually, Bob isn't even aware that he has caused hard feelings. He certainly hasn't intended to! He is the type of person who tends to look at situations factually, deal with them logically, and then make a decision and be done with it. He isn't alert to other people's feelings, unless they've been introduced as facts that must be accounted for in the logical reasoning process. Bob's ability to spot weaknesses in proposals is a real asset to the company—and to the task force—when he uses it in a way that still encourages the free flow of ideas.

Jerry, on the other hand, is the type of person who looks at situations from a contextual point of view, enjoys exploring many possibilities, makes decisions with people in mind, and values harmony. Although Jerry is aware his ideas are undeveloped, when Bob points out the gaps or weaknesses in them, he feels shot down. And, as a result, he shuts down, withdrawing into silence to protect his feelings and prevent conflict. Jerry's creativity, energy, and interpersonal sensitivity are important resources, but they don't do the company or the task force much good when he isn't willing to encounter and work with opposition.

Scott (1981) has suggested that education is the ultimate control mechanism, because associates who have been educated to produce decisions that align with top managers' values and goals will act predictably—and desirably—in unknown future situations. The purpose of coaching is to teach site managers to manage as the general manager would.

The most effective coaching, which produces high levels of performance from associates, follows this twelve-step process:

1. *Communicate Expectations in Action-Oriented Terms.* Describe the job—and excellent performance on the job—in terms of the specific, concrete results expected.

2. *Create a High-Performance Environment of Continuous Learning, Open Information, and the Recognition of Excellence.* Make problem solving part of everyone's job and assure that the information required for effective problem solving is widely shared. Create an environment that fosters learning, and always be on the lookout for excellence in any aspect of performance.

3. *Develop Positive Interpersonal Relationships.* Get to know the associate as a person. Learn as much as possible about how he feels and thinks about his daily work circumstances. Cultivate positive expectations about his capacity to learn and succeed.

4. *Evaluate Present Performance against Desired Performance.* Gather baseline data on the associate's current level of skill or performance, including information about both the associate's performance and his feelings and thoughts regarding his performance. Look at past performance as well as desired future performance.

5. *Give the Associate Feedback on Potential Areas for Performance Improvement.* Ask the associate to look at the difference between his actual performance and the performance required. Focus only on directly observable behavior he can change.

6. *Ensure That the Associate Has Free and Informed Choice Regarding whether to Commit to This Change.* Help the associate develop a commitment to change by allowing him to judge for himself whether the consequences of not changing are acceptable. Give him a sense of what will be involved in making a change.

7. *If He Decides to Do So, Help Him Develop a Performance Plan.* Together, determine general areas that could benefit from improvement and the levels of improvement required.

8. *Determine Learning Tasks and Resources Needed and Time Lines for Completion.* Together, determine specific learning tasks the associate will accomplish, time lines by which he will have accomplished them, and ways in which he will demonstrate mastery.

9. *Follow-up.* Help the associate make corrections during implementation of the plan. Use modeling and demonstrations, especially at the beginning of the learning program, to help the associate get a clear idea of what the changes in his management practice should look like.

10. *Building Responsibility.* A strong development plan encourages and enables the development of both self-esteem and self-efficacy through building responsibility.

11. *Accept Results, Not Excuses.* If the performance plan is a good one—specific, behaviorally anchored, and controllable—then don't accept excuses for failure. Keep trying to understand the causes of failure. Especially look for ways in which the coach may be ineffective.

12. *Allow Natural Consequences.* Don't protect the associate from the natural consequences of his failure if he does not improve after many opportunities and continued coaching. This step and the previous one emerge from the practice of reality therapy (Glasser, 1984).

For the long-distance manager, difficulties can arise in two areas during implementation of this coaching model: observation of and feedback on the associate's performance, and accommodating for differences in personal type.

Decision Log Observation. Because he has few opportunities to observe a site manager directly, the general manager can use supplementary techniques for capturing examples of his performance. One useful technique is the decision log—a record of specific decisions made, including the reasoning used to arrive at the decision, the alternatives considered, the outcome of the decision, and how the associate might have handled the decision differently, given the outcome. Figure 2 gives an example of a decision log entry.

The site manager can keep a journal of decisions made in his different areas of responsibility and periodically share them with the general manager, either by sending copies of journal entries through the mail or by reviewing them with him during site visits. The general manager is then not only informed about events at the remote site, but also is privy to the site manager's thoughts and feelings about those events. The general manager can then give the site manager feedback on the decisions and how they were made, indicating when he would have acted differently and why. In this way, both managers can gain insight into the other's reasoning processes and thereby understand how to make better—or perhaps simply more mutually acceptable—decisions in the future.

Face to face, the general manager and the site manager can explicitly acknowledge the similarities and mutually explore the differences in their values and assumptions about human behavior that have been revealed via the decision log. Not only will the general manager be able to help improve the site manager's performance through coaching, they both will have a means for developing greater trust for each other. Face-to-face discussion of the decision log should be used to

FIGURE 2
THE DECISION LOG

---

1. What was the decision?

I decided to dismiss the office manager.

2. What alternatives were considered?

I talked to the manager about her tardiness and frequent absences; I gave her notice of my intentions and a probationary time; I considered demoting her to a clerical position.

3. How was the decision made and communicated to others?

I reached the decision after she had missed her third day in a two-week period of the probationary period and after she had been late five times. I called her in and gave her two weeks' notice and told her that I would be holding a staff meeting that day to announce my decision and my plans to promote Jane to office manager. I then held the meeting and made this announcement. I did not offer any explanation because I felt it was obvious to everyone, and if it wasn't, then I didn't want to embarrass Mary further.

4. What was the outcome of the decision?

Mary left and Jane is now office manager. I have not been able to hire anyone to replace Jane yet. There was some bad feeling for a while among Mary's friends who felt I had just liked Jane better than Mary.

5. What would you do differently?

I would have explained what the problem was in objective terms, perhaps just listing the number of absences that Mary had and explaining that the office manager is often in charge and has to sign for me, which made her absences a hardship for me. I did explain all of this to Jane and she has gone out of her way to check with me when she has had to take time off. In retrospect, the rest of the staff would probably also have been more understanding had I explained it to them. As for Mary, the rest of her work was also suffering from her problems at home. I didn't feel that she would be able to be there enough even if I demoted her, so I don't think that I would have changed that part of this decision.

---

raise issues of substance, not as an opportunity to haggle over style, preference, or procedure. When building mutual trust, such matters are much less significant than shared values and shared beliefs about what is possible and what is meaningful in the context of their particular organization.

People Types. The Myers-Briggs Type Indicator (Myers, 1962) measures personal preferences in the way people perceive or gather information and in the way they judge or make decisions. These preferences are revealed through their patterns of behavior regarding four different factors:

- *Energy Patterns.* Does the person's interest flow mainly to the outer world of actions, objects, and persons (extraversion) or to the inner world of concepts and ideas (introversion)?

- *Data Gathering.* Does the person prefer to perceive the immediate, real, practical facts of experience and life (sensing) or the possibilities, relationships, and meanings of experiences (intuition)?

- *Decision Making.* Does the person prefer to make judgments or decisions objectively, impersonally considering causes of events and where decisions may lead (thinking), or subjectively and personally, weighing values of choices and how they matter to others (feeling)?

- *Time Management and Life-Style.* Does the person prefer mostly to live in a decisive, planned, and orderly way, aiming to regulate and control events (emphasizing judgment), or in a spontaneous, flexible way, aiming to understand life and adapt to it (emphasizing perception)?

According to the Myers-Briggs model, these patterns combine into one of sixteen possible personal types. Each type tends to operate in a characteristic manner, with characteristic strengths and weaknesses, positives and negatives. However, qualities that might be considered weaknesses in one context could be strengths in another, and vice versa.

As with representational systems and communication styles, personal types and working styles are closely connected. And, in a similar way, a mismatch in type between the general manager and the site manager can lead to unnecessary strain in the manager-associate relationship. For instance, a site manager who has an extroverted nature, an intuitive perceptual orientation, a tendency to make decisions based on feelings, and a preference for spontaneity might be a great leader and sound decision maker—but also might seem unconcerned about sharing factual information and have trouble meeting certain deadlines.

In such a case, the general manager might first ask himself, "Although I think Joe should provide me with more data, is this actually a performance problem? Perhaps it's just a difference in our personal styles." If indeed the general manager believes the behavior represents a performance problem, then he can use his knowledge of types when coaching his associate. For instance, knowing that to his associate details or facts don't seem meaningful in and of themselves—only as parts of larger patterns—the general manger can determine specifically what data he needs and work with the site manager to install a procedure or system to collect and report that data to him.

This article opened with the story of Carl and his difficulties with Gene and other site managers. It was Carl's experience that led this author to consider the effects of geographical separation on management relationships.

Carl know he had a problem—and he was deeply troubled by it—but he didn't know what the problem was. The situation could have continued to deteriorate to the point that it actually compromised the health of the organization—sapping morale, polluting the communication climate, leeching financial and human resources. However, quite by chance, Carl discovered what the problem was and used the services of the author to help resolve it.

Carl happened to attend a management seminar during which he was required to gather data from his subordinates regarding the degree to which they trusted him. When he received the feedback, Carl learned that his subordinates had very low trust in him and in his way of dealing with them. This information was disconcerting to this man who had every reason to feel confident of his managerial competence. However, the problem wasn't that Carl was untrustworthy. Nor were his associates. The problem was that the normal avenues and processes work associates use to build and maintain trust were simply not available or were seriously distorted *because of geographical separation.*

Managing from a distance is not business as usual. Managers must compensate for the informational and psychological barriers that arise when associates work at different locations. By sensitively attending to these highly delicate processes—aligning values, planning, communicating, and coaching—managers can maintain strong, positive work relationships, even across thousands of miles.

Oscar G. Mink and Barbara Mink
with Sheila Henderson

REFERENCES

Adler, A. 1979. *Superiority and social interest: A collection of later writing*. New York: W. W. Norton.

Allport, G. W. 1955. *Becoming*. New Haven: Yale University Press.

Argyris, C. 1990. *Overcoming organizational defenses: Facilitating organizational learning*. Sydney: Allyn and Bacon.

Argyris, C., R. Putnam, and D. M. Smith. 1985. *Action Science*. San Francisco: Jossey-Bass.

Ashby, R. W. 1956. *Introduction to cybernetics*. New York: Wiley.

Bandler, R., and J. Grinder, 1979. *Frogs into princes*. Moab, Utah: Real People Press.

Barker, J. 1985. *Discovering the future: The business of paradigms*. St. Paul, Minn.: I. L. I. Press.

Bean, R., and H. Clemes. 1978. *Elementary principal's handbook: New approaches to administrative action*. West Nyack, N. Y.: Parker Publishing Co.

Bennis, W. 1989. *On becoming a leader*. Reading, Mass.: Addison-Wesley.

Blanchard, K., and S. Johnson. 1982. *The one-minute manager*. New York: Morrow.

Brookfield, S. 1986. *Understanding and facilitating adult learning*. San Francisco: Jossey-Bass.

Carlsmith, J., and A. Gross. 1969. Some effects of guilt on compliance. *Journal of Personality and Social Psychology* 11 (3): 232–239.

Combs, D., and D. Snugg. 1959. *Individual behavior: A perceptual approach to behavior*. New York: Harper and Row.

Conant, R. C., and R. W. Ashby. 1970. Every good regulator of a system must be a model of that system. *International Journal of Systems Science* 1: 89–97.

Deming, W. E. 1982. *Quality, productivity, and competitive position*. Cambridge, Mass.: MIT Press.

Driekurs, R. 1957. *Psychology in the classroom*. New York: Harper and Row.

Erikson, E. H. 1979. *Identity and the life cycle*. New York: W. W. Norton.

Ernst, F. H. 1971. The OK corral: The grid for get-on with. *Transactional Analysis Journal* (October) 1 (4): 33–42.

Evered, R., and J. Selman. 1989. Coaching and the art of management. *Organizational Dynamics* 18 2: 16–32.

Fromm, E. 1956. *The art of loving.* New York: Harper and Row.

Fromm, E. 1947. *Man for himself: An inquiry into the psychology of ethics.* New York: Holt, Rinehart, and Winston.

Garfield, C. 1984. *Peak performance.* New York: Warner Books.

Gibb, J. R. 1978. *Trust: A new view of personal and organizational development.* Los Angeles: Guild of Tutors Press.

Glasser, W. 1984. *Control theory: A new explanation of how we control our lives.* New York: Harper and Row.

Goldman, K. 1980. *Basics of organizational openness.* Unpublished manuscript, University of Texas.

Harris, T. 1969. *I'm OK, you're OK: A practical guide to transactional analysis.* New York: Harper and Row.

Harvey, J. 1988. *The Abilene paradox and other meditations on management.* Lexington, Mass.: Lexington Books in association with University Associates.

Heider, F. 1958. *The psychology of interpersonal relations.* New York: John Wiley and Sons.

Hersey, P., and K. Blanchard. 1982. *Management of organizational behavior.* 4th ed. Englewood Cliffs, N.J.: Prentice-Hall.

Hersey, P., and K. Blanchard 1988. *Situational leadership: A summary.* San Diego, Calif.: University Associates.

Hiroto, D., and M. Seligman. 1975. Generality of learned helplessness in man. *Journal of Personality and Social Psychology* 31 (2): 311–327.

Hord, S. M., W. L. Rutherford, L. Huling-Austin, and G. E. Hall. 1987. *Taking charge of change.* Alexandria, Virg.: Association for Supervision and Curriculum Development.

Horney, K. 1945. *Our inner conflicts: A constructive theory of neurosis.* New York: W. W. Norton.

James, W. [1896] 1956. *The will to believe.* Reprint. New York: Dover.

Jung, C. [1945] 1979. *The development of personality.* Translated by R. Hull. Princeton, N.J.: Princeton University Press.

Levinson, D. 1978. *The seasons of a man's life.* New York: Alfred A. Knopf.

Lewin, K. 1969. Quasi-stationary social equilibria and the problem of permanent change. In *The planning of change,* edited by W. G. Bennis, K. D. Benne, and R. Chin. New York: Holt, Rinehart, and Winston, pp. 238–244.

Lippitt, G. 1979. Learning rhythms. *Training and Development Journal* (October): 12–28.

Luft, J. 1969. *Of human interaction.* Palo Alto, Calif.: National Press Books.

Luft, J., and H. Ingram. 1961. The Johari window. *Human Relations Training News* 5 (1). Washington, D.C.: National Eduction Association.

MacDonald, A., Jr., V. Kessel, and J. Fuller. 1972. Self-disclosure and two kinds of trust. *Psychological Reports* 30: 143–148.

Macher, K. 1988. Empowerment and the bureaucracy. *Training and Development Journal* 42 (9): 41–45.

Maslow, A. H. 1967. A theory of metamotivation: The biological rooting of the value-life. *Journal of Humanistic Psychology* 7: 93–127.

Maslow, A. 1971. *The farther reaches of human nature.* New York: Viking Press.

May, R. 1975. *The courage to create.* New York: W. W. Norton.

Mayeroff, M. 1971. *On caring.* San Francisco: Harper and Row.

Merton, R. 1948. The self-fulfilling prophecy. *Antioch Review* 8: 193–210.

Mink, O. G., J. M. Schultz, and B. P. Mink. [1979] 1991. *Open organizations.* 2d ed. Austin, Tex.: Catapult Press and The Somerset Consulting Group.

Moss-Kanter, R. M. 1989. *When giants learn to dance: Mastering the challenge of strategy, management, and careers in the 1990s.* New York: Simon and Schuster.

Myers, I. B. 1962. *The Myers-Briggs type indicator manual.* Princeton, N.J.: Educational Testing Service.

Nouwen, H. 1986. *Reaching out: The three movements of the spiritual life.* Garden City, N.Y.: Doubleday.

Peters, T. J., and N. K. Austin. 1985. *A passion for excellence: The leadership difference.* New York: Random House.

Peters, T. J., and R. H. Waterman, Jr. 1982. *In search of excellence: Lessons from America's best-run companies.* New York: Harper and Row.

Rogers, C. 1961. *On becoming a person: A therapist's view of psychotherapy.* Boston: Houghton Mifflin.

Rokeach, M. R. 1973. *The nature of human values.* New York: The Free Press.

Rosenthal, R. 1974. *On the social psychology of the self-fulfilling prophecy: Further evidence for Pygmalion effects and their mediating mechanisms* (Module 53). New York: MSS Modular Publications, pp. 1–28.

Rotter, J. B., M. Seeman, and S. Liverant. 1962. Internal versus external control of reinforcements: A major variable in behavior theory. In *Decisions, values, and groups,* edited by N. F. Washburne, vol. 2. New York: Pergamon Press, 473–516.

Rotter, J. B. 1966. Generalized expectancies for internal versus external control of reinforcement. *Psychological Monographs* 80 (1) (Whole No. 609).

Rotter, J. B., J. C. Chance, and E. J. Phares. 1972. *Applications of a social learning theory of personality.* New York: Holt, Rinehart, and Winston.

Roueche, J., and O. G. Mink. 1982. Overcoming learned helplessness in community college students. *Journal of Developmental and Remedial Education* 2 (3): 2–20.

Scott, W. R. 1987. *Organizations: Rational, natural and open systems.* 2d ed. Englewood Cliffs, N.J.: Prentice-Hall.

Seligman, M. 1975. *Helplessness: On depression, development, and death.* San Francisco: W. H. Freeman.

Senge, P. M. 1990. *The fifth discipline: The art and practice of the learning organization.* New York: Doubleday/Currency.

GLOSSARY

Achievement orientation. A great desire to achieve found in high performers, who have dreams about what they want for themselves, which creates the psychological need for achievement.

Adaptive learning. Learning that takes place in response to changes in the environment that demand changes in the operations of the individual, group, or organization.

Agency. The state of being in charge of your own life or life space (roles).

Andragogy. The art and science of teaching adults or facilitating adult learners.

Attribution. The psychological process of explaining the causes of events that have occurred in our lives.

The behavioral/environmental viewpoint of high performance. The point-of-view from which the challenge of achieving improved performance is simply a matter of eliciting and then reinforcing the right behaviors.

Climate. The social and interpersonal world in which you work. Empowering work climates need to be positive, supportive, and conducive to risk taking, and should provide the correct tools to do your job.

Coaching. The process by which one individual, the coach, creates enabling relationships with others that make it easier for them to learn.

Cohesiveness. A measure of the degree to which team members respond to one another—interpersonal attraction.

Commitment. The attribution of importance to an as yet uncreated future.

Common variation. A variation that affects all members of the work team and reduces meaningful communication; a variation that affects all units.

Competence. The knowledge, attitudes, and skills that enable you to produce positive outcomes through your own efforts.

Concerns-based adoption model (CBAM). A model that explains the stages of concern and levels of use that people go through when adopting new practices and innovations.

Congruity. Saying and doing as you say. Expressing outwardly what you are experiencing inwardly.

Connectedness. A sense of belonging or being a part of yourself and a part of another entity—the larger world in which you live and work.

Conscious competence. Being able to perform at an expected level or standard only when consciously concentrating on the work/task(s).

Conscious incompetence. Being aware of your incompetence to perform work/task(s) or use a particular skill.

Constancy. Degree to which you stay on course and maintain personal integrity.

Contractual trust. The confident anticipation (expectation) that people will do what they say they are going to do. Trust established through making and keeping simple agreements; being responsible.

Counseling. Relatively short-term interventions designed to remedy problems that interfere with job performance; enabling an associate to make changes consciously in her behavior.

Critical reflection. Reflecting on the assumptions that underlie your actions and changing these assumptions when evidence suggests change is appropriate.

Dispositional attribution. Attributing a failure to an internal characteristic of yourself or someone else.

Double-loop learning. Learning that challenges or examines the underlying goals, values, or variables that will lead to strategies that will produce desired results.

Efficacy. An effort that makes a difference in the quality of services and products delivered to the customer.

Empowerment. Enabling others to perform new tasks, to do more than they were doing, to do something entirely different, or even to perform at a higher level of complexity.

Expectancy theory. The theory that people learn when they believe that they can produce a desired result by coupling their skills with effort.

External responsiveness. Interaction with others that produces mutually beneficial results; exchanges of energy across system boundaries.

Feedthrough. Accurate information provided to people that relates what they are doing to the stated goals, and helps make adjustments before errors occur.

Force field analysis. A technique used to analyze change by examining the relationship between the *driving forces* pressing for a change versus the *restraining forces* blocking its momentum.

Framing goals. Describing the process by which (or the frame within which) a goal is to be achieved.

Galatea effect. A belief in yourself and your own ability to learn, grow, and achieve good results.

Generational or creative learning. A type of learning that leads to the development of new products and services that meet the needs of new markets in unique ways.

Halo effect. The tendency to see only what conforms to your preconceived perception of a person, once you have formed a theory about that individual's personality.

The individual/trait viewpoint of high performance. The point-of-view from which individual differences or traits are associated with excellence. From this perspective, high performance is an individual attribute. Accordingly, some people have the potential to achieve and some do not. The task of the organization is to choose those people who have the ability and the desire to achieve.

Innovative learning. Learning that involves critical reflection on the assumptions that underlie thoughts, feelings, and actions, then becoming open to discovering and experimenting with new modes of experiencing the world.

Integrated wholeness. Self-concept, organized by personal values.

Integrity. Doing what you have agreed to do.

Internal responsiveness. Awareness of your own wants and needs, and fulfilling them.

Locus of control. A belief (trait or characteristic) that you can couple your ability and skill with physical and mental effort to produce desired outcomes or results. This belief is exemplified by assuming personal responsibility for life's results as opposed to projecting blame onto someone or something else, like luck, chance, fate, or task difficulty. An internal locus of control is characterized by giving yourself permission to act, as opposed to seeking permission from external sources and having positive expectations that your action will produce positive results.

Maintenance learning. Learning in which you acquire new knowledge and skills to better adapt to an existing situation.

Mastery. The ability to take data from one's internal and external environments and to use them to design structures, create understanding and meaning, and ultimately to achieve a goal. Mastery is integrating many disparate functions and processes in a way that all become focused on achieving the organization's vision.

Mateship. The notion that we're in this together as friends.

Mentoring. Helping facilitate overall career growth and personal advancement. We believe that good mentors deal with the complete life space and life structure of the mentee—family (personal), career, and current work role.

Metalearning. Learning at increasingly higher and more complex levels. This involves freeing oneself from repetitive patterns of old learnings, which may be firmly imbedded in the unconscious, and adopting new mental operations—new mental models or structures that guide performance at work. Metalearning occurs when you have mastered the art and science of recognizing which of your values, goals, or contextual influences are governing your learning and performance. Learning how to learn.

Modeling. Coaching by example. The learner sees the coach meeting performance goals and copies the coach's behavior.

Pareto chart. Charts, typically in the form of vertical bar graphs, based on the Pareto Rule: 20 percent of work provides 80 percent of the payoff. Pareto charts help identify high-payoff activities. They can also be used to spot problems and to determine priorities for solutions.

Pedagogy. The art and science of teaching children.

Performance empowerment. The process of facilitating the development of skills and attitudes that allow a person to fulfill her potential.

The person-situation/interactionist perspective or applying systems theory to human systems. The concept that behavior is determined by both personal factors and environmental factors. From this viewpoint, behavior is a function of the person and the environment in interplay. This viewpoint assumes that every event or action in a human system has an impact on someone somewhere else in the system and that high performance is a process of creating environmental conditions that enable high performance.

Physical trust. The psychological feeling that you are safe in the current physical environment.

Pygmalion effect. The tendency of a person to act in accordance with another's expectations of her behavior.

Reality performance management (RPM). A general theory of motivation and performance designed to help leaders focus on key variables that influence performance.

Realization. The process during which the coach and the associate work together toward identified and shared goals.

Reliability. Being there when it counts, under every condition, not just when things are going well.

Responsibility. Making and keeping simple social agreements (see contractual trust).

Selective recognition. The process of praising competent behavior and ignoring incompetent behavior.

Self-disclosure trust. The willingness to share relevant information at the time it is needed.

Self-efficacy. The belief that you personally can make a difference by making a good product or providing a good service.

Sense of purpose. The framework that enables you to create meaning in your life, solve problems, make choices, and plan for the future.

Single-loop learning. Learning routine operations that are repeated automatically without examining governing values, goals, or other influences.

Situational attribution. Attributing a failure to an environmental barrier or to a certain set of circumstances.

Special variation. A variation that is a unique event.

Statistical process control. The statistical study of the variations in the output of an operation done to improve the process.

Symmetry breaking. Enabling a person to work through or break habitual patterns by creating disequilibrium and "unfreezing" or confronting these patterns.

Systemic thinking. The thought processes that enable one to see the interrelationships of a number of events and processes occurring simultaneously.

Total quality management (TQM). The process of getting all associates involved in continuous improvement of all systems and processes.

Transformation. Performing at increasingly higher and more complex levels. This involves freeing yourself from the repetitive patterns of old learnings, which may be firmly imbedded in the unconscious, and adopting new mental operations—new mental models or structures that guide performance at work. Transformation may be quantitative, as in when you are able to do more of what you were doing in the past. It may also be qualitative, as in when you are enabled to do something different, or when you leap from one level of performance to an entirely different level using an entirely new mental model or a significant modification(s) of an existing model(s).

Unconditional positive regard. Unconditional acceptance of the worth/value of another human being.

Unconscious competence. Being able to perform at the level of mastery without thinking about or concentrating on what must be done.

Unconscious incompetence. Being unaware of the need to learn a new skill and being unaware of the relationship between a lack of competence and failure.

Workscape. The totality of the environmental setting in which work takes place.

BIBLIOGRAPHY

Adler, A. 1979. *Superiority and social interest: A collection of later writing*. New York: W. W. Norton.

Argyris, C. 1982. *Reasoning, learning and action: Individual and organizational*. San Francisco: Jossey-Bass.

Argyris, C. 1990. *Overcoming organizational defenses: Facilitating organizational learning*. Boston: Allyn and Bacon.

Barker, J. 1985. *Discovering the future: The business of paradigms*. St. Paul, Minn.: I. L. I. Press.

Bennis, W. 1989. *On becoming a leader*. Reading, Mass.: Addison-Wesley.

Blanchard, K., and S. Johnson. 1982. *The one-minute manager*. New York: Morrow.

Brookfield, S. 1986. *Understanding and facilitating adult learning*. San Francisco: Jossey-Bass.

Burns, J. M. 1978. *Leadership*. New York: Harper and Row.

Carlsmith, J., and A. Gross. 1969. Some effects of guilt on compliance. *Journal of Personality and Social Psychology* 11 (3): 232–239.

Castaneda, C. 1972. *A separate reality: Further conversations with Don Juan*. New York: Pocket Books.

Cattell, R. *Sixteen personality factor questionnaire*. Champaign, Ill.: Institute for Personality & Ability Testing, Inc. (P.O. Box 188, Champaign, Ill., 61824-0188).

Combs, D., and D. Snugg. 1959. *Individual behavior: A perceptual approach to behavior*. New York: Harper and Row.

Coopersmith, S. 1967. *The antecedents of self-esteem*. San Francisco: Freeman.

Crawford, V. 1988. *From Confucius to Oz*. New York: Berkley Books.

Dailey, N. 1984. Adult learning and organizations. *Training and Development Journal* (December): 64–68.

Deming, W. E. 1982. *Quality, productivity, and competitive position*. Cambridge, Mass.: MIT Press.

Deming, W. E. 1982, 1986. *Out of the crisis*. Cambridge: Massachusetts Institute of Technology, Center for Advanced Engineering Study.

Driekurs, R. 1957. *Psychology in the classroom.* New York: Harper and Row.

Ellsworth, P., and J. Carlsmith. 1968. Effects of eye contact and verbal content on affective response to a dyadic interaction. *Journal of Personality and Social Psychology* 10 (1): 15–20.

Erikson, E. 1979. *Identity and the life cycle.* New York: W. W. Norton.

Ernst, F. H. 1971. The OK corral: The grid for get-on with. *Transactional Analysis Journal* (October) 1 (4): 33–42.

Evered, R., and J. Selman. 1989. Coaching and the art of management. *Organizational Dynamics* 18 (2): 16–32.

Fromm, E. 1947. *Man for himself: An inquiry into the psychology of ethics.* New York: Holt, Rinehart, and Winston.

Fromm, E. 1956. *The art of loving.* New York: Harper and Row.

Garfield, C. 1987. *Peak performance.* New York: Warner Books.

Geber, B. 1992. From manager to coach. *Training* 29 (2): 25–31.

Gibb, J. R. 1978. *Trust: A new view of personal and organizational development.* Los Angeles: Guild of Tutors Press.

Goldman, K. 1980. *Basics of organizational openness.* Unpublished manuscript, University of Texas.

Harris, T. 1969. *I'm OK, you're OK: A practical guide to transactional analysis.* New York: Harper and Row.

Harvey, J. 1988. *The Abilene paradox and other meditations on management.* Lexington, Mass.: Lexington Books in association with University Associates.

Hersey, P., and K. Blanchard. 1982. *Management of organizational behavior.* 4th ed. Englewood Cliffs, N.J.: Prentice-Hall.

Hersey, P., and K. Blanchard. 1988. *Situational leadership: A summary.* San Diego, Calif.: University Associates.

Herzberg, F. G., B. Mausner, and B. B. Snyderman. 1959. *The motivation to work.* New York: John Wiley and Sons.

Hiroto, D., and M. Seligman. 1975. Generality of learned helplessness in man. *Journal of Personality and Social Psychology* 31 (2): 311–327.

Hord, S., W. Rutherford, L. Huling-Austin, and G. Hall. 1987. *Taking charge of change.* Alexandria, Virg.: Association for Supervision in Curriculum Development.

Horney, K. 1945. *Our inner conflicts: A constructive theory of neurosis.* New York: W. W. Norton.

James, W. [1896] 1956. *The will to believe.* New York: Dover.

Jaques, E. 1976. *A general theory of bureaucracy.* London: Heinemann Educational Books.

Jung, C. [1945] 1979. *The development of personality.* Reprint. Translated by R. Hull. Princeton, N.J.: Princeton University Press.

Kuhn, T. 1970. *The structure of scientific revolutions*. 2d ed. Chicago: University of Chicago Press.

Levinson, D. 1978. *The seasons of a man's life*. New York: Alfred A. Knopf.

Lewin, K. 1969. Quasi-stationary social equilibria and the problem of permanent change. In *The planning of change*, edited by W. G. Bennis, K. D. Benne, and R. Chin. New York: Holt, Rinehart, and Winston, pp. 238–244.

Lippitt, G. 1979. Learning rhythms. *Training and Development Journal* (October): 12–28.

Lippitt, G. 1969. *Organizational renewal*. Englewood Cliffs, N.J.: Prentice-Hall.

Lippitt, G., and R. Lippitt. 1986. *The consulting process in action*. 2d ed. San Diego, Calif.: University Associates.

Lofland, J., and L. H. Lofland. 1984. *An analyzing social setting: A guide to qualitative observation and analysis*, 2d ed. Belmont, Calif.: Wadsworth.

Luft, J., and H. Ingram. 1961. The Johari window. *Human Relations Training News* 5(1). Washington, D.C.: National Education Association.

MacDonald, A., Jr., V. Kessel, and J. Fuller. 1972. Self-disclosure and two kinds of trust. *Psychological Reports* 30: 143–148.

Macher, K. 1988. Empowerment and the bureaucracy. *Training and Development Journal* 42 (9): 41–45.

Maslow, A. 1971. *The farther reaches of human nature*. New York: Viking Press.

May, R. 1975. *The courage to create*. New York: W. W. Norton.

Mayeroff, M. 1971. *On caring*. San Francisco: Harper and Row.

McGhee, P., and V. Crandall. 1968. Beliefs in internal-external control of reinforcements and academic performance. *Child Development* 39: 91–102.

McGregor D. 1960. *The human side of enterprise*. New York: McGraw-Hill.

Merton, R. 1948. The self-fulfilling prophecy. *Antioch Review* 8: 193–210.

Mink, O., B. Mink, and K. Owen. 1987. *Groups at work*. Englewood Cliffs, N.J.: Educational Technology Publications.

Mink, O. G., and J. E. Roueche. 1982. Combatting learned helplessness in community college students. *Journal of Developmental and Remedial Education* (Spring) 5 (3): 2–20.

Moss-Kanter, R. 1989. *When giants learn to dance: Mastering the challenge of strategy, management, and careers in the 1990s*. New York: Simon and Schuster.

Normann, R. 1985. Developing capabilities for organizational learning. In *Organizational strategy and change*, edited by J. M. Pennings and Associates. San Francisco: Jossey-Bass, pp. 217–248.

Nouwen, H. 1986. *Reaching out: The three movements of the spiritual life*. Garden City, N.Y.: Doubleday.

Owen, H. 1990. *Leadership is*. Potomac, Md.: Abbott Publishing.

Peters, T. 1988. *Thriving on chaos: A handbook for management revolution*. New York: Alfred A. Knopf.

Peters, T. J., and N. K. Austin. 1985. *A passion for excellence: The leadership difference*. New York: Random House.

Peters T. J., and R. H. Waterman, Jr. 1982. *In search of excellence: Lessons from America's best-run companies*. New York: Harper and Row.

Pitman, B. 1991. A systems analysis approach to reviewing completed projects. *Journal of Systems Management* (December): 6–9.

Rogers, C. 1961. *On becoming a person: A therapist's view of psychotherapy*. Boston: Houghton Mifflin.

Rogers, C. R. 1969. *Freedom to learn*. Columbus, Ohio: Charles E. Merrill Publishing Company.

Rosenthal, R. 1974. *On the social psychology of the self-fulfilling prophecy: Further evidence for Pygmalion effects and their mediating mechanisms* (Module 53). New York: MSS Modular Publications, pp. 1–28.

Rotter, J. 1954. *Social learning and clinical psychology*. Englewood Cliffs, N.J.: Prentice-Hall.

Rotter, J. 1966. Generalized expectancies for internal vs. external control of reinforcement. *Psychological Monographs* 80: 1–28.

Rotter, J. 1967. A new scale for the measurement of interpersonal trust. *Journal of Personality* 35: 651–655.

Rotter, J. 1975. A new scale for the measurement of interpersonal trust. *Journal of Personality* 35: 651–655.

Ryan, K. D., and D. K. Oestreich. 1991. *Driving fear out of the workplace*. San Francisco: Jossey-Bass.

Sashkin, M. 1986. True vision in leadership. *Training and Development Journal* 40 (5): 58–61.

Seligman, M. 1975. *Helplessness: On depression, development, and death*. San Francisco: W. H. Freeman.

Sellers, D. 1990. What customers really want. *Fortune* (June 4): 58–63.

Senge, P. 1990. *The fifth discipline: The art and practice of the learning organization*. New York: Doubleday/Currency.

Sheldon, A. 1980. Organizational paradigms: A theory of organizational change. *Organizational Dynamics*, American Management Association Publications, Winter: 61–80.

Tseng, M. 1970. Locus of control as a determinant of job proficiency, employability, and training satisfaction of vocational rehabilitation clients. *Journal of Counseling Psychology* 17: 487–491.

Waitley, D. 1984. *The psychology of winning*. Berkeley, Calif.: Berkeley Publishers.

Waitley, D. 1988. *Being the best*. Chicago: Nightingale-Conant.

Woodruff, D. 1990. A new era for auto quality. *Business Week* (October 12): pp. 86ff.

INDEX